D1154792

Ladies and Gentlemen
of the Civil Service

Ladies and Gentlemen of the Civil Service

Middle-Class Workers in Victorian America

Cindy Sondik Aron

New York   Oxford
Oxford University Press
1987

Oxford University Press

Oxford   New York   Toronto
Delhi   Bombay   Calcutta   Madras   Karachi
Petaling Jaya   Singapore   Hong Kong   Tokyo
Nairobi   Dar es Salaam   Cape Town
Melbourne   Auckland

and associated companies in
Beirut   Berlin   Ibadan   Nicosia

Library of Congress Cataloging-in-Publication Data
Aron, Cindy Sondik, 1945–
Ladies and gentlemen of the civil service.
Bibliography: p.   Includes index.
1. Civil service—United States—History—
19th century.   2. Women in civil service—
United States—History—19th century.   I. Title.
JK691.A76   1987   353.006'09   86–19974
ISBN 0-19-504874-1 (alk. paper)

2 4 6 8 9 7 5 3 1

Printed in the United States of America
on acid-free paper

For Mark and Samantha

Acknowledgments

I have incurred many debts over the years it has taken to write this book, and it is now a great pleasure for me to thank those people who have helped along the way.

The first debt is to James B. Gilbert. It was he who directed the dissertation from which this book grew. As teacher, advisor, and friend, he has always been ready with assistance and encouragement. While I was still a graduate student at the University of Maryland, Ira Berlin introduced me to the treasures of the National Archives. I was fortunate enough to spend one year working as a graduate assistant on his exemplary project where I learned a good bit about using the National Archives as a resource for the study of social history. When I began to search for a dissertation topic, Renée Jaussaud of the Natural Resources Branch of the National Archives used her extraordinary knowledge of the records to direct me to a wonderful cache of documents. Her efficiency and professionalism made years of research considerably easier. Terry Matchette of the Fiscal and Judicial Branch was also enormously helpful in keeping me supplied with records. This project owes much to the staff at the National Archives who searched for, delivered, and xeroxed truckloads of documents.

Numerous friends and colleagues were gracious enough to take time from their own work to help me with mine. Many thanks to Patricia Cooper, Alice Kessler-Harris, Linda Kerber, Page Miller, Gloria Moldow, and Leslie Rowland for reading various sections, working papers, and chapters. The late Herbert Gutman offered his always astute observations on two chapters of my dissertation. Fred Carstenson and Joseph Kett read the dissertation and helped me realize how important it was to revise my work on female clerks into a book that would study both female *and* male workers. Susan Porter Benson, Suzanne Lebsock, Barbara Melosh, Thomas Noble, and Olivier Zunz read the manuscript in its entirety and offered valuable suggestions that improved the final product theoretically, methodologically, and grammatically.

Three people read this work so many times that they can probably recite passages from memory. Edward Ayers, Cynthia Harrison, and Dorothy Ross worked over numerous drafts. I benefited not only from their insightful comments and their insistence that I confront difficult problems, but from their willingness to spend endless hours discussing my work. Their friendship and encouragement eased me through numerous difficult moments. This book is immeasurably better because of their assistance, and I am profoundly grateful.

I have received financial and institutional support which lightened many burdens. A dissertation grant from the Employment and Training Administration of the Department of Labor, a summer grant from the University of Virginia, and a fellowship from the American Council of Learned Societies all helped considerably at different stages of my work. The Department of History at the University of Virginia offered work-study assistance and leave time. Peder Garske and Sarah Ketchum—former students at the University of Virginia—coded data with care and precision. Graduate students Candice Bredbenner and Cathy McDonough gave much needed assistance with two research tasks. The clerical staff at the Department of History, Bonnie Blackwell, Lottie McCauley, Kathleen Miller, Elizabeth Stovall, and Ella Wood, taught me to use the word processor and cheerfully helped fix the errors I continually made.

It has been a pleasure to work with the people from Oxford University Press. Sheldon Meyer's good counsel, Stephanie Sakson-Ford's careful copy-editing, and Rachel Toor's ability to move this manuscript through production have more than proven Oxford's reputation for excellence.

My final debts are personal. My parents, Ethel and Leon Sondik, never ceased offering nurture and support. They, along with my sister, Barbara Perlmutter, and my brother, Rick Sondik, listened to my grousing and comforted me when I was low, then cheered my successes and shared pride in my accomplishments.

My husband, Mark Aron, and our daughter, Samantha, deserve perhaps the greatest thanks. Samantha has lived with this book for most of her dozen years, and has shown admirable patience with the demands on her mother's time. Moreover, she has given me the enormous pleasure of seeing her grow and flourish during the decade in which this book was written. Mark has offered the most. At a critical juncture in our lives, he altered his career so that I could pursue mine. But most important, he has always been there when I needed him, sustaining me with his humor and love. I could have asked for no better environment in which to work.

Richmond   C.S.A.
November 1986

Contents

Ladies and Gentlemen
of the Civil Service

CHAPTER ONE

Introduction

In 1859 only 1,268 employees worked in the federal government's offices in Washington, D.C.; at the turn of the century that number had mushroomed to more than 25,000 federal workers, nearly 9,000 of whom were clerks. The clerical workers laboring within these executive departments found themselves at the beginning of a major transition not only in the nature of the federal government, but of middle-class work generally. The ladies and gentlemen who worked for the federal civil service between 1860 and 1900 were forming part of the first white-collar bureaucracy in the United States. These were among the pioneering members of what C. Wright Mills would later call the "new middle class."[1]

In 1860, the year this study begins, most middle-class men worked as professionals, petty entrepreneurs, farmers, agents, or clerks within small businesses. The hallmark of nearly all these occupations was the independence they afforded. Farmers worked their own land; professionals managed their own practices; petty entrepreneurs ran their own businesses; and agents usually operated as their own bosses, buying goods from manufacturers or wholesalers and selling them to shopkeepers. Only those men who worked as clerks were actually employees, and these were, for the most part, businessmen in training—young men learning the ropes, aspiring to partnership or hoping to begin businesses of their own.[2]

In the same year, most middle-class women did not engage in any wage-earning occupation at all. The domestic ideology elaborated in the early nineteenth century instructed proper ladies to remain in a separate, domestic sphere and to refrain, unless absolutely necessary, from entering the labor force. Those middle-class women who did have to earn their own living—usually either widows or young, not yet married women—had access to only a few, limited fields of employment. A small number, discovering a lucrative market for their literary skills, made good money writing fiction. Many more women entered the teaching profession, filling the demand for low-paid teachers created by newly opened, tax-supported public schools. But such women usually remained in the classroom for only a few years before marrying and taking up the primary "occupation" of most nineteenth-century middle-class women—marriage to a middle-class man.[3]

Although new to the early nineteenth century, within a few decades after the Civil War this middle class began to undergo an important transformation, precipitated by a change in the nature of middle-class work. By 1900, the year this study ends, increasing numbers of middle-class men and women had moved into a variety of different occupations. In particular, they had joined the growing numbers of salaried, white-collar employees within burgeoning corporate and government bureaucracies. In the early decades of the twentieth century, white-collar employment within such organizations would become a typical and entirely acceptable middle-class pursuit for men and women alike.

This alteration in the nature of middle-class work hinged upon a change in the nature of American business. On the eve of the Civil War, most businesses were still small, family-operated establishments. Owners often knew their customers personally, handled much of the business face-to-face and had no need for lengthy correspondence or complicated record-keeping. Those entrepreneurs who needed clerical assistance could usually manage with one or two clerks—often relatives or young men aspiring to partnership.[4] For example, only four men—one cashier, one accountant, one teller, and one messenger—worked for the Massachusetts National Bank in 1864. Small scale, simple operations continued to characterize much of American business, in fact, through the 1880s. In the last decade of the century, the business affairs of the Pepperell Manufacturing Company, one of the half-dozen largest textile companies in the country, were still conducted by the treasurer and three clerks.[5]

There were a few important exceptions. By midcentury, the railroads were already large, complex business organizations employing thousands of people and requiring staffs of office workers. The Pennsylvania Railroad, for example, established departments of auditors to keep track of costs and expenditures involved in moving passengers and freight over great distances.[6] The vast majority of railroad workers, however, were stationmen, trainmen, shopmen, and trackmen rather than white-collar clerks. In 1880 less than 3 percent of railroad workers—in all 12,000 employees—held white-collar positions.[7] Mass retailing businesses, while much smaller than the railroads, were also beginning to employ increasing numbers of sales and clerical workers. In 1869, A. T. Stewart's retail establishment in New York employed as many as 1,500 people, 350 of whom were clerks. The entire staff of Macy's, however, still averaged only 198 employees in 1870.[8] During the twenty years following the Civil War, most American companies operated more like the Pepperell Manufacturing Company than like the Pennsylvania Railroad or A. T. Stewart. Consequently, the numbers of white-collar clerks in the United States remained small. In 1880 only 0.9 percent of Americans worked in clerical occupations.[9]

In the mid-1880s, however, the face of American business began to change dramatically. The creation of what business historian Alfred Chandler has called "integrated, multidepartmental enterprises," such as Swift, American Tobacco, and Standard Oil, required virtual revolutions in business methods. No longer could the owner and a few trusted clerks run the company. Instead, growing corporations operating within national markets required armies of office workers, managers, and salespeople. As companies like these hired people to fill their offices, more and more middle-class Americans experienced salaried work within white-collar bureaucracies.[10]

The executive departments of the national government were, however, decades ahead of the private sector. As early as 1870, when most American businesses still needed only a handful of clerks, more than 5,800 people—nearly 1,000 of them women—labored in government offices in Washington, D.C., alone. And in the twenty years after 1880 the number of employees in federal offices in the nation's capital increased by more than 300 percent, to over 25,000 workers. (See Table 1.1.) The federal government thus became the first large, sexually integrated, white-collar bureaucracy in America, and the people it employed became the first Americans to experience a new kind of middle-class work.

TABLE 1.1
Number of Male and Female Employees in
the Executive Departments in
Washington, D.C.

Year	Women	Men	Total
1859	0	1,268	1,268
1870	958	4,866	5,824
1880	1,773	6,093	7,866
1893	5,637	11,667	17,304
1903	6,882	18,793	25,675

Sources: U.S., Department of State, *Register of Officers and Agents, Civil Military, and Naval, in the Service of the United States, 1859;* U.S., Census Office, *Statistics of the Population of the United States . . . Compiled from the Original Returns of the Ninth Census (1870),* p. 727; U.S., Census Office, *Statistics on the Population of the United States at the Tenth Census (1880),* p. 816; U.S., Congress, House of Representatives, *Organization of the Executive Departments and Other Government Establishments at the National Capital, and Information Concerning the Persons Employed Therein,* H. Rept. no. 88, 53d Cong., 1st sess., 1893, p. 208; U.S., Department of Commerce and Labor, Bureau of the Census, *The Executive Civil Service of the United States,* Bulletin 12 (1904), p. 9.[11]

This book will study, at close range, the men and women who worked as clerks in the federal government during the last four decades of the nineteenth century. It will examine who these clerks were, why they chose to become federal employees, the nature of the work they performed, the problems they encountered in finding jobs and procuring promotions, and the types of relationships they formed with supervisors and coworkers.

While federal clerks are the subjects of this study, its goal is broader: to describe and explain the important transition in middle-class labor that began as increasing numbers of middle-class men and women assumed positions within an expanding government bureaucracy in the years following the Civil War. An examination of government employment reveals what happened as members of the "old" middle class moved into new occupations as salaried, white-collar employees. Indeed, the federal workplace offers an ideal laboratory in which to study the creation of a modern, middle-class work force. For while certain aspects of government employment were specific to the federal bureaucracy, much that we consider commonplace within our contemporary white-collar work world began as innovations introduced in late nineteenth-century government offices.

The mixing of the sexes within offices, for example, while customary in the twentieth century, represented a bold "experiment" when the Treasury Department first hired female clerks in 1861. At the time such an idea was not only avant-garde, but bordering upon scandalous. Bringing women into government departments challenged some of the most sacred tenets of Victorian, middle-class culture. In 1861 proper middle-class ladies rarely ventured into public male spaces, much less did they work for wages at the same jobs as men. Indeed, nowhere else in nineteenth-century America did large numbers of middle-class men and women labor together. The presence of women in federal departments represented a direct and flagrant violation of the code that kept men and women in separate spheres. More than a few eyebrows were raised.

The government's decision to hire female clerks opened new employment opportunities for women. During the 1880s, private industry, motivated by a pressing need for more clerical services and encouraged by the success of the federal example, began to turn to female labor. Between 1880 and 1900, the number of women employed in clerical occupations grew from 7,000 to more than 187,000. By the turn of the century, women constituted between 25 and 30 percent of the nation's clerical labor force.[12] No longer restricted to teaching school, middle-class women in need of work found another occupation to which they could turn—one that held definite advantages, financial and otherwise, over working in the classroom.

This book will examine why the government decided to employ women and how that decision was implemented. Recent scholarship has linked women's introduction into white-collar jobs to the increasing demand for clerical work generated by an expanding corporate, capitalist economy. These studies have emphasized how the availability of a cheap, female labor force encouraged businessmen to rationalize and mechanize office work, leaving most women clerical workers in routinized, sex-segregated, dead-end jobs.[13] The federal example, however, suggests other possibilities. Women's experience in government offices reveals that many enjoyed highly paid and diversified work. And offices that did rationalize work procedures were not necessarily responding to the influx of women workers, but had in some cases already initiated such changes before the government began to employ female clerks. Feminization, then, did not necessarily lead to rationalization and mechanization. Women's presence, rather, had varying effects upon the organization of work in government departments.

While government employment created a host of opportunities for women, it also posed a host of problems, not only for the new female employees but also for the men with whom they worked. The nature of those problems and the manner in which federal clerks handled them are major concerns of this study. These men and women were middle-class Victorians, used to dealing with members of the opposite sex in domestic or social gatherings. Federal employment required men and women to face each other on the job and treat each other as coworkers. Male and female cultures squared off. Accommodations were made and new rules—both written and unwritten—were established. The men and women who clerked in Washington offices succeeded in creating a neutral zone—a space between the two separate spheres—habitable by both middle-class men and women. Women's entrance into government offices brought middle-class women's influence from the home and the church into the work world and changed the physical, social, and economic complexion of white-collar labor. But in the process the women themselves and the men with whom they worked also began to change. People who characterized themselves as middle-class began to alter their behavior, their attitudes, and their expectations in ways that reflected, in part, the impact of work in a sexually integrated environment.

Sexual integration was the most dramatic, but certainly not the only innovation that middle-class men and women encountered in federal employ. During the Gilded Age the government began to eschew personal, informal, and political methods of management in favor of more rational and bureaucratic administrative techniques. Bureaucratic settings were new to the nineteenth century, and the manner in which government workers adjusted to them is another issue addressed in this work. While much about the operation of the federal government in the nineteenth century remained irrational and idiosyncratic, federal clerks nevertheless found that the nature of the work they performed and their chances for success hinged largely upon their ability to function within and manipulate an environment that was slowly and haphazardly becoming more bureaucratic.

Working within a bureaucracy clearly made different demands than had other types of middle-class labor. Middle-class workers had traditionally been answerable primarily to themselves, whether they managed their own businesses, professions, classrooms, or households. But men and women who worked in an increasingly bureaucratic environment needed to follow directions, obey regulations, and accept the decisions of those above them in the hierarchy. Federal clerks had to learn to behave in ways not heretofore required of most nineteenth-century middle-class workers. Middle-class men responded by taking the traditional, individualistic, and competitive work ethic and tailoring it to the needs of the federal workplace. Middle-class women, new to the competitive world of work, adopted some of what had previously been regarded as "male" behavior and adapted other, traditionally "female" modes of conduct to fit new circumstances. The federal example reveals not only how these men and women accommodated to a new bureaucratically organized work environment, but speaks as well to other important questions—the advantages and disadvantages that bureaucratization held for middle-class workers generally and whether men or women, specifically, benefited as bureaucracy replaced more informal modes of office management.

Why did members of the "old" middle class choose to embark upon this new kind of work? I was able to answer this question by mining detailed, voluminous files kept by the Department of the Interior and the Treasury Department in the late nineteenth century. Although labelled "application files," these records are, in fact, nineteenth-century personnel dossiers. It is difficult to describe a "typical file," since they vary considerably—some incredibly rich and others quite thin. But most contained, at a minimum, a letter from the applicant requesting work. In such letters, job-seekers presented their qualifications for the positions, often furnishing information on their education and former work experience. These letters revealed much about the applicants' backgrounds, frequently discussing family and financial problems as well as the specific situations or crises that brought them into the federal labor market. It was possible to use these documents not only to create a social and demographic profile of would-be government workers, but to discover these men's and women's motivations for entering government employment and their attitudes about this new kind of middle-class work. Most of the files also include letters of recommendation from congressmen, community leaders, or friends of the family. Such letters were sometimes straightforward, even *pro forma*, endorsements, but in other instances imparted much personal information about the applicant.[14]

These records disclose not only the workings of the federal departments, but offer as well an unusually close look at the personal histories of large numbers of middle-class men and women. And what the data make clear is that many members of the old entrepreneurial and professional middle class faced a variety of financial and family crises in late nineteenth-century America—crises severe enough to bring them to the verge of economic disaster. Such men and women looked to the federal government as a means of reestablishing their footing and halting a precipitous slide down the socioeconomic ladder.

For both men and women, however, the decision to enter Washington offices posed a fundamental dilemma: how to square employment as federal clerks with their status as members of the middle class. Men who worked in federal agencies had moved from being self-employed to salaried workers, in the process placing at risk the independence that lay at the core of middle-class male values. The women who worked for the government, on the other hand, assumed a kind of independence that threatened their positions as delicate, middle-class ladies deserving the protection and care of men. These represented more than minor irritants. Indeed, it was critically important to federal workers that they maintain their positions as middle-class ladies and gentlemen. The assumption of government positions thus required more of these men and women than their adjustment to a new type of work, their abilities to manage within bureaucratically organized offices, and their willingness to work in sexually integrated environments. The clerks themselves considered it essential, as well, to make such behavior seem congruent with traditional middle-class values. They found, however, that many of the old norms could not fit the demands of the white-collar world. Left with a void, these government workers responded not only by helping to create a new style of middle-class work, but by beginning to shape new definitions of what it meant to be middle-class in America.

My effort to recreate the white-collar world of these middle-class workers began as a study of the female clerks alone. But it was, I found, impossible to understand the transition in middle-class labor and the emergence of this "new" middle class without considering both women and men together. Ever since Barbara Welter's 1966 article outlining the contours of the cult of true womanhood, historians have seen the nineteenth century as a world bifurcated by gender.[15] Indeed, women's exclusion from much of the public male arena—politics, higher education, most professions—and their dominance of domestic, charitable, and many reform activities meant that, in fact, much of women's and men's lives did take place in separate spaces. Consequently historians attempting to describe and explain the social fabric of nineteenth-century America have, for the most part, examined men and women separately.[16]

Recent studies of clerical work are no exception. Much important scholarship on the history of white-collar labor has concentrated upon how and why women assumed clerical occupations. These are, certainly, critical issues—questions with which this book, as well, will deal. But it is essential to emphasize that women's entrance into white-collar occupations did not result in an immediate exodus of men from the profession. Rather, clerical work remained an occupation in which both men and women engaged for more than half a century. Much can be learned by analyzing clerical work as a sexually integrated occupation.

Indeed, considering both male and female office workers together offers new insights not only into the history of white-collar labor, but a new window on the nineteenth century generally, revealing things about late Victorian America that we could not learn by studying women clerks alone. First, it demonstrates that there were interstices between the separate sexual spheres, and that the white-collar workplace was one of them. Moreover, analyzing how both men and women behaved within this sexually integrated environment suggests much about the strengths and weaknesses of the domestic ideology and about how this important prescriptive code actually figured in the everyday lives of middle-class American men and women. Finally, this vantage point allows us to witness men and women beginning to fashion, within this narrow zone between the two separate spheres, a new kind of middle-class culture—one that, as it expanded, would help create a twentieth-century world less divided by gender.

This book begins by introducing the characters. Chapters Two and Three explore the social and demographic characteristics of male and female clerks and discuss their motivation for entering government work. Chapter Four turns more specifically to these men and women as workers, detailing the nature of their work and attempting to explain the impact of feminization on the work processes. Chapter Five deals with the hiring, firing, and promotion procedures of the federal government, using these as a means of illustrating the slow process of bureaucratization and the ways in which middle-class workers functioned within an increasingly bureaucratic work environment. The last third of the book considers the interpersonal aspects of office life and the kind of work culture that middle-class men and women devised within government departments. Chapter Six discusses competition and conflict among workers, while Chapter Seven turns to more informal matters such as sex, manners, and money-lending in the office.

The story takes place in the nation's capital, and that seems the appropriate place to begin.

PART ONE

Reluctant Pioneers

A prospective federal employee, arriving in Washington, D.C., in 1860 might have been struck by how unimpressive the city was. With a population of only 75,000, Washington, the twelfth largest city in the nation, offered little in the way of grandeur. Congress had begun during the 1850s to appropriate money to spruce up the city's public facade, but much work remained to be done. Construction to enlarge the Capitol building and erect an impressive dome was underway, but still incomplete. Visitors and congressmen alike had to maneuver around huge marble blocks that cluttered the area near the Capitol. The city had abandoned work on the Washington monument five years earlier for lack of money, and what would one day become the famous, towering obelisk remained a stump, blighting rather than improving the landscape.[1]

Washington in 1860 was not only an unimpressive city to look at, but an inconvenient and often unhealthy one in which to live. While some efforts had been made to improve streets and to lay sewers, gravel surfaces still raised clouds of dust or became bogs of mud, depending upon the weather. Pigs wallowed, flies swarmed, and rats multiplied in the streets, while odors from garbage and nearby slaughterhouses wafted through the city. Gas lamps adorned only main thoroughfares, and even these lamps remained dark except on moonless nights. Unlit streets held numerous dangers. The incidence of vandalism, arson, prostitution, robbery, and assault increased every year after 1850.[2]

Four decades later, Washington's population had grown nearly fourfold and the city could command considerably more respect. In 1900, the 278,000 residents enjoyed improved sewer and water services. Not only had more streets been paved, but, as a columnist for the Cleveland *Leader* reported in 1883, they were being swept daily "by a patent twig brush run by horses." The city's appearance had definitely begun to improve. A few statues of public figures dotted the open squares, and the Washington Monument, finally completed in 1885, brought Washington some of the stateliness due a national capital. In 1899, Congress passed a law that would help insure the architectural integrity of the city. The new ordinance limited the height of private buildings, thereby preventing the erection of skyscrapers that "would dwarf public edifices and darken the streets."[3]

Washington may still have seemed a sleepy Southern town compared to bustling commercial and industrial centers like New York and Baltimore, but it could nevertheless boast its share of powerful people and important cultural institutions. On the way to work, government clerks might catch a glimpse of one of the numerous politicians who stayed in Washington for the congressional "season" and returned home during the hot summer months. Federal workers might pass their leisure hours visiting the Corcoran Gallery or the Library of Congress, while those less culturally inclined could take in the political spectacle on Capitol Hill or join the throng that gathered on Saturday afternoons on the White House lawn.[4]

Life in the nation's capital, then, held numerous possibilities for those who ventured into federal employ in Gilded Age America. Men and women who clerked in Washington departments would find novelty, however, not only in the city in which they lived, but in the offices in which they worked. Indeed, here they would encounter a world unlike any other that the nineteenth-century had yet produced.

CHAPTER TWO

The Gentlemen

In 1890, at the age of twenty-nine, Fred Dickerson applied for a clerkship in the U.S. Census Office. Dickerson had spent two years in high school and two years in a Boston business college before becoming a clerk in a small fruit and confectionery business in 1881. Apparently a good worker who earned the trust of his boss, within six years he had been made a junior partner. Thus far, Dickerson's career seemed to fit a classic early nineteenth-century pattern. In antebellum America, where most businesses were small enterprises employing only a few clerks, clerking had been one of the traditional routes to a proprietorship. An employee in such an establishment could reasonably hope to learn the ropes, become a partner, or start a business of his own. But by 1887, when Fred Dickerson was made a junior partner, the chances of advancing along such a path had diminished. The growth of larger corporations doing business in a national market was making it increasingly difficult for small businesses to survive, and the repeated depressions of the Gilded Age were bringing financial ruin to many a small entrepreneur. Indeed, things did not turn out at all as the young Dickerson had hoped, for in 1890 he recounted, "Mr. Brook, the proprietor, or senior member, decided to retire, and rent the store and building which we occupied. Not feeling able to pay the enormous rent exacted, as the business would not warrant it,...I decided on making this change."[1] In moving into the federal labor force, Dickerson was doing more than merely switching jobs. He was exchanging the work of a nineteenth-century middle-class man—a petty entrepreneurship—for the work of a twentieth-century middle-class man—a salaried position within a large white-collar bureaucracy.

Not all the men who entered the government's offices had been aspiring proprietors like Dickerson, but most had come from one or more of the varied occupations that, in nineteenth-century America, defined middle-class work. Professionals, small businessmen, clerks, agents, salesmen, and a smattering of skilled manual laborers all became federal clerks in the four post-Civil War decades. These men served as the cutting edge of a transition in middle-class labor. For while professionals and entre- preneurs continued to fill the ranks of the middle class, by the early twen- tieth century a large and growing proportion of middle-class men would earn their livings as clerks and managers within corporate bureaucracies. The federal government, however, was already employing thousands of clerical employees by the late 1860s.[2]

The middle-class men who filled the ranks of this first, large white-col- lar bureaucracy did so for a variety of reasons. Examination of their back- grounds and motivations suggests much about the trials and problems that middle-class men faced in the Gilded Age. But even more, it indicates that these men were often reluctant pioneers. Indeed, the move to bureaucratic white-collar jobs proved difficult, for it altered the basic structure of middle-class male labor in late nineteenth-century America and challenged men to create new definitions of successful middle-class work.

BEFORE ENTERING GOVERNMENT employment, most would-be male clerks had occupied that amorphous and ill-defined part of the nineteenth-century social landscape called the "middle class." Some had been professionals—primarily lawyers, ministers, or school teachers—be- fore assuming government positions. Others had made their living as merchants, small businessmen, or agents, and in some instances, as jour- nalists or editors. A third group came to the government from other cler- ical jobs—usually with small businesses, banks, or insurance agencies. Only a small minority had formerly been manual laborers, and of these most came from the ranks of the skilled. (See Table 2.1.)

At the midpoint of the nineteenth century, this middle class was, itself, a relatively new social construct. A half-century earlier, when most white American men were still property-owning farmers or artisans, the term "middle class" had little meaning. The vast majority of men who made their living growing or producing what they needed and exchanging within a local market might have been referred to as the "middling sort," sandwiched between the small, elite mercantile community of the coastal cities and a growing but still unthreatening number of dependent poor and day laborers.

During the second quarter of the nineteenth century, changes in the economy began to shape both a working class and a middle class in the United States. The growth of mercantile and industrial capitalism made working-class wage earners out of mechanics and artisans who had once been included within the middling sector of society. These same eco- nomic changes simultaneously encouraged the formation of a middle class. The products generated in factories and workshops required distri- bution within an enlarged domestic market, thereby opening a whole

TABLE 2.1
Prior Occupation of Male Clerks and Applicants

Prior occupations	Year			
	1861	1871	1880	1890
Professionals	40	13	13	18
Semi-professionals, small businessmen, agents	30	13	20	17
Clerical workers	14	26	39	33
Manual laborers	3	2	3	11
Unemployed	11	5	11	5
Farmers	0	0	3	4
Students	0	0	9	13
Connected with army (clerk or soldier)	3	41	2	0
	100%	100%	100%	100%
Number	37	119	175	307

Sources: Computed from sample of Application Files of Treasury Department (Record Group 56) and Interior Department (Record Group 48), National Archives Building, Washington, D.C.[3]

range of new business opportunities for shopkeepers, wholesalers, jobbers, and agents. Seeing a market for their agricultural goods in the growing number of small cities that dotted the new transportation network, farmers who once produced primarily for their own consumption became entrepreneurs. At the same time the population inhabiting these cities created a need for expanded professional and commercial services. The men who filled these various positions became the seedbed of the nineteenth-century middle class.[4]

Only lately have historians begun to examine the formation of this middle class. In a recent essay Stuart Blumin has noted that the existence of a self-conscious, distinct nineteenth-century middle class remains a "hypothesis," not yet recognized or acknowledged by many historians. A long-standing liberal tradition that perceives all Americans as belonging to the same class, political historians who view ethnicity and religion as the major divisions in American society, and Marxists who maintain that there are only two real classes—workers and capitalists—all question whether a middle class existed in nineteenth-century America. Burton Bledstein and others have noted that even the term "middle class" remained an unfamiliar one during much of the nineteenth century, not appearing in the dictionary until 1889.[5] Contemporaries used a variety of other terms—middling sort, middle classes, middling interests—to identify what historians are attempting to define as a middle class. Such problems and skepticism notwithstanding, scholars have lately made convincing attempts to locate an early nineteenth-century middle class—not only as a strata between the rich and the poor, but as a group that shared attitudes, beliefs, and a way of life.

Mary Ryan's study of Oneida County, New York, *The Cradle of the Middle Class*, offers one of the most comprehensive analyses of middle-class formation in early nineteenth-century America. According to Ryan, the middle class emerged not only from changes in the economy of an expanding commercial and early industrial capitalism, but also from specific changes within the family. The patriarchal and community-oriented family of the eighteenth century gave way to a more privatized, Victorian family. These families began to limit their size, therefore offering their children greater financial and educational resources. Within the borders of such households, mothers, increasingly responsible for the nurture of their children, inculcated in sons the values of prudence, honesty, and hard work—values necessary for becoming successful and respectable small businessmen.[6]

Stuart Blumin has devised a more general framework within which historians can begin to study middle-class formation in the early nineteenth century. Taking off from the work of Anthony Giddens, Blumin has suggested that class can be perceived as a "social and cultural reality" and can manifest itself in shared experiences. The expression of class consciousness may even, according to Blumin, be a matter of "secondary importance," especially amongst a group that is "most likely to express awareness of its common attitudes and beliefs as a denial of the significance of class."[7] Historians might, Blumin offers, be well served to hunt for these patterns of shared experience as a means of identifying a coherent group with, at least, a middle-class "awareness" if not yet a fully developed class consciousness. Blumin has identified a variety of experiences—a move to non-manual work, consumption patterns that reveal an interest in comfortable accouterments, participation in voluntary organizations, a tendency to live in what were becoming "visibly middle-class residential milieux," and the development of new family strategies—as some of the important foci around which a middle-class "social and cultural reality" might have coalesced in the nineteenth century.

New attitudes—specifically a desire for self-improvement and self-aggrandizement—seemed both to fuel and result from the new experiences which middle-class people encountered in the decades before the Civil War. Indeed, the middle class emerging in the early nineteenth century quickly developed a reputation for being restless and competitive. Alexis de Tocqueville commented upon the consuming desire for wealth and material possessions that he observed amongst Americans in the 1830s. The American, according to Tocqueville, "clings to this world's goods as if he were certain never to die; and he is so hasty in grasping at all within his reach that one would suppose he was constantly afraid of not living long enough to enjoy them. He clutches everything, he holds nothing fast, but soon loosens his grasp to pursue fresh gratifications."[8] While the poor dreamed of wealth and the rich feared its loss, the "middle classes,"

Tocqueville discovered, displayed the greatest appetite for material possessions. "The passion for physical comforts is essentially a passion of the
middle classes; with those classes it grows and spreads, with them it pre-
ponderates."[9]

Certainly much about this middle class still remains elusive. The problems historians have encountered in identifying the nineteenth-century
middle class may, however, stem not from our attempt to locate what did
not exist, but from our efforts to understand a class that, before it was
barely formed, was already being transformed. The middle class described by Ryan, Blumin, and others emerged from changes within a
commercial and early industrial capitalist economy. Nevertheless, these
changes happened slowly and the process was, by the mid-nineteenth
century, still incomplete. Yet within two decades after the Civil War,
members of this middle class would begin to face a variety of new situations. Thus even before an "old" entrepreneurial and professional middle
class was firmly established in this country, much about its shared "social
and cultural reality" had begun to change. One of the critical areas in
which such change occurred lay in the realm of work. Not only the shift
to non-manual labor, but the move to bureaucratic white-collar employment became a part of the middle-class experience. And, indeed, these
changes may well have been as important in reshaping the middle class
as were those that had initially created it from a world of one-time artisans
and farmers.

It is from this "old" middle class of acquisitive, individualistic professionals, small businessmen, and clerks that the federal government drew
its labor force in the postbellum decades. It seems possible to identify such
men as middle-class for a number of reasons. First, they worked at occupations that, if not necessarily guaranteeing security or wealth, nevertheless relieved them of the burdens of manual or industrial labor.
Moreover, in their applications for government positions, such men displayed characteristics that differentiated them from a working class which
comprised growing numbers of foreign-born laborers. Potential federal
employees revealed that they had mastered the rules of grammar and
spelling, knew the correct conventions of business correspondence, could
write a legible and sometimes even exquisite hand, and, in some instances,
keep financial accounts as well.

The social and demographic characteristics of federal male clerks point
not only to their position within this entrepreneurial and professional
middle class, but also suggest the changes which that class would begin to
undergo in the late decades of the nineteenth century. The former occupations of government workers, for example, underwent a subtle but important shift toward the end of the century. Increasing numbers of government workers came to federal offices from clerical positions rather
than from professional occupations. Indeed, the Washington bureaucracy seemed to be filled by more men from what would, in the twentieth
century, be designated as the lower end of the middle-class spectrum. The

percentage of male federal office workers who had formerly been professionals or small businessmen dropped from 70 percent in 1861 to 35 percent thirty years later. During the same period, the percentage of clerks
seeking federal jobs more than doubled. Limitations of the data make
these findings, by themselves, more suggestive than definitive. Only 30
of the 212 men in the 1861 sample revealed their former occupation.
Moreover, the figures for 1871 are distorted because so many of these
men came to the government directly from the military. Evidence on education of male clerks, however, helps to corroborate the picture suggested
by occupational data. (See Table 2.2.)

Most of the men working in government offices had benefited from
educational advantages that were, in the nineteenth century, not enjoyed
by the growing numbers of working-class people. The great majority of
would-be federal clerks had received—at a minimum—secondary education, and many had attended universities, business schools, or professional schools. Fewer than one-third had attended only public elementary
school. By 1890, however, a smaller proportion of men with college or
university backgrounds entered government offices, while a growing
number of men with public-school education became part of the federal
work force. Like the data on occupation, the information on schooling
indicates both that these men came from middle-class backgrounds and
that the nature of that middle class was, by the end of the nineteenth century, beginning to be transformed.

This changing profile of federal workers reflects important structural
alterations in the American economy—specifically, the growing strength
of the clerical sector of the labor force during the last decades of the century. Between 1880 and 1900, as the expansion of American business
generated a demand for more clerical labor, the number of men working
in clerical occupations expanded from 153,000 to 550,000—an increase

TABLE 2.2
Education of Male Clerks and Applicants

Type of school	Year		
	1871	1880	1890
Common	10	32	31
High school (public)	3	0	14
Private	27	16	14
Normal or business	7	4	15
University or college	50	27	18
Graduate, medical, legal	0	19	4
Military, parochial	3	1	4
	100%	100%	100%
Number	30	81	300

Sources: Computed from sample of Application Files of Treasury Department (Record Group 56) and Interior Department (Record Group 48), National Archives Building, Washington, D.C.[10]

of more than 300 percent. At the same time the male labor force as a whole grew by less than 65 percent.[11] Having already had some clerical experience, these men became candidates for government employment, and by the 1880s represented a little more than one-third of the applicants for federal clerkships.

The declining number of professionals and entrepreneurs and the increasing number of clerical workers within federal offices did not, however, alter the fundamentally middle-class nature of government employment. Indeed, federal clerks throughout the nineteenth century continued to share important characteristics with other members of the middle class. The men who worked in government offices came overwhelmingly, for example, from the ranks of the native-born. Between 88 and 92 percent of these men had been born in the United States, and those who were immigrants had come predominantly from northern or western Europe or Canada. Most federal clerks were even sons of native-born mothers and fathers.[12]

Federal jobs attracted middle-class men of all ages; neither the very young nor the very old predominated. In 1860 as many as 13 percent of male clerks were still teenagers, and in both 1860 and 1870 about one-third were over the age of forty. But over the course of the century, government offices began to include greater numbers of middle-aged men. At least half of the men clerking in government offices during the last twenty years of the century were well into their middle years. (See Table 2.3.)

The aging of the federal labor force resulted not from young men abandoning government employment. The age distribution of male applicants, as distinct from employees, reveals that, in fact, younger men continued to find government work attractive. Approximately one-half of the men applying for work in the Interior Department in 1880 and 1890 were under the age of thirty.[13] It was, rather, the presence of a

TABLE 2.3
Age of Federal Male Clerks

Age	Year			
	1860	1870	1880	1900
Under 20	13	2	2	2
20–29	30	29	16	22
30–39	20	34	32	20
40–49	17	17	28	19
50–59	11	11	13	21
60 or older	9	6	9	17
	100%	100%	100%	100%
Number	710	509	438	626

Sources: Computed from samples drawn from the U.S. manuscript censuses for Washington, D.C., 1860, 1870, 1880, and 1900. For a discussion of sampling methods, see Appendix.

group of clerks who entered the government while still young and remained federal employees for a number of years that explains the increasing percentage of older men within the federal work force over the late years of the century.[14] For a growing number of these middle-class men, clerical jobs apparently were no longer the first step on the road to proprietorships. Those who grew old in government service had, instead, become permanent members of a white-collar work force.

Federal clerks were family men. From 1870 until the end of the century, approximately two-thirds were married. (See Table 2.4.) Only in 1860, when an unusually large percentage of very young men clerked in the government, did single men represent more than half of the male employees in Washington departments. By the 1870s, however, a substantial majority of men in government employment were not only married, but heading their own households as well.[15] A little more than one-quarter of male federal clerks boarded in the households of non-relatives, while a small percentage still lived in the households of their parents.[16] Yet even the boarders were not necessarily free from family obligations, for approximately one-third of such men had other family members living as boarders in the same household. Indeed, the vast majority of male clerks—82 percent in 1880 and 77 percent in 1900—lived with at least one other family member.

For a middle-class man, having a family often meant shouldering the primary burden of that family's support. And in this way federal clerks appeared little different from other men of their class. Indeed, government employment promised salaries that were high enough to allow for only one wage earner in the family. The government pay scale, instituted in 1853, classified all clerks as first-, second-, third-, or fourth-class. First-class clerks earned $1200 per year, with salaries increasing by two-hundred-dollar increments in each of the next three categories. Male clerks began their careers at the bottom of the pay scale, and earned access to higher paid positions through promotions up the ladder.[17]

On these wages, the majority of men working in government offices became sole providers for their families. In 1880 as many as 74 percent of male government clerks supported themselves or their families with

TABLE 2.4
Marital Status of Male Federal Clerks

Marital status	1860	1870	1880	1900
Married	47	66	71	63
Single	53	34	24	31
Widowed	0	0	5	6
	100%	100%	100%	100%
Number	699	502	483	626

Source: Computed from samples of the U.S. manuscript censuses for Washington, D.C., 1860, 1870, 1880, and 1900.

no other assistance. By 1900 more such men were receiving help from other members of the family, for the percentage of men carrying the entire financial burden of the household dropped to 63 percent. (See Table 2.5.)

In a minority of households, wives helped to supplement the family income. Between 1880 and 1900, from 15 to 20 percent of male clerks' wives contributed to the families' coffers—nearly all by taking in boarders.[18] When adult sons lived at home, men turned to them for assistance as well. In 1880, 11 percent of male clerks lived with adult sons, and 56 percent of those sons were employed. Twenty years later, 15 percent of these men lived in households with adult sons, and three-quarters of such sons were employed. Middle-class male clerks were less willing to allow their adult daughters to work outside their homes, yet on occasion even daughters contributed to the family economy. In 1880, 15 percent of the men clerking within federal offices had adult daughters, but only 20 percent of those daughters were employed. Over the next twenty years, however, such men grew more likely to turn to adult daughters for help with household finances. In 1900, 18 percent of male clerks lived with adult daughters, and 31 percent of those women worked for wages.[19] By the end of the century, middle-class male clerks more frequently shared financial responsibilities with other members of their families—even, in a small but growing number of cases, with their adult daughters.

The difficulties of maintaining a middle-class standard of living, even on what were comparatively high government salaries, may have prompted such men to relinquish their traditional position as sole support of the family. The $1200 annual average salary of a federal male clerk constituted a handsome sum in nineteenth-century America, exceeding not only the wages of industrial workers but of most clerks in the private sector as well. Clerical salaries varied sharply in the postbellum decades, and although some private companies could afford to pay their most skilled clerks $1000 or $1200 per year, others paid only half that much. In Detroit, for example, railroad clerks earned only $500 per year, while men who clerked for the city averaged $916.[20]

TABLE 2.5
Household Composition of Families of Male Clerks,
1880 and 1900

Number of wage earners	1880	1900
Male clerk living alone	19	23
Male clerk is sole wage earner in family	55	40
Two wage earners in family	18	22
Three or more wage earners in family	8	14
	100%	100%
Number	483	626

Sources: Computed from samples drawn from the U.S. manuscript censuses for Washington, D.C., 1880 and 1900.

The relatively high salaries they earned did not, however, make federal clerks wealthy. Approximately one-quarter of the men working in Washington offices in 1860 and 1870 had accumulated some real estate, although in most cases these holdings were worth $5000 or less. (See Table 2.6.) A greater proportion of these men (39 to 52 percent) reported owning personal property. Studies of other cities reveal that in their personal wealth, federal workers differed only moderately from clerks elsewhere. Real property holdings of clerks in Washington, D.C., were remarkably similar in 1860 to those of men clerking in Boston, for example. About three-quarters of Boston clerks owned no real property, while one-tenth reported real property worth under $5000, and one-twentieth owned property valued between $5000 and $11,000.[21] At the turn of the century, 16 percent of federal clerks owned their homes free and clear, while another 9 percent owned their residences with mortgages. An almost identical proportion of native white men living in Detroit the same year owned or mortgaged their homes.[22]

These data suggest surprisingly limited resources for people whom we have identified as middle-class. Before drawing firm conclusions, however, it is important to look at these men's wealth and age simultaneously. It takes time, after all, to accumulate property or money, and young men rarely hold the same kind of wealth as those farther along in their careers. And, indeed, the greatest proportion of those government clerks without wealth tended to be young men, under the age of thirty. Moreover, wealth holdings increased with age amongst this population of government workers. (See Table 2.7.) Thus, a considerable majority of the men under thirty—more than two-thirds—held no personal property, while fewer than one-third of the men in their fifties were so poorly situated. Real estate holdings revealed a similar pattern. At least 90 percent of the men in their late teens or early twenties held no real property, but that proportion had dropped to between 57 and 64 percent for men in their fifties.

TABLE 2.6
Percentage of Federal Male Clerks Holding Personal and Real Property,
1860 and 1870

	Real property			Personal property	
Dollars	1860	1870	Dollars	1860	1870
0	79	76	0	61	48
200–5,000	14	18	50–1,000	31	42
5,001–10,000	5	5	1,001–5,000	6	8
10,001 +	2	1	5,001–10,000	1	1
			10,001 +	1	1
	100%	100%		100%	100%
Number	710	503		710	506

Sources: Computed from samples drawn from the U.S. manuscript censuses for Washington, D.C., 1860 and 1870.

TABLE 2.7
Percentage of Male Clerks Who Held No Real or Personal
Property, by Age, 1860 and 1870

Age	Percentage holding no real property		Percentage holding no personal property	
	1860	1870	1860	1870
Under 20	98	92	99	85
20–29	94	90	88	69
30–39	79	76	49	41
40–49	61	65	41	34
50–59	64	57	29	30
60 and older	51	62	28	41

Sources: Computed from samples drawn from the U.S. manuscript censuses for Washington, D.C., 1860 and 1870.

The fact that men who were younger than thirty accounted for one-third of the federal work force during these years partly explains the meager financial holdings of these clerks.

But only partly. There is no ignoring the substantial number of federal clerks who had accumulated few, if any, financial assets or reserves. A number of circumstances might account for their dilemma. Washington was a high-priced city, one that severely taxed the resources of even these well-paid government workers. Monthly expenses for a government clerk with a wife and three children included $30 for rent, $15 for staple groceries, $27 for perishable foods, and $9.50 for wood, coal, and gas.[23] At these prices, the necessities would cost nearly $1000 per year, but considerably more would be required if the family were to pay for clothing, education, doctors' bills, transportation, and entertainment. M.D. Montis, a $1200-per-year clerk in the Treasury Department, requested a raise in 1867, explaining that the cost of living and "high rents" made it, he said, "impossible, with my large family, to make my present salary pay my expenses."[24]

The numerous federal clerks finding themselves in the same position as Mr. Montis used a variety of techniques to solve their financial worries. Many bought on credit and were less than prompt in paying bills. In response, angry creditors—landladies, doctors, merchants, grocers—wrote to federal officials requesting assistance in collecting debts owed them by government clerks. When Tasker Dulany, for example, bought a new suit of clothes from tailor George Keen in 1871, he arranged to pay for it in installments of $10 a month. Six months later the tailor, not yet having received a dollar, wrote to the Treasury Department asking for help in the collection of the debt.[25] James Collins explained in detail why he had not paid an outstanding $80 bill to his former landlady. He could barely, he claimed, maintain his wife and two children on the $75 per month he earned from the Census Office: "[F]or my wife, myself and daughter I pay $50 per month, for my son who I was obliged to send away to school as keeping him here was much more expensive I pay $20 per month including board tuition washing mending etc., and for my family washing I pay $4.00 per month. My daughter attends the parochial school which is taught at the Convent and I don't pay a cent for tuition. These expenses leave me only one dollar per month to clothe four people."[26] Collins and Dulaney earned $900 and $1200 per year, respectively, but men making higher salaries also ran into debt. William Mertz, a $1600-per-year employee in the Treasury Department, owed a former servant $4.50 for half a month's pay, while Oscar Woodward, a $2500-per-year examiner in the Patent Office, owed $21 to a landlady and $27 to the music teacher who gave his wife singing lessons.[27]

Besides buying on credit, male clerks also borrowed money to meet their needs. Indeed, money-lending occurred extensively within federal agencies. Some clerks borrowed casually—and quite regularly—from each other to tide them over until payday. In 1865 the young Lester Frank Ward, then a clerk in the Treasury Department, described his financial troubles in his dairy. He noted that he had to borrow $40 to buy furniture for his house, but still found himself short. "It will be necessary," he wrote, "also to secure more money from someone before the end of the month." During his first summer's work in the government, Ward made a valiant effort to climb out of debt. By late August he was finally able to write, "I shall pay my last debt at the end of this month, and then our salary is all ours." Such was not, however, to be the case. Throughout the next few years Ward continued to borrow money from fellow employees in his office.[28] Other clerks—needing larger sums—turned to professional moneylenders who circulated within the departments offering much-needed cash at usurious rates of interest.[29]

The prevalence of both money-lending and credit-buying suggests that the men who clerked in government offices were having a hard time maintaining a middle-class standard of living on their substantial government salaries. Moreover, the numerous, dunning letters from creditors reveal that male clerks were unwilling to sacrifice amenities, despite their inability to afford them. James Collins did not expect his son to forego an expensive education, Tasker Dulaney got his new suit of clothes, the Mertz family enjoyed the benefits of a domestic servant, and Mrs. Woodward learned to sing. Perhaps nothing speaks so eloquently to the middle-class status of federal clerks as their apparent belief that these were necessities, not amenities. Indeed, these men seemed to subordinate the accumulation of property and savings to the comforts they required in their day-to-day lives. Security—something that we perceive as a critical part of middle-class culture today—may have been less important within the middle-class world of the nineteenth century. And if, as the data presented earlier suggest, more men from the lower ranks of the middle class were beginning to enter federal employment, such men were nevertheless holding fast to the material circumstances that seemed to define middle-class life.

GIVEN THE FINANCIAL PROBLEMS that plagued government workers, why would middle-class men have chosen to apply for federal clerkships? Answering this question requires a closer examination of the lives of federal clerks before they entered Washington offices. We can bring these men into much sharper focus by considering what motivated them to apply for government work. Indeed, it is possible not only to distinguish fairly discrete categories of applicants, but also to suggest that these groups reveal something about the problems, challenges, and changes that middle-class men faced in post-Civil War America.

Businessmen and professionals suffering from declining financial and career prospects composed one group of government workers. These men applied for federal jobs in an effort to combat or at least postpone imminent financial problems. Indeed, the federal government seemed to serve as a safety net for a large number of downwardly mobile middle-class men.

Some such men were victims of the general upheaval brought by the Civil War. John Clark, for example, applied for work in 1862 from his home in Exeter, New Hampshire, explaining, "The war has seriously diminished my business, in fact ruined it."[30] Silas Merchant, "long engaged in manufacturing for the Southern trade" sustained "heavy losses" during the early 1860s. A letter from his wife revealed that her husband's "means and business [have] been lost through the difficulties" which surrounded them.[31] G. W. Williams, applying for a position in 1862, did not attribute his business failures specifically to the war. He simply stated: "I have been engaged in the Union Bank (in Massilon, Ohio) as teller and bookkeeper for 10 years previous to 1859. When I went into the Milling business and got *ground out*."[32]

Some of these men had achieved only marginal successes in their businesses, but others had been men of considerable means. G. W. L. Kiddell's entrance into Washington offices in 1860 resulted from a precipitous decline in family fortune. Both he and his wife had been raised "in easy circumstances," but a "succession of singular misfortunes" had reduced them to being "utterly dependent" on themselves.[33] Garrett Luff had once commanded an "extensive mercantile business," but had suffered financial reverses that brought him into government employment.[34]

Business problems did not, of course, stop plaguing such men when the war ended. Throughout the last three decades of the century, middle-class businessmen facing financial ruin turned to the government as an alternative means of livelihood. William Webster had been employed as a clerk before becoming the proprietor of a small merchandizing firm. The venture lasted two years before folding. Out of work and without other prospects, Webster decided in 1880 to apply for a government po-

sition.[35] Horatio Dorr's problems lay not with his own shortcomings as a
businessman, but with the fault of the companies for which he worked.
Dorr held clerical or bookkeeping positions with nine different establishments—most of them insurance agencies—in the years between 1885 and
1890. Each company failed. Dorr's brother described him as "one of these
unfortunate men, who, without any bad habits, and with a good deal of
ability, especially in clerical work, seems always to ally himself to concerns
which, though seemingly prosperous, shortly after go out of business and
leave him stranded." After this string of bad luck, Dorr decided to try business for himself and formed a partnership with another man in the
photo-engraving business. The result, he explained, did not "prove prof-
itable, [and] I sold out and closed out entirely."[36]

Such men sometimes looked to the government not as a permanent solution to their problems, but as a place where they could retreat for a short
period of time, regroup, and start again. E. Lac Hawkins applied for a
position in the Census Office in 1890 claiming that he wanted a government job because, he said, "I have not been lucky in late years in my transactions and need it again to gain another footing. I want to go forward
again—to go honestly—and it is asked *not* from preference but because
at 49 years old I have nearly lost my capital and *must* work as employee
instead of doing business for self."[37] Similarly George Ransdell had "recently had an unfortunate turn of luck in mining matters" and found
himself "in need of employment to aid him in bridging over a year or
two."[38] Occasionally a man already employed within the government
would leave, strike out on his own, and then attempt to come back when
his business venture failed. George Wellman was one such man. Wellman
had worked in the insurance business for four years before entering the
Census Office in 1890. After two years as a government clerk he resigned
to try to make a go of it in the private sector, but "utterly failed" and within
two months was applying for reinstatement within the department.[39]

Only the solution that these would-be federal employees sought to their
business failures, not the failures themselves, made them atypical. The
much-heralded success myth notwithstanding, small businesses folded
with great frequency in nineteenth-century America. In their study of
Poughkeepsie, New York, Clyde and Sally Griffen found, for example,
that from 30 to 60 percent of business lasted three years or less, and those
that survived were often volatile and insecure—turning a profit one year
and tottering on the edge of bankruptcy the next.[40] Bankruptcy was not
new to late nineteenth-century America, but the economic conditions of
the Gilded Age often aggravated the problems that plagued petty entrepreneurs. The repeated and prolonged depressions during the two decades after 1873 wreaked havoc with small businesses, forcing many to
close. Then, in the late decades of the century, the growth of large, national corporations able to implement cost-cutting and money-saving procedures exacerbated already difficult conditions. Recent research has revealed that in both Poughkeepsie and Boston it was primarily establish-

ments serving a local clientele—groceries, bakeries, and saloons—that survived. Those small businessmen engaged in other ventures such as dry goods, millinery, and small wares frequently found themselves unable to compete and closed their doors.[41] Some regrouped and plunged back into other potentially unsuccessful ventures, but by the end of the century many had begun to assume salaried jobs within government and corporate bureaucracies.[42]

Small entrepreneurs were not the only middle-class men to encounter economic troubles. Professionals as well often found that mere survival, much less success or prosperity, proved difficult in the volatile economy of post-Civil War America. Different professions faced different problems, but lawyers, doctors, school teachers, and ministers, all realizing that their professional status did not necessarily provide protection from financial crises, turned to the federal government for employment

Many a teacher wrote saying that the seasonal nature of his work and the low salaries attached to his position had moved him to seek other employment. Preston Sherrad, for example, applied for a clerkship in the Department of the Interior in 1882. "I am a teacher of twenty years standing, holding a Professional certificate of a high grade," he wrote, "but the unsteady employment and meagre wages incident to the profession have compelled me to abandon it."[43] Even men like Lucien Colliere who ran their own schools found the going rough. The friend writing on Colliere's behalf described the dilemma: "Professor Colliere is without pupils during the summer months; being compelled to keep his house for the fall and winter terms, his rent goes on for the entire year, and, in fact, the rent in summer eats up the profits of the school in the winter."[44] Indeed, in the postbellum decades male teachers like Sherrad and Colliere were facing diminishing opportunities as school districts began to hire large numbers of lower paid female teachers. Between 1870 and 1900 the proportion of male teachers declined from 41 percent to 30 percent. While such men still earned considerably more than their female counterparts, their salaries were by no means grandiose. In the 1860s male principals in St. Louis earned $800, while most of the male teachers in Poughkeepsie—other than those owning their own private academies or teaching at Eastman's business college—made less than $600 per year. Teachers in other locations did better. Average weekly earnings of men teaching in city schools ranged from $35 per week in 1870 to $32 per week in 1900.[45] Many male school teachers, however, caught in the midst of a declining male profession, changed their occupations and entered Washington offices.

Lawyers, plagued by persistent financial troubles, also chose government employment. For some, the Civil War disrupted a once lucrative practice.[46] Others shared the predicament of teachers—seasonal employment. John Murphy, for example, explained that in Trenton, New Jersey, where he lived in 1880, the court was "virtually closed by the absence of the Chancellor, who [was] in Europe...." Consequently, he continued, "I am unemployed a great part of the time."[47] Most, however, simply claimed that it was too difficult to build successful practices. John Clark applied for a government job because the legal business in his small country town had become "trifling in quantity and unremunerative."[48] Charles Wesson, a lawyer who had enjoyed the benefits of a university education, found it difficult even to support his family. He consequently wrote to the Secretary of the Interior from his home in Powhatan, Virginia, in 1890 and asked for a position: "Now I ask you if it is not possible to give me a clerkship? My qualifications are—a graduate of the University of Virginia as well as an education in Europe and I will give you the best vouchers for sobriety and integrity. I find here at my old home [it is] almost impossible to make a living at Law. We are so poor that it makes life very hard for me and my three children."[49]

These men were not anomalies within their profession. For while the legal profession, as a whole, grew and prospered during the late nineteenth century, the changes it underwent brought considerable upheaval to many practitioners. Those men who entered the new and remunerative specialty of corporate law became rich handling the legal problems of developing American businesses. But small-town and country lawyers in Gilded Age America were rarely so fortunate. Confronting competition from new companies specializing in what used to be lawyer's work—debt collection and title searches—attorneys scrambled to expand their practices. According to historian Lawrence Friedman, many a country lawyer only "eked out a bare living at the law." As law schools opened at a rapid rate in the decades after 1860, practitioners who had learned the law by clerking in a small law office saw rivals in a new crop of academically trained lawyers. The small-town lawyers who did become successful often made their fortunes by expanding into other fields—real estate, local business, politics, or government.[50]

It seems clear that in Gilded Age America the ability to achieve professional status offered no guarantee of prosperity or even security. Professionals and businessmen alike faced potential economic problems at numerous times in their lives. If middle-class men were fueled by the idea that they could rise to great heights, they were equally aware of the ever-present possibility of failure. Indeed, the disruptions of the Civil War, the depressions of the postwar decades, and the growth and consolidation of large national corporations brought many a middle-class man to the brink of economic ruin. Employment within the government presented one solution. For these men, federal clerkships were a last resort—one means of staving off disaster.

A SECOND GROUP of government employees saw federal jobs in an entirely different light—as a first rather than a last chance. Many Washington clerks were, in fact, men who perceived the government as a source of great opportunity. Different from those federal clerks who had tried their hand at business or professional life and failed, these were primarily younger men just beginning their careers. Moreover, it was not until the last two decades of the century that the attraction of government work became apparent to young middle-class men on the way up. Most assumed that their stay in government would be short, and they harbored varying plans for how best to reap the benefits of federal employment.

Young men with professional aspirations often saw a few years' stint in the bureaucracy as an ideal way to achieve their goal. Government salaries allowed those men with limited family obligations the financial means necessary to attend medical school or law school. Howard M. Smith, who had already spent two years at Emory College in Georgia and had graduated from Mercer University, wanted to enroll in a regular course of law. In 1880 he applied for a government position because it would allow him to accumulate the necessary funds.[51] Similarly Harry Parker wrote in 1881 explaining why he desired a clerkship in the Interior Department: "I am a young man left wholly upon my own resources and I seek this position that I may obtain the means to fit me for a legal profession."[52]

As important as the money was the opportunity for education that government employment provided. Numerous professional schools operated in the District of Columbia, many of which offered their courses at night. Columbian College, for example, established its law school in the late 1860s with the specific purpose of attracting government clerks who worked during the day and attended classes in the evening.[53] The plan succeeded. Men like Charles Collins applied for work in the government not only because of their general "desire to make honest headway against the world," but also because they wanted to take specific advantage of "the opportunity Washington City affords to attend (at night or leisure times) law lectures."[54] Potential physicians, as well as lawyers, saw the nation's capital as the place to learn their future professions. In 1890, Frederick Okie unsuccessfully sought a job from his home in rural Wyoming. He desired the position "in order to be able to take a course in the evening sessions of the Columbian Medical College."[55] Requests like those from Okie and Collins came to federal offices with increasing frequency during the last two decades of the century, reflecting the response of young men to changing requirements of professional life. Training for law or medicine had in the early nineteenth century been haphazard and informal, often requiring only a short clerkship in a lawyer's office or a few months' apprenticeship with a physician. But during the late nineteenth century, professional men began forming associations, lobbying for licensing requirements, and attempting to keep unqualified men from practicing. In such an environment it was becoming more critical for would-be professionals to obtain certification from the growing number of formal institutions of learning.[56] Many young men hoped to receive the necessary academic training while they clerked in government offices. For the young and ambitious, a short stay within government employment seemed to promise a springboard to the professions.

The existence of both Howard University and the federal bureaucracy in the nation's capital made Washington an attractive place for black men who sought professional status. A few black men did procure clerkships in Washington offices, although they amounted to only a tiny fraction of the government's clerical work force.[57] Some young blacks, already students at Howard, applied for federal jobs when their money ran short. Albert Johnson, a medical student at Howard, wrote in 1890 requesting immediate appointment to the Department of the Interior: "I am forced to ask that something be done *now*. I am in need of means *now* to meet my current expenses in college for the present month."[58] James Wormley had attended a normal school in Massachusetts before beginning to work as a desk clerk in his father's hotel. He desired a government position because his present job required that he work evenings and prevented him from attending medical lectures.[59] While there is no evidence that Johnson ever received the appointment he so desperately needed, Wormley worked as a clerk in the Census Office for three and a half years, in that time winning promotion from a $720- to a $1000-per-year position. The very small number of blacks who achieved federal jobs was testimony to the racism endemic in Washington. The few black men who did, however, manage to obtain government appointments were not, during the nineteenth century, segregated from white coworkers. Not until the Wilson administration did federal officials openly suggest establishing racially segregated offices within the Washington agencies.[60]

Federal jobs provided middle-class men with another chance for career advancement: on-the-job training. Men realized that clerking in the government could afford them skills and knowledge that would smooth the way to professional careers. Would-be patent attorneys or pension lawyers could learn much by working in the Patent Office or the Pension Bureau. Eugene William, an employee in the Census Office in 1882, requested transfer to the Patent Office because he was "anxious to gain a knowledge of the Patent business."[61] Edward Foote Waite took advantage of all the potential career and educational benefits that federal employment proffered. Waite, a graduate of Madison University, earned his law degree from Columbian Law School during three years while he clerked in the Pension Office. His schooling did not, apparently, prevent him from giving his job considerable attention, for during those years he won promotion from a $720-per-year copyist position to the high-status $2000-per-year job of principal examiner. In 1884 he requested transfer to the office of the Assistant Attorney General for the Interior Department. The reason for the transfer was that he wanted, he maintained, "to fit myself as speedily and as thoroughly as possible for the practice of the law in the West, and I believe that the experience which this position would afford, in the adjudication of cases rising under the U.S. Public Land Laws, would be of great value to me." The new position was so important, that he was willing to take the job "even at a considerable sacrifice in salary."[62]

Government work offered more modest prospects for upward mobility to yet another group of federal applicants. Men who applied for positions from clerical jobs with small businesses or local government sought the larger salaries that clerkships in Washington promised. George Shire, for example, had held a variety of clerical positions—in the Central National Bank of New York, in various insurance and real estate offices in Pennsylvania, and, from 1875 to 1879, as bookkeeper in the Scranton office of the General Real Estate Agent of the Delaware and Hudson Canal Company. The salary in this last position, he explained in 1879, was too small and he wanted a federal job in order to "improve [his] condition."[63] William Robinson was nineteen years old when he began to work in 1879 as clerk for a lawyer and claims agent "at the small salary of $3 per week." Robinson had graduated from high school and spent one winter attending medical lectures at a university in the nation's capital by the time he began his clerking career. In less than a year the small firm for which he worked was sold to a larger real estate and claims agency. The new owners apparently liked Robinson, for they kept him on and even raised his salary to $8 per week. Robinson, however, was dissatisfied with his position, despite the new promotion, and he accepted a job in the Census Office at a salary of $50 a month—a handsome increase over his former income. Moreover, within a year he won promotion to a position paying $1000 per year. When the census work ran out near the end of 1881, Robinson applied for a job elsewhere in the Interior Department. There is no evidence that he obtained such a position, but it is clear that Robinson recognized the financial benefits of working in the Washington bureaucracy.[64]

Whether they saw government as a refuge from financial failure or as an avenue for career advancement, many of the applicants for federal jobs had held numerous positions and had moved frequently from one job to another. Some had worked at more than five different places within as many years. George Flint, for example, left his job as manager's assistant with a British engineering firm in 1886 to visit a relative in Ohio. Over the next five years he moved continually from one clerical job to another: "During part of the year 1886 I employed myself as a Stenographer in the Newark [Ohio] Law Courts. Early in 1887 I came to Washington, where I worked as a Stenographer reporting in the Law Courts, Sermons, etc. In the latter part of 1887 I entered the service of Senator Stanford, of California, as Stenographer. In June 1888 I was in the employ of the Southern Pacific Company, in San Francisco, Cal., as Stenographer....In July 1889 I left this employ to visit friends in Washington. In October 1889 I left with the U.S. Eclipse Expedition to West Africa doing secretarial work for the Expedition, which Expedition I left at Cape Town, Africa, the purposes of the Expedition being fulfilled."[65] Behavior like George Flint's was not in the least atypical of middle-class, nineteenth-century men. Not only clerks, but professionals and businessmen as well moved frequently from one position to another, alternately running their own businesses or practices and working in other men's firms. Lawyers took up farming, farmers published country news-papers, doctors tried operating small businesses, ministers became teachers, salesmen moved into clerical jobs, and clerks attempted to ac-quire professional credentials. Only their decision to make one more change and enter government offices distinguished federal employees from other men of their class.[66]

Various explanations account for the peripatetic behavior of would-be government workers. Some changed jobs because they had no choice—the businesses they operated, the professional practices in which they were engaged, or the companies for which they worked had failed. In-deed, the histories of these men are replete with business defeats and per-sonal disappointments. Many men were apparently having enormous dif-ficulty succeeding at what had traditionally been middle-class work—in-dependent proprietorships, professional careers, or upwardly mobile clerkships. It would be simple to dismiss such men as a tiny minority—so-ciety's failures. But set against the backdrop of frequent business failures and upheaval within the professions, their stories suggest a considerable zone of insecurity within the nineteenth-century middle class. Determin-ing the width of that zone is a problem that merits investigation by future historians.

Not all federal applicants had been chased from job to job by failure. Many, dissatisfied with their current situations and salaries, had moved around in search of "improvement." These men appeared more than will-ing to leave positions even when they had no immediate prospect of other work. Joseph C. Calhoun, for example, applied for a clerkship in the Cen-sus Office in 1890 at the age of twenty-four. For the previous four years he had been a clerk in a small New York City business, but he left that job "because of insufficient remuneration." Calhoun then spent a year with-out any regular employment, except for a few month's work as a census enumerator.[67] Similarly, Charles Isham left the Singer Manufacturing Company in 1888 after three years' employment because, he said, "I did not like the business." It took four months of unemployment before he was able to find a place with an insurance company in Minneapolis.[68] Allen Fowler had been vice president and general manager of the Batch-elder Egg Case Company, until the failure of the business led him into a variety of clerical jobs—one with an insurance company, one with an elec-tric utility company, one with the Chicago Board of Trade, and one with the William Deering Harvester Works. Each of these he "left by resigna-tion with the idea of improving [his] income."[69] David O. Floyd held three different positions between 1885 and 1889, moving from a proprietor-ship of a small business to a clerkship in a utility company: "[I] kept a family hotel about three years, was manager of a restaurant in the large store of Houghton and Dutton, nearly a year, until they sold the business, which was the reason I left them....The next six months I was in the West in Washington Territory and Dakota looking for business, but found none satisfactory and returned to Boston in March and engaged with the concern I am at present with, as bookkeeper, the Boston Electric Gas Lighting Company." He found "the pay small," however, and, wishing "to better [his] condition," sought a clerkship in the government.[70] Men like Calhoun and Fowler and Floyd were, on the one hand, unable to make it as petty entrepreneurs or professionals, and, on the other hand, dissatisfied with the jobs available to them—modestly paid clerical positions in a variety of small, private business enterprises.

The career of Carl Stark illustrates the problem most eloquently. Stark had worked at a series of clerical positions—as bookkeeper for a large commission firm in Mississippi, as city collector for a coal company in Indiana, and then as bookkeeper for private banks in Indiana and Illinois. The last position he held for two and a half years until "growing tired of working on salary" he decided to learn photography and go into business for himself. In 1885 he opened a photo gallery in a small city in Kentucky, but, finding it "unprofitable," sold the business and moved to Arkansas. There he "made a Homestead Entry" and opened a "fruit ranch." This last venture apparently also failed to meet his expectations, for in 1890 he applied for and accepted a position in the Census Office.[71] Stark had moved from one clerical position to another, in search no doubt of better opportunity. Then, his unhappiness with "working on salary" impelled him to attempt business for himself. When that business, too, failed, he resorted again to salaried work—this time within the government.

What propelled Carl Stark and others from one position to another was not only the search for higher wages, but the desire for self-employment. Indeed, the letters of these would-be government workers suggest that free-labor ideas—part of late artisanal culture of antebellum America— were still of concern to men who had, by the late decades of the nineteenth century, become part of a middle class. The free-labor ideology had glorified the economic independence of men who controlled their own labor. It was perfectly consonant with free-labor beliefs for a young man to spend a few years in the employ of another until he had earned enough to start his own business or buy his own farm. But a permanent wage earner was considered "almost as unfree as the southern slave."[72]

Such ideas seemed to carry an especially important message to those men within the middle-class. For as increasing numbers of artisans and mechanics were being reduced to wage workers, self-employment was becoming an important part of what defined middle-class work and differentiated it from the labor of the working class. The expression of these free-labor ideas reveals that, even as the worlds of the middle and working class were becoming increasingly distinct, they shared roots within the commercial capitalist culture of antebellum America.

A commitment to free labor and a desire for self-employment did not prevent middle-class men from working for someone else. As long as their jobs were temporary, such men were willing to work as employees in small businesses or professional offices. But these men guarded their autonomy closely. Remaining too long within any one job might have made them feel uncomfortably like permanent employees. The frenetic movement so characteristic of middle-class male employment patterns in the nineteenth century suggests more than economic instability and a perpetual quest for self-aggrandizement. It also may reveal a prevalent fear that long-term attachment to any one job would threaten their autonomy and eclipse the economic independence that lay at the core of nineteenth-century middle-class values.

If middle-class men felt uneasy about remaining too long in the employ of any one small business, they were openly defensive about working within the large federal bureaucracy. Would-be federal office workers repeatedly apologized for seeking government clerkships, implying that to do so was somehow less than admirable. The numerous young men who claimed that they had become government clerks only as a means of acquiring a professional education were telling the truth, but still attempting to justify their decisions. Many other men rationalized their actions by explaining that only the dearth of choices had driven them to Washington. Webster Elmes was typical: "I am compelled from present circumstances to seek a situation in one of the Departments at Washington....In seeking an appointment of this nature I go contrary to my feelings and would much rather stay here in the practice of law and battle it out were no one but myself concerned."[73] Elmes applied for work in 1861, close in time to the era when farmers, professionals, entrepreneurs, and artisans still defined the parameters of middle-class work in America. But even men who became government employees a generation later displayed similar misgivings. A. S. Taylor, applying in 1893, wrote: "I am a young man with no family....I would not ask for work from the Government but I had the misfortune to fail in business and lost all I made in ten years' hard work."[74]

Those federal clerks who had left the government to strike out on their own and who had failed felt especially apologetic about their wishes to be reinstated. Herman Seligson, for example, had worked as a government clerk in the early 1870s, but had resigned to "take an interest in a Music Store in New York." The "great business depression" of that decade forced him to "retire" from this venture, and Seligson was compelled to work as a vocalist in a traveling opera "at low and uncertain salaries." His wife, sick and unable to accompany him, stayed behind in the city running up large doctor bills and sending Seligson deeper into debt. "Notwithstanding all this," he wrote, "I tried to keep out of Government employment," but concern for the health of his wife convinced him once again to become a government clerk.[75]

These extremely defensive attitudes suggest that the men who clerked in government offices in the late nineteenth century considered autonomy and independence as key components of middle-class status. Such men had grown up in a world where free-labor ideas were still prevalent and had witnessed the creation of a wage-earning working-class from self-employed artisans who had once been considered within the middling ranks of society.[76] Federal clerks may well have feared that their turn was next. Middle-class men who clerked in small businesses in late nineteenth-century America could still view such work as a temporary stop along the road to self-employment and economic independence. But positions as federal employees differed markedly in that they no longer offered the traditional route from clerkships to proprietorships. Government clerks realized that their jobs held no potential for marrying the boss's daughter or advancing to partnership. Near the end of the century some of the younger federal workers began to discover in government clerkships new possibilities for upward mobility—primarily education or training for professional careers. But for many federal applicants, entering government offices may well have felt like a permanent move into the ranks of salaried employees.

To be a government clerk smacked of dependence—not only the economic dependence feared by the free-labor advocate, but even physical dependence. Indeed, many of the men who applied for federal clerkships did so, they claimed, only because they were physically unfit to perform other kinds of work. Some suffered from Civil War injuries that prevented them from engaging in strenuous labor. S. S. Stearn, for example, applied for work in 1865, explaining that he had been taken prisoner at Gettysburg during the war and, he wrote, "the hardship of my confinement disabled me from active and laborious duties."[77] The disability that drove Henry Fried to government employment, he said, was a result of his having been kicked off his horse during his wartime tour of duty.[78] John Johnson lost his right arm serving in the war, and became a Treasury Department clerk right after his release from the army in 1865.[79]

Since the government assumed an obligation to hire disabled veterans, it is no surprise that such men would apply for federal jobs. But a number of male applicants claimed non-war-related ailments and disabilities as their excuse or reason for entering Washington offices. Milton Durnall turned to federal clerical work in 1869 when a partial loss of his voice prevented him from pursuing the teaching profession any longer.[80] Arthur Weston had lost his left arm in an accident on his father's farm. When he applied for a government clerkship in 1880 the state senator writing on his behalf explained that the accident "prevented [him] from pursuing any other calling than that of a clerk or other light employment, and but for this fact he would not be an applicant for a position under the government."[81]

A frequent refrain runs through the letters of applicants and their patrons—that clerical work generally was the appropriate calling for men who were physically unable to perform manual labor, and that government clerkships specifically were the best jobs for such men. These jobs were considered what men should do when they were incapable of earning their living the way "real men" should—by the sweat of their brow and the strength of their back. That most such middle-class men never aspired to manual labor did not seem to upset the equation. Thomas J. Staley was perceived as "illy qualified to make a living in the ordinary avocations of life" because he had only one arm, regardless of the education he had received at Ohio Wesleyan University or his professional position as a lawyer.[82] Although the occupations that middle-class men followed required more brain than brawn, the inability to perform manual labor was nevertheless a mark of weakness.

Disabled men often found it painful to admit such weakness, as the words of James Brown poignantly demonstrate. Brown, who applied for work in 1880, explained, "[I was] wounded in the head, by a minie ball, at Atlanta Georgia 1864, which has, and is now troubling me so much that I am unable to perform manual labor of any kind." With more than a note of sadness and resignation he continued, "[I] am forced to give up all ambitious hope, and ask the Government to support me."[83] How much more difficult it might have been, then, for strong, healthy men to apply for government work, thereby risking an identification with the disabled and the dependent. Fear of being tainted by such an association no doubt contributed to these men's seemingly obsessive need to defend their decisions to become federal applicants.

But the stigma attached to government jobs stemmed from more than the association with wage work and physical disability. In the years after 1860 the men who entered federal offices were engaging in labor that was also being performed by women. According to prevailing Victorian wisdom, women were quintessentially dependent. The increasing proportion of women in government offices heightened the connection between federal jobs and weakness, contributing to the unease with which middle-class men assumed these positions.[84]

The popular literature of the late nineteenth century made explicit what the defensive attitudes of male clerks often only implied. Where in antebellum America clerking was usually regarded as a good place for an upwardly mobile man to get his start, by the postwar years writers were advising men to stay away from clerical jobs—especially clerkships in the government.[85] In 1873, James McCabe wrote a book which purported to reveal what occurred *Behind the Scenes in Washington*. In it, he warned potential male clerks that their salaries would be small and their tenure uncertain. A government employee faced "at least twenty rivals constantly working against him, each one hoping to have him discharged and be appointed in his stead." Even worse, according to McCabe, was a clerk's subordinate—and virtually powerless—position within the bureaucracy. "He has no independence while in office, no true manhood. If his opinions differ from those of the Chief of his bureau or department, he dare not express them, for his Chief tolerates no such liberty on the part of his subordinates. He must openly avow his implicit faith in all his superiors, on pain of dismissal, and must cringe and fawn upon them...."[86] Writers and journalists pictured the men working in government offices as feebleminded and emasculated, as well as sycophantic. Mary Clemmer Ames, for example, commented upon the "weak-limbed and wizened" men who spent their days behind desks in the Treasury Department.[87]

Government employment was also deemed unsuitable for men because it inhibited the entrepreneurial spirit. Harriet Earhart Monroe's book, *Washington, Its Sights and Insights*, decried the "hundreds of fine young men, well educated" who willingly sought government clerkships when they should "be in the manufacturing business of our country." Men who received government salaries, rather than trying to earn their fortunes, were considered too unambitious or lazy to engage in the important struggles.[88]

In the view of most members of the late nineteenth-century middle class, enterprising and successful men did not take jobs in the federal government. Rather they followed the kind of path that Frederick Chase pursued upon his graduation from Dartmouth College in 1860. The young Chase moved to Tennessee where, in the words of his uncle, he "expected to follow the stereotyped series by which many a Yankee boy has risen to honor and usefulness among men, viz. first, teaching, and saving his wages, then the study of law and its practice." Chase, like many others, found his plans upset by events outside his control. A Northerner by birth and sentiment, he refused to remain in the South. Chase was, however, still eager to become a lawyer, and he sought a clerkship in Washington where he hoped to save enough money to open a successful legal practice. Since Chase's father was dead, a friend of the family wrote to Secretary of the Treasury Salmon Chase requesting a clerkship for Frederick. The sponsor made it clear, however, that he only endorsed the application on the grounds that the young man's foray into clerical employment would be a temporary one: "[I]f young Chase had any idea of permanent occupation at Washington, I should not want him to succeed, for I recollect very well your telling me what your uncle Dudley Chase told you under similar circumstances, and I believe that to make a bookkeeper or government clerk out of a bright young man, except for some temporary purpose, is to waste half his brains."[89] Frederick Chase's patron apparently knew Secretary of Treasury Salmon Chase well enough to realize that they shared a disdain for men who chose clerical positions for their permanent careers. This disapproving attitude persisted throughout the Gilded Age. In 1889, when Winfield S. Gardner, a thirty-four-year-old bookkeeper, applied for a job in the Interior Department, he asked a prominent man in his town to write a letter to the Secretary of the Interior on his behalf. George Crumb obliged, writing that he knew of "no more deserving or promising young man in Southeast Missouri." Crumb continued, however, "I sincerely regret to see him apply for a clerkship for he is fitted to take a higher position with a brighter future."[90]

By the early years of the twentieth century the disdain had turned to a lament, one directed not only at government clerks but at middle-class male clerks generally and even at society at large. In 1904, Henry Stimson wrote an article for the *Atlantic Monthly* in which he mourned the passing of one-time small businessmen into the ranks of clerical employees. Stimson recalled that when A. T. Stewart opened his large dry-goods store in New York, it "soon became known...that when any failure occurred in the dry-goods district, the principal man in the broken firm would be quickly invited by Mr. Stewart to enter his employ." Before long, it was possible to recognize a change in the numerous one-time businessmen who now worked as Stewart's employees: "They no longer had either the responsibilities or the dignity of their former position....They were no longer businessmen in the old sense. They were servants, in that their powers were obedient to the decisions of another...." Since that time, Stimson continued, corporations with large staffs of clerical employees had "unquestionably" become "the necessity of the hour." While accepting the benefits that the new corporations bestowed, Stimson still felt it necessary to recognize their limitations: "Among them all none is more serious than this radical one of the effect upon the character of many employees who, under former conditions, would have been either managing their own businesses or ambitious for the opportunity of doing so." Stimson recognized that the men laboring in large corporations may very well lead more stable and even more affluent lives, but he wondered what would "take the place of the old discipline, with its insistent demand for those traits of character which have made the merchant and the manufacturer the sturdy, thoughtful, self-respecting men they always have been." Eventually, he warned, the system might bring its own demise, for men trained only as clerks could never acquire the "character and intellectual stamina which are necessary in the management of the great corporations."[91] While Stimson offered no solution to the problem, his words reveal the influence of somewhat altered free-labor ideas. Rather than addressing artisans and craftsmen who had sunk to industrial wage workers, he instead directed his concerns toward middle-class men who faced a loss of autonomy as they moved into permanent, salaried positions within white-collar bureaucracies.

The irony is that despite all the bad press, the men who entered this new white-collar world could have found much to recommend it. The vast majority of the men in government offices, for example, earned at least $1200 per year, despite a decline in male salaries near the end of the century.[92] At a minimum, most government clerks could be assured of a regular monthly paycheck—something not necessarily true for many small businessmen, professionals, or even clerks working in marginal enterprises. The regularity of their incomes allowed such men not only to plan their lives accordingly, but to obtain credit, borrow money, and purchase items that enhanced their standard of living. Government work also promised some job stability. While civil service regulations did not, in the nineteenth century, protect government workers from arbitrary dismissal, large numbers of federal employees remained within Washington offices for decades—thereby achieving the security that eluded many of their professional or entrepreneurial counterparts.[93] It is possible, of course, that in applying for government positions these men had decided to exchange autonomy for security. But if such was the case, they were less than proud of their choice. Indeed, the work histories of these men—the peripatetic movement from one job to another, the apparent willingness to leave a position before obtaining employment elsewhere, and the defensive posture of federal applicants—suggests that nineteenth-century middle-class men valued economic independence above security or stability. Federal clerks may, however, have slowly come to view the benefits of security as consolation for the loss of autonomy that they experienced upon becoming government employees.[94]

Nineteenth-century federal clerks—some of the first middle-class men to work in a large white-collar bureaucracy—seemed caught in an increasingly untenable position. In post-Civil War America the rightful work for middle-class men was still perceived to be independent work—labor that allowed men to be the "architects of their own fortunes."[95] A man could fit this mold if he remained self-employed as a professional, small businessman, jobber, agent, or farmer—or if his work still at least theoretically held the potential for autonomy, as did that of the clerk working his way up to partnership within a small business. But the men who followed the middle-class prescription and went out on their own as businessmen or professionals often met with financial failure. Those who chose a different path—what they hoped would be temporary employment within another man's firm—were dissatisfied not only by the income derived from their jobs but by the whole notion of "working on salary." Government workers were trapped between an ethic that encouraged them to make it as independent, autonomous professionals and entrepreneurs and an economic reality that required them to take their place within an increasingly white-collar world.

They moved into that world reluctantly. Indeed, these men's stories suggest the substantial psychological sacrifice required of middle-class men as they assumed federal positions. Becoming government employees seemed, to many, to signal an eclipse of independence and the surrendering of "all ambitious hope." The peculiar nature of the federal bureaucracy no doubt fostered some of this despair. The requirements of the patronage system, for example, exaggerated the dependence and deference that federal applicants and employees were required to demonstrate.[96] But employment within any bureaucracy would raise similar problems for men who cherished their autonomy. Bureaucratic labor required a middle-class man not only to subordinate himself but to ingratiate himself to his boss, to curb his desire for independence, and to work as a team player rather than as a rugged individual. In the twentieth century the kind of work that middle-class men would increasingly come to do would demand a different ethic, one that defined success in terms of security, income, and the ability to inch up a bureaucratic ladder. But this first generation of salaried white-collar workers continued to cling to the old definitions of middle-class labor as they ventured defensively into what would become the work world of the twentieth-century middle class.

CHAPTER THREE

The Ladies

Josephine Waller, a member of "one of the first and leading families of Pennsylvania," entered the government's clerical labor force in 1890. She had been born in 1861 and, as the daughter of a prominent Philadelphia physician, had received her education in a female seminary. Waller completed school at the age of eighteen, but some time thereafter the death of her father radically altered her family's economic status and forced Josephine to earn her own living. Waller turned to the primary occupation available to women of her class—teaching. She taught first in a girl's academy in Georgia and then traveled to Rhode Island to work as a governess. Apparently dissatisfied with these positions, she decided to try a different kind of work, and in 1890 became a $720-per-year clerk in the Census Office in Washington, D.C. Four years later, still a Census Office employee, she married a Mr. Grogan, but requested permission to retain her job. Two U.S. Senators intervened on her behalf, explaining: "[The] health of her husband on account of his having been buried alive in the wreck of Ford's Theater...has been rendered so precarious as to preclude his continuance in office life but a short while." Moreover, they noted, the new Mrs. Grogan still supported her sister and they felt therefore "that [her] salary...is, under the circumstances, much needed." Mrs. Grogan only held the job for a few months after her marriage, claiming ill health as the reason for her resignation.[1]

Josephine Waller Grogan in many ways represented a "typical" nineteenth-century female federal clerk. Her social origins resembled those of many of her coworkers—women from respectable middle-class families that had fallen into some kind of financial trouble. Prompted primarily by economic necessity, Waller and thousands of other nineteenth-century women turned to the federal bureaucracy for their livelihood.

The knowledge that women like Josephine Waller typified the government's female labor force offers a new source of insight into the role of middle-class women in the nineteenth century. Over the last twenty years, historians who have dealt with Victorian middle-class women have been concerned largely with domesticity, religion, and reform, but almost never with work. Scholars have noted how, in the early nineteenth century, the wives and daughters of an emerging middle class were released from much of the productive labor that had characterized women's work in the past. While working-class and immigrant women continued to contribute to the family economy by taking in boarders or by working outside the home as domestic servants or factory operatives, native-born middle-class women were filling their time with other concerns—nurturing and educating their children, infusing moral and civic virtue into their homes and communities, and strengthening religion within their churches. Wage-earning labor, however, was clearly a part of the public male sphere, something that was becoming increasingly foreign to the world of the middle-class lady. The domestic ideology expounded in the early nineteenth century did its best to remove middle-class women from the locus of economic activity and to exclude them from the wage-earning world.[2]

Indeed, by midcentury the presence of leisured women within the household had become a benchmark of middle-class status.[3] Translated into everyday life, leisure often meant not necessarily the absence of work, but the absence of wage-earning work. Many a "leisured" middle-class woman in nineteenth-century America worked long and hard at domestic chores within her home—despite the availability of some primitive labor-saving devices and the ability of some families to afford a servant. But other than perhaps a few years spent as a school teacher in the years between her own schooling and marriage, a middle-class woman expected to be relieved of the necessity of entering the labor force.

An examination of the social origins of women who entered government employment reveals, however, the variety of circumstances under which middle-class women became critical to the economic survival of their families. In the four decades after the Civil War, thousands of middle-class families called upon their daughters and wives and mothers to assume roles as wage earners. But there were precious few places in Gilded Age America where the wages paid to a woman could support a middle-class life-style. When the government began to hire female clerks, middle-class women—recognizing the economic potential—flocked to fill the positions. These women became government employees not only to support themselves, but frequently to help shoulder the financial burdens of their families as well.

The pioneering women who clerked in Washington offices shared a place with their male coworkers on the cutting edge of the transition in middle-class labor. For just as male federal workers had begun to create salaried, bureaucratic labor as an option for middle-class men, female federal workers were doing the same for women. The transition, of course, was different for the two sexes. For men it involved a change from self-employment to salaried work. But for women, it required first, justifying the employment of middle-class women at all and, second, opening a new, hitherto male field to members of the female sex. The white-collar work of the new middle class would be different not only because it was salaried, but because it was sexually integrated, as well.

Like their male counterparts, potential female clerks approached government employment with considerable reluctance. The specific fears and hesitations of women differed from those of men, but both realized that the assumption of government positions threatened to set them apart from other members of their class. The women who clerked in government offices devised their own rationales and defenses and used them to push forward, however hesitantly, into the emerging white-collar work world.

IN THE LAST HALF of the nineteenth century, most women who worked for wages in the United States came from working-class or immigrant families, and the kinds of work in which they primarily engaged were domestic service or industrial labor.[4] In contrast, the women who clerked in federal offices were predominantly members of native-born white American families.[5] Their parents had been born in this country and had achieved respectable middle-class status. Daughters, widows, and occasionally even wives of doctors, lawyers, ministers, and other government clerks formed the government's female clerical labor force. The great majority of these women's fathers worked either as professionals, white-collar workers, small businessmen, or federal clerks. Less than one-fifth of their fathers labored at manual jobs, and of these nearly all were skilled craftsmen such as carpenters, stonecutters, or engravers. (See Table 3.1.) Some of these women came from influential, established, or at one time very wealthy families: the granddaughter of Francis Scott Key, the widow of one of Washington's former mayors, and daughters or widows of one-time senators, congressmen, and generals all applied for jobs during these decades. Others came from less illustrious yet still decidedly middle-class backgrounds.

In the years after 1880, the social origins of women seeking federal positions changed somewhat. (See Table 3.1.) A declining percentage of women from professional or business families and an increasing percentage of women whose fathers labored at salaried clerical or administrative positions within the government applied for federal clerkships. The growing proportion of women from the lower edge of the middle class mirrored changes in the social origins of male government employees. Government offices began to attract not only more male members of the new white-collar middle class, but their daughters as well.

The presence of the federal bureaucracy and the absence of heavy industry may have made Washington a city with a large number of white-

TABLE 3.1
Occupation of Fathers of Women Applicants for Federal Jobs

Father's occupation	Year			
	1862/63	1870	1880	1890
Professional	40	50	32	22
Semi-professional; small businessman	10	21	14	5
Clerical (non-govt.)	0	7	6	1
Government clerk	30	21	29	15
Government job (unspecified)	0	0	0	51
Manual laborer	10	0	18	3
Farmer	10	0	1	2
	100%	100%	100%	100%
Number	10	14	111	144

Source: Computed from sample of Application Files of Treasury and Interior Departments and U.S. manuscript census for Washington, D.C., 1880.[6]

collar workers, but the special occupational structure of the city does not entirely explain the social-class background of the women who entered government offices. Forty-three percent of the women who joined the government's clerical work force in the late nineteenth century lived elsewhere than Washington prior to accepting government jobs. This was true throughout the post-Civil War decades as women came to the nation's capital to work as clerks. While one in every five had previously lived in neighboring states of Maryland, New York, Pennsylvania, and Virginia, all other regions of the country—New England, the South, the Midwest, and the Far West—contributed women to the government's clerical labor force.[7]

By nineteenth-century standards female clerks had received uncommonly long educations, most having enjoyed the advantage of secondary schooling. Only 6 percent had left school before reaching the age of sixteen; 81 percent remained in school until some time between the ages of sixteen and nineteen; and an impressive 13 percent continued their education into their twenties. By comparison, published census statistics on school attendance for the year 1890 reveal that only 42 percent of native white teenagers, ages fifteen to nineteen, were attending school. Moreover, about one-quarter of the women applying for government positions had spent some time in a private school, usually a seminary or female academy.[8] These statistics indicate that the women who worked in the Washington bureaucracy came from families that at one time had been able to forgo the wages of their female children and in some instances to pay for their daughters' private education as well. But, typical of the education of most nineteenth-century women, this schooling was directed toward the accomplishments rather than toward rigorous academic or career goals. So it is no surprise that Ellen Page, a thirty-year-old widow of an eminent physician, would explain that although she had been well educated, it was, she said, "not…with a view of supporting myself." Consequently, she noted, "[I have] no training for any special work."[9]

While women from all age groups worked in the Washington departments, female federal employees tended to be considerably younger than their male coworkers. (See Table 3.2.) In 1880, when about one-quarter of the women in government offices were over the age of forty, half of the men fell in this age bracket. The federal government continued to employ more older men than older women throughout the post-Civil War decades, although the gap had narrowed somewhat by the end of the century.

But these women were not, by any means, all youngsters. In fact, what is most striking about the age distribution of female federal clerks is how old they were compared to women workers generally and to female clerks in other cities and situations. The overwhelming proportion of female wage earners in late nineteenth-century America were young women. Published census statistics reveal that between 49 and 55 percent of women workers were under the age of twenty-five, while even greater proportions of young women filled the ranks of clerical employees in the United States. (See Table 3.3.) By comparison, the percentage of women under the age of 25 clerking in government offices ranged from 35 percent in 1870 to 13 percent in 1900. (See Table 3.4.) By 1900 more than half of the women in Washington offices were thirty-five or older, while only 12 percent of other women clerks and about one-quarter of women workers were from this age bracket. The presence of so many older female government clerks suggests that such women were not working to fill a short hiatus between school and marriage, a pattern that historians have recognized in many nineteenth-century working women.[10] The fi-

TABLE 3.2
Age of Federal Female and Male Clerks

	Year					
	Women			Men		
Age	1870	1880	1900	1870	1880	1900
Under 20	10	2	1	2	2	2
20–29	49	35	27	29	16	22
30–39	25	36	28	34	32	20
40–49	13	19	21	17	28	19
50–59	2	6	16	11	13	21
60+	2	1	7	6	9	17
	100%	100%	100%	100%	100%	100%
Number	303	488	624	509	438	626

Sources: Computed from samples drawn from the U.S. manuscript censuses for Washington, D.C., 1870, 1880, and 1900.

TABLE 3.3
Age Distribution of All Women Non-Agricultural
Workers and of Women Clerks in the United States,
1890 and 1900

| | 1890 | | 1900 | |
Age	Women clerks	All women workers	Women clerks	All women workers
10–14	2	4	3	6
15–24	67	51	57	43
25–34	23	22	27	24
35 +	9	23	12	26
	100%	100%	100%	100%
Number	82,205	3,219,225	177,311	4,333,987

Sources: U.S., Census Office, *Report on Population of the Eleventh Census (1890)*, pt. 2, p. 372; U.S., Department of Commerce and Labor, Bureau of the Census, *Occupations of the Twelfth Census (1900)*, pp. 16-17.[11]

nancial and family problems that prompted thousands of women to seek government positions could occur at any time during a life cycle.

Traditionally, school teaching had been the occupation to which middle-class women in need of economic assistance had turned, but numerous genteel yet impoverished middle-class ladies found the profession wanting in several respects. Teaching positions frequently promised only seasonal employment and inadequate pay.[12] Sallie Shane, an applicant for a federal position in 1881, explained: "Having been favored with a liberal Education, a graduate of Patapsco Female Institute, I sought a place as a teacher but the salary is small, and often the teachers are without employment as is my case at this time."[13] Josephine Placide tried to procure a clerkship in 1886 and claimed similar reasons for approaching the government: "It is only lately that I have had to battle with the world, and I am not fitted for all kinds of employment....Teaching and music which are my principal resources are very difficult to obtain and when obtained pay such miserable prices that it is almost starvation."[14]

Women expressed dissatisfaction not only with the low salaries of teachers, but with the job itself. Numerous applicants for federal jobs— refugees from the teaching profession—held that their experiences as school teachers had left them physically or emotionally exhausted. Sue Jones spent several years "leading a laborious life teaching in public schools" in rural Virginia, but found that "such close confinement continued so long brought on delicate health."[15] Amelia Rowland hailed her 1881 appointment to the Pension Office because it released her "from the trying duties of a teacher's life."[16]

Discontented with both their incomes and their lives as school teachers, yet needing to earn their livings, these women began to search for alternatives—only to discover the dearth of opportunities. Lizzie Bachelder, a resident of Georgia, explained the problem that she and other Southern women faced in the late 1860s. Bachelder's father had lost his fortune

TABLE 3.4
Age Distribution of Women Federal Clerks
1870, 1880, and 1900

Ages	1870	1880	1900
Under 25	35	20	13
25–34	39	37	31
35+	26	43	56
	100%	100%	100%
Number	303	488	624

Sources: Computed from samples drawn from the U.S. manuscript censuses for Washington, D.C., for 1870, 1880, and 1900.

during the war and she, along with two unmarried sisters, now bore the responsibility for supporting themselves, their mother, and two widowed sisters. The three unmarried sisters all tried to procure jobs but found, Bachelder wrote, "[A]las in our war-smitten and impoverished South, the demand for work exceeds the supply, then too here in the country there are so few avenues open to [a] woman, only teaching and sewing, whereby she can make a living."[17]

The problem of limited opportunities for female employment was restricted neither to the South nor to the immediate postwar years. In 1880, Lillie Stratton applied for a job in the Census Office from her home in Elizabeth, New Jersey, and expressed despair at the lack of employment prospects: "If you only knew what it is to watch and wait, week after week, and month after month, for the arrival of the mail, hoping it would bring to you the good news that a place had been given you where you could earn an honest living, [especially] if you were a woman to whom so few avenues for so doing were open...."[18] Anger and resentment occasionally accompanied the note of desperation in these women's letters. Prospective female clerks began to discover, in the words of one of them, "how it hurts a girl to be a two-legged stool, as far as usefulness goes."[19] The difficult and disheartening experience of seeking employment may have forced such women to a rude realization that the traditional domestic ideology was an unrealistic ideal to guide the material conditions of their lives.

Government employment, with its relatively high pay scale, offered a potential solution to the financial problems of these women's families. The middle-class women who became federal clerks did so because they and their families needed the wages they could earn. What constituted need, however, varied greatly, ranging from procuring food and shelter to securing the middle-class status of parents, siblings, or children.

When necessary, middle-class families called upon their daughters, sisters, wives, and even mothers to become federal workers. Not surprisingly, however, the majority—usually as many as two-thirds—of women working in government clerkships were single.[20] Most often single women entered the federal labor force when their fathers died, fell ill, or lost their jobs. Many of their fathers had provided comfortable middle-class lives, but had never accumulated enough money to guarantee financial security in the event of their own death or illness. Typical was Ellen Neale who applied for a job in the Interior Department in 1890, one month after the death of her father. She was nineteen years old at the time and explained: "I am the daughter of the late Judge Neale of Virginia and at his death...I was left the sole support of a helpless, invalid mother and invalid sister, with two little sisters and little brothers to support and educate. Being a large family we lived up to my Father's income during his life, so that we are left with absolutely nothing, excepting the heritage of his noble name and memory."[21] Hattie Towne's father had held a position as a clerk in the Pension Office for ten years, but because of the "long sickness of his wife before her death, and his own long ill health, he was not able to save any money even for his own burial." Consequently, when he died in 1890, his eldest daughter, age twenty-three, immediately entered the Census Office so that she could support her three younger sisters.[22]

Even in families where the male breadwinner had earned a considerable income and had bequeathed a comfortable estate, unforeseen economic reversals could leave the women in penury. The Civil War precipitated many such sudden financial problems. Cordelia Emmons, who became a clerk in the Treasury Department in 1865, described her family's unfortunate situation: "I have been, during the last four years, reduced from ease and comfort to destitution. I am a Marylander by birth, but have spent half my life in the city of Philadelphia. There my father died, but from time to time before his death he invested his means advantageously [in] the South. From a part of this I received my maintenance, but with the breaking out of the war my income ceased and it is very doubtful if I ever again [will] derive any benefit from it."[23] Her father dead, and with no male wage earners in her family, the sudden loss of her income propelled Emmons into government employ where she remained for more than ten years.

The presence of a healthy father did not, however, in all cases guarantee the leisure status of a middle-class daughter. A small minority of women—about 10 percent—clerked in the government although they resided with able and healthy fathers.[24] In the early post-Civil War years such women were more likely to be daughters of manual laborers, but by 1880 a majority of their fathers worked in white-collar, professional, or business occupations. Many of these men held jobs which placed them on the lower edge of the middle class: positions as clerks or bookkeepers drawing salaries insufficient to support families adequately in high-cost Washington. (See Table 3.5.) The small numbers within each category of Table 3.5 clearly show that these nineteenth-century middle-class fathers only rarely turned to daughters for financial assistance. Nevertheless, such cases merit consideration for the variety of situations they encom-

TABLE 3.5
Father's Occupation of Female Clerks Who Are Living with Fathers

	Year		
Father's occupation	1870	1880	1900
Professional	4	17	8
Semi-professional, self-employed, small businessman	8	17	19
Clerical	23	23	24
Manual	65	29	35
Farmer	0	2	0
Unemployed	0	13	9
Unspecified govt. or military job	0	0	4
	100%	100%	100%
Number	26	48	86

Sources: Computed from samples drawn from the U.S. manuscript censuses for Washington, D.C., 1870, 1880, and 1900.

passed. Middle-class families seemed increasingly willing to meet a wide range of financial problems—not only the direst economic crises—by sending their daughters into the government's clerical work force.

A father who lost his job or his money in an unlucky business venture could cause his family severe distress and force the women within the family to take on heavy financial responsibilities. Such was the case in the Rhea family when sixteen-year-old Lillie, the eldest of six children, asked for a job. Her father, a bookkeeper by profession, had worked as a clerk in the Census Office. At the present, however, he was "undecided as to his future," and his family lacked the money "to purchase daily necessaries."[25] The Robinson family faced a similar problem and looked to a similar solution, as Laura Robinson explained in her 1881 letter of application: "A few years ago I enjoyed all the luxuries of an elegant home, but commercial disaster, which as you know has ruined so many men, compels me now to seek assistance from strangers."[26] Laura Robinson and Lillie Rhea were offering a daughter's perspective on the kind of financial problems that numerous male federal clerks had described. Not only did these crises drive many a middle-class man to seek his own position in the government, under certain circumstances they also impelled female members of middle-class families to apply for federal clerkships. Such situations reveal the precarious financial status of many middle-class, nineteenth-century families—comfortable and successful one year, reduced to poverty the next.

Some middle-class fathers were willing to rely upon daughters not only as a last resort but as a supplement to the family income. Women like Mamie Sandidge, for example, entered government offices in order to contribute to the support and education of younger brothers and sisters. Sandidge began clerking in 1890 while her father also worked in the government. She did so in order to help her parents "rear and educate" her siblings.[27] Indeed, in families like these, it was frequently the labor of a daughter that allowed the family to maintain its respectable social and economic standing or even to improve its status. The income from a daughter's salary sometimes permitted the family to purchase property or accumulate savings. When Maggie Loftus faced possible loss of her $720-per-year job in the Census Office, she wrote explaining why she needed to retain her clerkship: "My father was a Union soldier having served his country faithfully in the late war, and we have but recently purchased a little home, and if I am deprived of my position this we must lose...."[28] Maggie's salary allowed the Loftus family the added security and status of property ownership.

More comfortably placed middle-class men also, upon occasion, relied upon the wage-earning capabilities of the women in their families. Some women whose fathers held better paid or more prestigious jobs claimed they needed government positions to help extricate the family from a crisis. Ada Collins's father, an editor of the *Washington Evening Star*, wrote to the Superintendent of the Census in 1880 asking employment for his daughter to relieve him "from a temporary but uncomfortable financial squeeze."[29] Similarly, twenty-year-old Mary McKee, daughter of the Assistant Librarian of the U.S. Senate, applied for work in 1889. An influential friend, intervening on her behalf, noted, "[her father] is now financially embarrassed...and desires to get a position for his Daughter in your Bureau. He only desires a place for a short time for her...."[30] Mary McKee worked in the Census Office for four years to help her father overcome his financial "embarrassment."

The presence of an adult brother did not necessarily mean that a middle-class woman would be freed of family obligations. For in some cases it was the daughter who assumed financial responsibilities so that a brother might attend college or professional school. Gertrude Bourne, for example, described her family's situation in 1890:

> I am twenty years of age and am anxious to earn something for my support and to assist my family. My father was recently a sergeant in the 2nd Rhode Island regiment and has recently obtained employment at the Springfield armory. He has a large family to support—there are nine of us—and the pay he receives barely provides the necessaries of life. I also have a brother in the War Department but he is over twenty-one years of age and is studying law, so the principal help he can give us at present is in relieving my father of the cost of his support; and I am anxious to be employed in Washington so as to be near him and do what I can do to help educate my brothers and sisters.[31]

While Marion Porter's father held a more clearly defined middle-class position, she found herself in a similar situation. In 1885, at the age of eighteen, Porter graduated from a private seminary in Washington, D.C. Her father worked in the Adjutant General's Office, but in early 1889 he allegedly suffered a severe mental breakdown and deserted his wife and four children, leaving them nearly destitute. That summer the young Marion began to work for the government. Her seventeen-year-old brother, however, "continued studying for the University, friends having secured him a scholarship and...are supporting him." The other daughters remained "absolutely without support save from Miss Marion's salary."[32] The labor of unmarried daughters not only supported the family, but offered the promise of intergenerational upward mobility.

The death of a wage-earning husband, like the loss of a father, created severe crises for middle-class women, and often reduced them from comfortable situations to immediate penury. During the post-Civil War decades, widows comprised between 13 and 28 percent of the women who applied for clerical jobs in government offices.[33] Mrs. William Pemberton's distress, although more eloquently expressed than most, was typical:

> I, like many others, although surrounded by poverty and its blasting effects, was neither born nor reared in poverty, nor was my early married life seared by such a curse. I never knew want or never had a wish ungratified....I have sacrificed piece after piece of furniture (which was very dear to me from association) to pay rent and to buy bread. Now to day finds me even worse off. I have neither money, coal or wood, and nothing to eat but mush without meat or butter, what is left for me to do. I will not beg, I cannot steal, I cannot depend on what the world calls friends for help, they might for a while aid me, but how soon would they too grow weary. I never until now thought there was an excuse for women to barter their souls for gold, it is such an hour as this when the strongest become weak, make one fearful leap, accepting the present, postponing the future. What is sadder than widowhood.[34]

Mrs. Pemberton's words reveal more than her sorry financial state. They also show pride in her late husband's ability to provide and humiliation at having to "sacrifice" her worldly goods. But even more, they indicate the extreme despair such a woman felt at having been reduced to the status of a wage earner.

The hope of anchoring their families within the middle class moved less desperate widows to become government clerks, just as it had pushed young single women into the work force. Many widows recognized that maintaining the status of the family required that they try at all costs to keep their children in school. Amanda Doty, for instance, worked in the Census Office in 1881, but lost her job within the year. In 1882 she asked to be reinstated, saying, "I have been waiting for more than a year for a position....I have been dependent on the charity of friends since my husband's death three years ago. I have three children to educate and provide for." Without employment, she noted, she could not purchase the necessary Latin and Greek books for her son to prepare for Princeton.[35] Similarly, Fannie Dorsey explained in 1880 that her husband had died recently, leaving her with two dependent daughters. "The wish nearest my heart," she wrote, "is to give them a finished education, and I could in no way better secure its accomplishment, than by obtaining a position under the government."[36] These widows held fast to their middle-class values and tried valiantly to maintain their families' social status.

Federal clerical jobs also attracted married women, although it is difficult, if not impossible, to determine their numbers with much certainty.

Apparently, some women lied about their marital status. Long-held social norms questioning the propriety of married women's employment, as well as departmental nepotism restrictions, prompted many wives to apply for jobs as single women. Rumors in the Patent Office in the mid-1870s hinted that many of the allegedly unmarried women workers were wives of clerks in the same office. Mrs. Whittlesey, the wife of clerk R. H. Whittlesey, had accepted her $900-per-year job under the name of Miss E. M. Fisk. The official who investigated the scandal reported: "Mr. Whittlesey says that his wife signs this name although it is the name of her sister. He also says that it was placed on the roll at the suggestion of the Commissioner [of Patents] who thought it would be better to appear by that name than to have it appear that two in the same family were drawing pay from the office."[37] Anonymous letters sent to Treasury Department officials in the late 1860s and 1870s suggest that this practice was not limited to the Patent Office.[38] Since there is no way to know how many women lied, the data on marital status are inexact: married female clerks represented a minimum of 4 percent and perhaps as many as 18 percent of the women applying for clerical jobs in any one year during the Gilded Age.[39] Like the daughters of employed or able-bodied fathers, these married working women suggest that middle-class families were devising alternate means of meeting economic responsibilities—schemes that relied upon the wage-earning capabilities of female family members.

Married women who desired government clerkships encountered problems that did not so significantly affect their unmarried coworkers. Although all women faced prohibitions against entering the public sphere, married women who relinquished their domestic roles received special condemnation. An anonymous accuser enumerated these charges against Mrs. Swan, an employee in the Treasury Department in the mid-1870s: "1st. Her husband is in the Navy Department and is competent to care for her family. 2nd. She has an infant at home about one year old which requires the care of a mother. 3. Her husband owns the property which they occupy at present. 4. Children four in number growing up without the care of either parent during the day. 5. All the cares of her house including the washing and ironing etc. are imposed on her husband's mother an old lady 65 years old. 6. She holds the place in the Office against her husband's will."[40] One wonders whether the over-worked mother-in-law penned this anonymous note, hoping thereby to get some domestic help from her errant daughter-in-law. Regardless of the author, the letter reveals some of the obstacles that married middle-class women faced as they attempted to move into the federal workplace.

Married women workers were more frequently indicted for depriving widows, orphans, and male breadwinners of jobs. This was the complaint against Mollie Greene: "The fact that one Wm. B. Greene...is a clerk at $1800 per year in the Pension Office and his wife Mollie Greene...is a clerk in the Bureau of Education at $900 per year, we are of the opinion that when the government gives employment to the head of a family we are justifiable in asking for the removal of Mollie Greene, wife of Wm. B.

Greene."[41] Competition for jobs in Washington added economic justification and intensity to the widespread moral and social sanctions against the employment of married women.[42]

In the mid-1870s various federal departments responded to such complaints by prohibiting the employment of more than one member of a family. The government did not, however, specifically exclude married women from its work force. Instead the judgment, or whim, of a particular department head or bureau chief determined whether or not a married woman could be hired. In many offices married women were the first to lose their jobs in the event of a reduction of the work force, and single women often found their positions in jeopardy if they married. The Third Auditor of the Treasury Department wrote to the Secretary of the Treasury in 1877, reporting that Emma Fuller, a high-paid $1600-per-year clerk in his office, had married a clerk in the Patent Office. Moreover, he continued, "being further advised that it is not Miss Fuller's intention to resign, I have the honor to recommend her removal." Under threat of dismissal, Fuller quit her job a few days later.[43] But not all officials were so eager to fire married women, and some wives continued to work after marriage. Widow E. A. McPheeters feared in 1868 that if she remarried she would lose her job, but when she explained to Treasurer Francis Spinner that her future husband could not afford to educate her son, she said, "[he] advised me to marry and promised that my name should be changed on the payroll and my place secured."[44] Throughout this period the government's ambiguous policy, rather than outright prohibition, added to job-hunting difficulties for married women.[45]

Married women may have faced unique problems, but their motivations for working usually paralleled those of single women and widows. Financial crises within the family compelled many of them to exchange their domestic roles for positions within the clerical labor force. Most married women who entered government offices did so when their husbands suffered illness or unemployment. For example, Nellie Grant was twenty-seven years old when she began to work in the Census Office in the summer of 1890. She lost her job in a reduction of the work force ten months later and within a year applied for reinstatement on the following grounds: "My husband is in Ill health having consumption and heart disease and is not able to work...but little....[As] a wife it is my duty to help him which compels me to seek work to help support us."[46] A husband's business reversals or chronic unemployment could also precipitate a wife's entrance into the labor force. In a few cases couples initially came to Washington to seek work for the husband but found job opportunities for the wife instead. Other women had worked for the government before marriage and reentered federal employment when their husbands fell ill or lost their jobs.

Even so, acute financial stress does not entirely account for the presence of married women in clerical jobs. The relationship between work and marriage appears to have been complex, with a variety of situations inducing married women to work. In a few cases the ultimate financial success of a middle-class man rested on the ability of his wife to succeed as a government worker. Sometimes the wife assumed responsibility for supporting the family during those lean years while her husband was establishing himself within a profession. Mary Whitehead, for example, had worked in the General Land Office for ten years when, in 1892, she married an attorney. She argued that although now married, she could not afford to lose her $1000-per-year job because her husband, she wrote, "is laboring to build up a practice that we hope will, in time, enable me to resign my position."[47]

In one unusual case a woman used the expertise gained in her government position, as well as her income, to assist her husband. In 1879, Carrie Hopkins entered the Patent Office because her husband, a lawyer, had fallen ill and was unable to support their two children. Mrs. Hopkins proved a skillful clerk and within six years had advanced to a $1200-per-year position. Soon thereafter she began to campaign for another raise, claiming that she performed more work than other $1200-per-year clerks. In 1887, Mr. Hopkins wrote to his wife's supervisor explaining that he was recovering from his illness and starting a patent law business. His wife had, for the last year, been studying a regular course of law so that she could soon leave her government job and help him in his new office. In the meantime, however, Mr. Hopkins requested that Mrs. Hopkins be transferred to the examiner's rooms where she could learn more about the practical workings of the patent business. The records don't reveal if Carrie Hopkins obtained the position she sought, but she remained in the Patent Office for another five years before resigning in 1892.[48]

Some married women worked in government offices not only to help husbands or children, but to provide financial assistance to parents, siblings, or more distant relatives. Marriage did not necessarily relieve middle-class women of the economic burden of their families of origin. Mrs. M. A. Naylor, dismissed in 1868 from a $900-per-year job in the Register's Office, petitioned for reappointment. She contended that she needed the position although her husband was currently working in the Pension Office: "[My] mother and five children are left without support since the death of my father in 1867 [and] look to us for assistance. My salary since entering the department has been exclusively devoted to them, by my discharge their support is cut off."[49] Emma Whelply worked in the Treasury Department for more than nine years while her husband also clerked in the Pension Office. She explained, "I applied for the position in order to provide for my [widowed] Sister and her children and my entire salary has been applied to their support—being their only legitimate means."[50]

A man was not necessarily more likely to assume his future wife's personal debts than to undertake her family's support. Financial obligations incurred while still single kept a few women in the labor force after they had married. Kate Wing, daughter of a judge, had worked in the Treasury Department for eight years when she married a Mr. Hunter in 1891.

Before her marriage she notified officials that she needed to retain her position in order to pay off certain debts. Although informed she could stay on, she did not learn until after the wedding that her salary would be reduced from $900 to $720 and that her job would be changed from copyist to the less desirable position of paper-counter. A Senator intervened on her behalf explaining that "[if] she had not been told she would retain her place, she would have *postponed* her marriage till she could have paid off her debts—which were caused by the long and severe sickness of her sister."[51]

Other married women entered federal offices with an entirely different motivation: to gain sufficient financial independence to separate permanently from their husbands. The $900 annual average salary paid to female clerks, while still below what most male clerks earned, allowed a thrifty woman to live respectably, if not luxuriously. To women trapped in unhappy marriages, federal employ held out the possibility of self-support and the option of separation or divorce. Twenty-four-year-old Charlotte Cross, for example, applied in 1866 for a job in the Treasury Department. Her husband had joined the army in 1863 and she had spent the war years teaching school in Buffalo, New York. When he returned at the end of the war, she found that he had changed: "Warm-hearted, social and easily influenced he proved too susceptible to the temptations and many allurements of camp life, and like many of our brave and noble soldiers yielded to the demon intemperance, rendering him unfit for work, for society, and too soon unworthy of a wife's care, forgiveness, or endurance." She decided to leave "home, friends, position, and occupation" to rid herself of him: "I have become fully convinced that while I live with him I shall have him to support, and this I can never think my duty. I should feel unworthy the name of woman to support a husband who is able and capable to support himself and wife, and shall never do so, even though I should come to beggary, no never." Cross journeyed to Washington where she began a fifteen-year stint as a government clerk.[52]

The arrangements made by these numerous families were still, no doubt, unusual in late nineteenth-century America, for only a minority of middle-class men encouraged or even allowed their wives and daughters to enter the labor force. The daughters who contributed to the support of younger siblings, the wives who helped to establish their husbands in business, and the women who tried to earn enough to separate from unsuitable husbands all seem, however, to be typical of more modern middle-class women. The families that chose these options suggest how the increasing availability of respectable employment for women began to alter middle-class people's approach to economic problems. These families—especially those within the new white-collar class—were taking advantage of expanding clerical opportunities to restructure the household economy so that women shared a greater proportion of the financial responsibilities.

An examination of the manuscript census confirms the picture presented in these women's letters. The composition of the households in which female clerks lived reveals that most such women were not entering government offices to achieve autonomy and independence or to escape from the demands or watchful eyes of parents or relatives. (See Table 3.6.) While female clerks were more likely than their male counterparts to be living without other members of their families, two-thirds of female clerks still resided with at least one other relative. Those who lived alone were presumably responsible for their own support, while those living with other family members were making substantial economic contributions to their households. Approximately half of female clerks had no other family members present with whom they could share economic burdens, while at least two-thirds of male clerks were in similar situations. That fewer middle-class women than men singlehandedly assumed financial family responsibilities does not, however, diminish the importance of these women's economic roles.

The critical economic function female government employees performed suggests that our understanding of the workings of the middle-class family requires some re-examination. Much recent scholarship has focused upon the collective orientation of working-class families, stressing the necessity of each family member's contribution to the economic survival of all. Different immigrant and ethnic groups devised variants of the "family economy" that fit their cultural and financial needs. Many Italian families, for example, refused to allow their daughters out to work without close supervision by another family member, while Irish families frequently sent their daughters into domestic service or factory work. Children of French-Canadian and Irish immigrant families labored long hours in textile mills so that their mothers could remain at home, while black women worked for wages so that their children could stay in school.[53] Compared to this wealth of material on working-class families in the Gilded Age, we know relatively little about the workings of the middle-class family. Historians have assumed that middle-class families operated in a more individualistic mode—father holding the entire responsibility for the family's support, mother nurturing offspring and caring for the home, and children in school. The middle-class people who labored in government offices, however, often devised other arrangements. They tapped the wage-earning potential of women in the family—adult daughters, wives, and widowed mothers—in order to meet a variety of financial needs. Often adults within these families would share the economic burdens by passing a single government job from one member to another. It was common for a woman to resign her position in favor of her sister, brother, adult daughter, or mother. Such families did, however, make every effort to keep their children in school—even when threatened with severe financial crises. In relieving children of economic responsibilities, government workers revealed their commitment to the kind of individual quest for mobility and advancement so characteristic of middle-class values. Nevertheless, these same families realized that in order to achieve those ends they had to seek a collective solution to the stresses of the late nineteenth century.

TABLE 3.6
Household Composition of Families of Female and Male Clerks, 1880 and 1900

	Female clerks		Male clerks	
Number of wage earners	1880	1900	1880	1900
Clerk living alone	36	33	19	23
Clerk is sole wage earner in family	22	16	55	40
Two wage earners in family	28	30	18	22
Three or more wage earners in family	14	22	8	14
	100%	100%	100%	100%
Number	488	623	483	626

Sources: Computed from samples drawn from the U.S. manuscript censuses for Washington, D.C., 1880 and 1900.

IF ECONOMIC NECESSITY drove middle-class women into the government's labor force, the decision to become federal clerks was nevertheless a difficult one. Just as middle-class men had felt defensive about their foray into government, so too did middle-class women approach these positions with trepidation. For both sexes, the assumption of government clerkships meant behaving in ways that contradicted the accepted standards of middle-class behavior. Men, we saw, felt that they would be surrendering the autonomy and independence that was a central feature of middle-class male work. Women had even more to fear. The simple act of becoming a wage earner was enough to question a woman's standing within the middle class. But these pioneering female clerks were doing more than simply entering the labor force; they were assuming a male occupation within the public male sphere. Such women were products of a social class and culture that restricted women's activity primarily to the domestic realm, and for the most part they had tried to conform to society's standards. While it is impossible to know how ardently each woman had accepted and internalized the ideology of separate sexual spheres, female clerks undoubtedly understood that entering federal offices meant violating long-held, dominant social norms. At the time when women began to clerk in government offices, applying for a "man's" job constituted at best an unconventional, and at worst a revolutionary act. Indeed, women who chose to become federal employees might well have felt that they were jeopardizing not only their class status, but their gender identity as well.

Female applicants for government positions used various means of dealing with the apparent contradiction between their need for lucrative jobs and society's expectation that they would remain within the domestic sphere. While these women's actions bespoke an unorthodox entry into the public male world, their words attempted to construct an image of themselves as proper nineteenth-century ladies. Potential female clerks often took great pains in their letters of application to display the requisite passivity, reserve, and helplessness demanded of well-bred, nineteenth-century ladies. For example, lest officials misinterpret her actions, Anna S. Parsons assured them that she had "always shrunk from bringing [her]self before the public needlessly."[54] Miss M. L. Burroughs described the painful process of making application for a federal clerkship: "If you only knew how long I've been trying for a position, without success, and still persevering, I am sure you would through pity and compassion help me—It is so embarrassing (at least I find it so) for a girl to be compelled to seek employment alone. I sometimes wish that my eyes could close in silent death."[55]

These extravagantly emotional statements, echoing the dominant nineteenth-century concept of "true womanhood," may have reflected such women's genuine feelings, or they may have been means of compensating for an unconventional, and by definition unwomanly, entry into the public arena. Alternatively, applicants might, with good reason, have felt that a shy, helpless woman stood a better chance of obtaining a job than a coarse, aggressive one. In fact, all of these interpretations are probably valid. Women undoubtedly knew what characteristics were most likely to win them jobs, and also were genuinely concerned that they maintain their status and reputations as proper, middle-class ladies.

In accommodating to their new positions as government workers, female clerks neither entirely rejected nor completely embraced the ideology that dictated women's separate sphere. Although such women altered their behavior, moving out of the domestic realm and into federal offices, they nevertheless attempted to fit such actions within the confines of proper domestic activities. Many struggled to minimize the contradiction between their roles as respectable middle-class wives, daughters, and mothers and their roles as government clerks by presenting clerical work as an extension of their domestic responsibilities: they worked to help their families. Belle Edelin claimed selfless devotion to family as her excuse for stepping outside women's sphere when she wrote: "I long for the quiet shelter of my home life, but I feel glad to think I can put aside self to be helpful to my dear ones."[56] Ann Sheffey explained that her widowed sister required assistance in caring for an invalid daughter and, she said, "[I]t is *chiefly* for the comfort of my Niece that I wish to obtain some considerable addition to our narrow income."[57] In so doing Sheffey performed the role of the traditional maiden aunt—living with and helping a married or widowed sister, and sometimes contributing to the family income by teaching school. In another sense, however, Sheffey had seriously modified and transformed that role: in order to fulfill her responsibilities as a maiden aunt, she needed to step outside the female arena and enter government service. Hannah Meade's position ostensibly violated the strongest tenet of the domestic ideology—that which confined married women to their homes. Meade, a married Treasury Department employee, worked in order to help support the family while her husband built up his business practice. Yet she offered reasons for her apparently deviant behavior that most members of society would have applauded. "I

see no [other] way," she explained, "to keep my little family together
under the same roof, and if the choice were given me to-day I would
sooner die than see our little home broken up."[58]

Such frequent expressions of familial and financial need, like the over-
blown rhetoric that filled their letters, suggest various motivations. First,
most women did require the income to support themselves and their
families, and their statements reflected the objective reality of their situations. Second, applicants understood that the government's policy favored needy women—especially those who had lost male breadwinners
in the war—and they hoped that their protestations of need would help
win them jobs.[59] Third, and perhaps less consciously, such women sought
some means for making their behavior fit within the boundaries of accepted, nineteenth-century female activities. They tried to stretch the
domestic ideology as far as possible by claiming that the problems of their
families justified even so bold an action as entering government offices.
But by pushing the domestic ideology to its limits, they were exposing
one of its major contradictions: it was becoming increasingly difficult
even for some middle-class women to care for their families without entering the public sphere.[60]

In becoming government clerks these women had placed themselves in
an ambiguous position. The very act of entering the paid labor force—
especially in a previously male occupation—threatened to invalidate a
woman's claim to middle-class status, for proper ladies only worked for
wages within a few circumscribed and often poorly paid endeavors. At
the same time, the wages such women earned as government clerks were
often all that allowed them and their families to maintain anything like a
middle-class life-style. Indeed, at an average salary of $900 per year, the
women employed in Washington departments were not only some of the
best-paid women in nineteenth-century America, but commanded
salaries equal to or better than many middle-class men.[61] In order to secure their economic position within the middle class, female clerks found
it necessary to jeopardize their social status as middle-class ladies.

Faced with this dilemma, the women who worked in government offices tried to alter the standards of what constituted suitable middle-class
female behavior. They attempted to use the language of domesticity to
carve out a new role for middle-class women—one that would allow them
to enter a previously all-male occupation without feeling that they had
forsaken their position as "true women." So, amid a flurry of verbal
apologies and protestations, these middle-class women took on simultaneously the burdens of supporting themselves and their families, and
the risks that such burdens imposed.

By the last decade of the century, a small number of female clerks appeared somewhat less conflicted about their decisions to enter Washington offices and more willing to accept and prepare for new, more public roles within the wage-earning world. While the purple prose and emphasis on economic problems never disappear from the letters of female

applicants, women who applied for work in 1890 more often argued their competence and offered assurances of their abilities than did the pioneering female clerks of a generation earlier. Part of this shift can be attributed to the increasing bureaucratization of the government itself. The hundreds of women who applied for jobs in the Census Office in 1890, for example, were required to fill out detailed forms that specified qualifications for the job. As the federal government grew, its hiring practices became more bureaucratic and less personal, and job seekers had to alter their applications accordingly.[62]

But more had changed than the bureaucratization of federal procedures since the first women entered government departments. The clerical needs of expanding American businesses had, in the decade after 1880, increased the number of clerical women in this country tenfold, until by 1890 more than 77,000 women worked in offices.[63] A lady clerk was no longer the oddity in 1890 that she had been a generation or even a decade earlier. The tone and content of letters from female federal applicants revealed that some of these women had begun to become acquainted with the ways of the business world.

Expanding educational opportunities partly explain the new, more confident tone manifested in women's letters during the last decade of the century. In the years after 1880, private commercial and business schools—recognizing the growing corporate demand for women clerks—saw potential profits in a large female market and began to open their doors to women. In 1890, 23,000 women attended private business schools, and by the turn of the century, public secondary schools were adding commercial courses to their curricula.[64] Women applying for government jobs during the last decade of the century often claimed certification from such courses, or in other instances explained that they had rented typewriters, practiced at home, and gained expertise. Julia O'Connor, for example, attended parochial school until the age of sixteen, and four years later applied for work in the Census Office. Although she had never held a clerical position, she asserted, "I have had three hours of dictation in Shorthand and the same in Typewriting for the past four months." She felt herself "fully capable of mastering both...arts."[65] By 1890 many female applicants had already clerked in either government or private offices, and pointed to their work experience as ample qualification for federal positions. No such opportunities, for either business education or work experience, had existed for the first female clerks of the 1860s and 1870s.

Near the end of the century, more women mentioned that they had expected to spend a portion of their adult lives as wage earners and had consequently prepared themselves for such eventualities. A few applicants even expressed the desire for upward career mobility as their motivation for entering government employment. Carrie King, for example, worked as a law clerk and stenographer in a large Michigan law office and in 1890 applied for work in the government. Her current employer

explained that King sought a federal job in order to obtain "more responsibility and correspondingly better pay" than she could find in Michigan.
King worked in the Census Office for eighteen months before applying
for work in one of the permanent bureaus. She declined the first job offered her in the Patent Office because, she explained, "I have specially
fitted myself for stenographic work and prefer that to type-writing alone,
particularly at the salary [$720 per year] above named." At the time, work
within the Census Office was nearing completion and most clerks, both
male and female, were scrambling for any job they could grab within one
of the permanent offices. King, however, waited until she was offered a
position she wanted—a $900 place within the Office of Indian Affairs.
She held the place until her resignation in 1896, by which time she had
earned promotion to $1200.[66] Lizzie Shannon's 1893 letter of application
made no attempt to hide either her motivations or her credentials. She
described herself as "well and strong," and honestly admitted, "I do not
plead poverty, but ambition." She wanted the job because, she explained,
"I am tired of being dependent." Such straightforward attitudes did not,
however, prevent Shannon from reminding the Secretary of the Interior:
"You are a Southern man, show your Southern chivalry by making your
1st appointment—a lady."[67]

Those women who were prepared to enter the government's work
force and were confident of their abilities remained, in the nineteenth
century, the exceptions. Most women seeking federal employment still
approached the public sphere with great hesitation. Throughout the last
decades of the century, a defensive tone continued to pervade the letters
of women clerks, suggesting the ambivalence and trepidation with which
they embarked upon this new undertaking. Women like Carrie King and
Lizzie Shannon nevertheless represented a critically important minority,
for they presaged the attitudes of a future generation of women who
would, as a matter of course, turn to white-collar jobs.

MOST OF THE WOMEN who became federal clerks in the late nineteenth
century did so when unforeseen problems created economic need within
their families. The upheaval of the Civil War followed by decades of repeated depressions brought respectable, comfortable, and even established families to the brink of economic disaster and pushed thousands
of middle-class women to look for wage-earning labor. For other women
"need" took on a different meaning. Educating children or siblings or allowing the family to accrue savings or purchase property were all needs
that more and more middle-class women felt called upon to meet. Despite
the prohibitions against women's entry into the public sphere, large numbers of middle-class women responded immediately when opportunities
for lucrative employment opened in Washington, D.C. Indeed, once
white-collar jobs became available to women, middle-class families
seemed increasingly willing to alter their financial arrangements accord-

ingly, allowing female family members to take on more economic responsibility.

The men who worked in Washington offices came from similar social backgrounds, and many had suffered from similar economic crises. A large number of male clerks entered government employment in an effort to stop what appeared to be a calamitous decline. Professionals whose practices proved unprofitable, small businessmen facing bankruptcy, and clerks whose employers were going under all turned to the government for employment. Other men, however, looked to federal jobs as a means of upward mobility—a way of acquiring professional education in one of Washington's universities, professional expertise within one of the government's agencies, or higher salaries than their current positions allowed.

The men and women who worked in Washington departments in the late nineteenth century were marking out new turf for middle-class workers. Yet it seems clear that entering government offices proved a difficult step for male and female applicants alike, and that both sexes took that step with reluctance. Prospective female clerks made great efforts to cloak their actions in the rhetoric of domesticity, attempting thereby to protect their status as middle-class ladies even while they ventured beyond women's sphere. Male clerks attempted to rationalize their desire for salaried work by citing extreme financial hardship, physical disability, or the professional aspirations that they hoped such positions would allow them to realize. Amidst the apologies and the rhetoric, however, these men and women began to create new work roles for middle-class people. Henceforth proper and respectable middle-class ladies would have access to the public male world of the office, and middle-class men would begin to contemplate careers as salaried workers within large white-collar bureaucracies.

PART TWO

A Developing Bureaucracy

CHAPTER FOUR

Feminization, Rationalization, Mechanization

Over the last four decades of the nineteenth century the federal government introduced a variety of innovations in personnel, technology, and work routines into its Washington departments. Women, office machines, and new, more rationalized methods of work organization became, during these years, an integral part of the federal workplace. By the end of the nineteenth century, growing corporations within the private sector would begin to follow similar paths. While the federal bureaucracy cannot be construed as a microcosm of all bureaucracies, it nevertheless reveals, at close range, the emergence of a new kind of middle-class work in late nineteenth-century America. Examining the evolution of federal employment during the Gilded Age, specifically the varying nature of both men's and women's work within government offices, allows us to analyze both the causes and the consequences of these important changes in middle-class work. How such changes affected the everyday work lives of male and female clerks is one part of the story. Another is how the ladies and gentlemen of the federal civil service influenced the processes of feminization, mechanization, and rationalization and helped to shape the contours of middle-class labor.

It is impossible to determine how federal office work changed in the postbellum decades without first looking briefly at the nature of federal clerical labor before the Civil War. The story begins there.

THE MEN WHO CLERKED in antebellum Washington offices—and they would have all been men—performed jobs that today would be considered far beyond the scope of a mere "clerk." These clerks did legal and accounting work, examined substantive problems in a variety of fields, and made policy recommendations. For example, C. E. Mix, a $1600-per-year clerk within the Indian Office in 1842, explained that his job required him to collect evidence and prepare all reports and correspondence "in regard to the condition of any particular claim or class of claims to land set apart as an individual [Indian] reservation." Such reports were prepared in response to inquiries from the Secretary of War, both houses of Congress, and the President.[1] Other clerks, such as those working within various offices of the Treasury Department, were kept busy auditing and adjusting accounts, while those in other agencies performed work that required "a knowledge of law, and a proper application of evidence."[2]

There were, however, more strictly clerical chores that accompanied these diverse, substantive duties. Letters had to be written, briefed, and registered in books, and a variety of documents had to be copied for the file. How such tasks were accomplished depended upon how specific supervisors chose to organize the work within their offices. And an 1842 congressional investigation of the executive departments revealed considerable variety from one office to the next.

In some offices the same clerk performed all aspects of a specific job—from the most complex to the most mundane. There were, for example, fifteen clerks in the Second Auditor's Office, earning from $800 to $1700 per year, who were engaged in "examination of accounts or claims against the government." All of them, the auditor explained, "write their own letters in relation to the business referred to them."[3] In other offices such duties were handled differently. C. E. Mix, the $1600-per-year clerk whose work required considerable thought and expertise within the Indian Office, explained that an assistant worked with him copying "letters, reports, and records[,] deeds, &c., at a salary of $1,000 per annum."[4]

Supervisors sometimes chose to subdivide the work more narrowly, assigning a few clerks most of the clerical chores and keeping others on substantive, legal, or technical duties. For example, nine men were employed as clerks within the Fifth Auditor's Office: a chief clerk in charge of the other eight; five men who were "engaged in the adjustment of accounts"; one man who did some accounting and also had responsibility for "recording letters written from the office in relation to the accounts"; and two clerks who carried out more strictly clerical chores such as recording and copying.[5] In such offices all clerks were engaged in a variety of tasks; some of these men performed diverse clerical duties, while others combined clerical labor with more substantive and intellectually demanding work.

But as early as the 1840s there were already a few offices where the work had become highly rationalized and where clerks were relegated to routine, repetitive jobs. In the recording division of the General Land Office twenty men performed strictly clerical, not terribly demanding jobs—the writing and recording of land patents. Similarly, the Patent Office hired a few men whom they paid piece rates—"ten cents per every hundred words"—and whose jobs required only that they copy other documents.[6] The Patent Office continued this practice for more than a decade, by the early 1860s employing twenty-two men in this capacity, many of whom had been on the payroll for a number of years.[7]

Men working on salary and earning good pay also performed routine, repetitive labor. Four such male clerks employed in the note-signing room of the Treasury Department were recommended for promotion from $1200- to $1400-per-year jobs in 1861. Their supervisor noted: "These gentlemen have been signing U.S. Notes for the last three months. The Secretary made 3000 signatures a day's work; these gentlemen have each done 4000 a day." He based his recommendation for promotion not only on the amount, but on the nature of the work these men had performed: "The work on which they are engaged is very confining and laborious; these gentlemen are industrious and efficient and I respectfully submit that the increase of their salaries is well deserved." Thus, the routine and rationalized nature of some male labor did not necessarily degrade men's status or diminish their salaries. Instead, some antebellum officials recognized the unpleasantness of such jobs and rewarded the men who had been required to perform them.[8]

During the twenty years prior to the Civil War, the duties of federal clerks varied considerably—ranging from routine clerical tasks to complex, technical work. Most such men, however, worked in environments where the labor remained largely undifferentiated. Many, moreover, performed jobs that required considerably more than clerical expertise, although often these clerks had to add to their substantive duties whatever clerical chores were necessary to get the work done.

Salaries, too, ranged widely during these decades. Throughout most of the antebellum years, men in government offices earned anywhere from $800 to $1800 per year. But after 1853, the government instituted a new pay scale that upgraded the salaries of federal clerks. Henceforth most male clerical employees began their government careers as "first-class clerks" at salaries of $1200 per year—whether they performed primarily clerical labor or more substantive, intellectually demanding work. The only exceptions to this rule were the clerks who did copying for piece rates within the Patent Office. Moreover, men who worked conscientiously and did reasonably well—whatever the nature of their work—were able to receive promotions up the federal ladder to second-, third-, or fourth-class clerkships which paid $1400, $1600, and $1800 respectively.[9]

A man's salary did not, however, necessarily reflect how demanding or difficult was his job. In some offices those men performing the most exacting, substantive work received less pay than men whose jobs required considerably less knowledge or expertise. George Head's case is a good example. In 1842 the chief of one division within the Fourth Auditor's Office died, and the Auditor assigned Head to take over those duties. Head complained that while he had assumed the extra work, the salary attached to that work had been given to another clerk. "Superadded to my duties as superintendent and corresponding Clerk," Head explained, "I am also charged with the settlement of the accounts of foreign Navy Agents." Such "exceedingly complicated and difficult" accounts required an "acquaintance with the laws, regulations, and usages applicable to them." He was, therefore, decidedly angry that his salary had remained $1200 while Mr. Cheever, "a clerk in a subordinate position and totally unacquainted with the duties assigned to him receiv[ed] a higher salary than his superintendent, on whom he was, of necessity, dependent for instruction at every step."[10] Samuel Bootes complained of a similar problem within his office in 1850: "[T]he disparity of the duties and compensation, performed by myself and Mr. Jackson, is a theme of general remark in the Office, that a change has not been made, and the injustice done me—the most important and responsible duties as Book-Keeper of the Office performed by me at $1200—and his incompetency being such, that 3/4ths of his duties, has been assigned to others, yet he is receiving $1400."[11] Thus, while all federal clerks were paid according to the classification system established in 1853, the correlation between work and salary varied widely from office to office. As a result, antebellum government offices contained some well paid male clerks—earning as much as $1400 or $1600 per year—who labored primarily with their pens, while others, earning the same salaries, were required to use their brains as well.

IN THE YEARS after the Civil War the federal government expanded dramatically, assuming a whole range of new responsibilities and making a variety of critical changes in the operation of the federal departments in the nation's capital. Some of this growth resulted from the nationalizing effects of the Civil War, although widened federal jurisdiction often persisted after the conflict had ended. For example, in 1862, Congress passed the Legal Tender Act to help finance the war, legislation that set up a new national banking system and created the first federal paper currency. Pension applications, initially occasioned by the war, continued to mount in the postwar years. Other legislation was not so directly linked to the war. The passage of the Homestead Act and the creation of the Department of Agriculture signaled heightened federal interest in western land development and the problems of the nation's farmers.

Broadened federal authority accompanied an increase in the government's existing responsibilities. In part this expansion was tied to the growth of the U.S. population. Taking the census, for example, became a more complex job as the number of Americans swelled from 31 million people in 1860 to over 76 million in 1900. The expanding American populace required other kinds of assistance from the federal government. The number of patent applications to the Patent Office rose from 5,133 in 1863 to almost 21,000 by 1880. Besides this dramatic increase in quantity of its work load, the Patent Office also examined an increasingly complex array of inventions. In 1885 the Commissioner of Patents explained that the "field of inventions is widening so wonderfully and the lines have become so finely drawn in most instances, that the greatest care and skill are required to determine accurately what is new and what is old."[12] Similarly, federal land policy increased the burdens on the General Land Office. In 1872 the head of that bureau described the heavy responsibilities that his office shouldered: "There is not an owner of a home in many of the states in the prosperous valley of the Mississippi, nor in the rapidly growing regions beyond that river, who does not depend upon the records of this Bureau for evidence to complete the chain of title by which his home is held."[13]

The executive departments that existed at midcentury were able, for the most part, to absorb these new and expanded tasks. Six of the eight cabinet level agencies—State, Treasury, War, Navy, Post Office, and Justice—had been established prior to 1800 and persisted into the twentieth century. The seventh, the Department of the Interior, was created in 1849 in order, in the words of historian Leonard White, "to relieve the existing departments of some of their unwanted baggage." The Department of Agriculture, first organized in 1862 but not elevated to cabinet rank until 1889, was the only cabinet-level agency to be created during the postbellum decades. During the 1880s two independent commissions—the Civil Service Commission and the Interstate Commerce Commission—and one non-cabinet-level agency, the Department of Labor, became part of the executive branch.[14]

Throughout the nineteenth century these agencies remained divided into numerous bureaus, each responsible for another aspect of the agency's work. Six auditor's offices, two comptroller's offices, and the Commissioner of Customs, for example, were among the bureaus of the Treasury Department. The Department of the Interior included bureaus as diverse as the General Land Office, the Pension Bureau, the Patent Office, and the Office of Indian Affairs, amongst others.

The substantial expansion of federal responsibility brought, of course, some changes to the executive branch. Departments added bureaus as the work became more plentiful and more complex in the postbellum years. The Department of the Interior, for example, grew to contain twenty bureaus by the turn of the twentieth century, including offices such as the Bureau of Education and the U.S. Geological Survey. It was, however, the increase in the size of the work force within these bureaus that signaled the greatest change. Officials repeatedly petitioned for more employees in order to keep up with all the work. In 1862, U.S. Treasurer Francis Spinner proclaimed the "necessity for an entire reconstruction of personnel in this office. The work has been performed by devoting not only almost every hour of each day, (Sundays not excepted,) but many hours of night, to continuous labor beyond the endurance of most men."[15] Throughout the next four decades many officials would make similar claims. The Commissioner of Education complained in 1875: "In a word, while the work of the statistical branch has increased more than fourfold since 1870, there has been no corresponding increase in its clerical force under law."[16] In 1880 the First Auditor of the Treasury Department protested that while his clerical force had merely doubled, the work in his office had increased by more than 300 percent.[17] Ten years later, numerous offices within the Treasury Department were still reporting a need for more clerks in order to keep the work current.[18] Under these and similar protests, the executive departments began to expand. By 1903 the small, 1,268-person work force of 1859 had grown to include more than 25,000 workers.

This dramatic growth in the size of the federal workplace could not, however, happen without other changes as well. Congress, which appropriated funds for each department, was reluctant to increase the budget sufficiently to accommodate the numerous supervisors clamoring for more clerical help. Continual and pressing demand for more workers, combined with the ever-present problem of tight budgets, motivated federal bureaucrats to look for ways to save money. Women fit the bill perfectly.

Federal officials first hired female clerks in 1861, a year in which the Treasury Department faced an unprecedented and sudden expansion of its work load. The government had begun to print money as a means of financing the War, and handling the new paper currency was time-consuming and labor-intensive. The new notes had to be clipped and counted before being released, and old, worn-out notes had to be checked for counterfeit and recounted before being destroyed.[19] Male clerks earning $1200 a year had been put to work performing the necessary tasks, but the office was falling behind.

It was U.S. Treasurer Francis Spinner who decided to expedite the work by hiring women. Before coming to the nation's capital, Spinner had been a banker in New York where his wife and daughter had assisted in trimming bank notes. Spinner arrived in Washington and, finding a "score or more of hale and hearty young men, armed with small shears, busy clipping notes," chided Secretary of Treasury Salmon Chase that "these young men should have muskets instead of shears placed in their hands and should be sent to the front, and their places filled by women, who would do more and better work, at half the pay that was given to these 'men milliners.' " Chase hesitated, fearing that employing women as clerks would "demoralize" the department, but consented to try out one woman. Her first day on the job, this young woman, according to Spinner, "did more work than any one of the clerks....[T]his decided the whole matter." Thereafter, only female clerks were hired to clip currency.[20] Spinner's successful "experiment" precipitated Congress's enactment of a Deficiency Act authorizing the hiring of women at $600 per year—exactly half the salary given to the lowest-paid male clerk.

Despite Spinner's suggestion that women's entry into government offices would make more men available for enlistment in the Union Army, the primary motive for hiring female clerks was economic rather than military: women offered a way to solve the continual and pressing demand for more workers without overextending the budget. In 1861 two women could be hired for the price of one man, and even when Congress, in 1865, raised women's salaries to $900, female clerks continued to represent a considerable saving.[21] Senator Frederick Sawyer of South Carolina, speaking at an 1870 congressional debate on the merits of equalizing men's and women's salaries, summed it up this way: "The truth is that those ladies were put into the Departments of the Government as clerks because they were cheaper."[22] While women's salaries continued to lag behind those of men, Congress changed the regulations in 1870 and opened "men's" positions to female clerks, allowing women to compete for promotion to positions paying from $1000 to $1800. All women continued to enter government offices at starting salaries of $600 to $900, but supervisors were permitted, after 1870, to promote female clerks to higher paid positions.

Financial considerations prompted the initial hiring of female clerks, but charity offered a convenient rationale for this new departure. Numerous officials maintained that the government had an obligation to support those who had lost husbands or fathers during the Civil War. There were a few who believed that even widows who drew government pensions should be allowed to work in Washington offices. Senator Lyman Trumbull of Illinois, for example, insisted: "The women who have given up their husbands to the country, and have children to support, may very properly be in the Departments, though they get a pension of eight or twelve or sixteen dollars a month, a very inadequate compensation to a soldier's widow left with a family of children, and without property to support them."[23] In the hope of improving their chances for securing clerkships, women went to great lengths to validate their claims as dependents of men who had been injured or killed in the war. The existence of this large supply of qualified women, desperately in need of income and willing to work for as little as half of men's wages, moved government officials to look more favorably upon the idea of hiring female clerks.

In addition, women's initial entrance into Washington offices was facilitated by the kind of work that the pioneering female clerks were hired to perform. The women who first worked in government offices only clipped currency—a job that, prior to 1861, did not exist within the Washington departments. These women thus did not assume jobs that had traditionally been viewed as "male" work. It was easier to hire women for the first time, and to justify paying them lower wages, when they were expected to perform a new kind of work.

Within a year of women's entry into federal employ, the Treasury Department introduced machines that cut the long sheets of money into bills. This innovation did not, however, put an end to the hiring of female clerks. Officials quickly recognized that the government could profit from more than women's abilities to handle scissors. Some female note clippers lost their jobs, but others were transferred to different work—counting the newly cut currency.[24]

Counting currency remained exclusively women's work for the remainder of the century. It also constituted one of the most routine, low-paying clerical jobs within the federal departments. Counting was tiring, repetitive work, requiring both concentration and attention to detail. The women who counted redeemed silver and gold certificates, for example, would have to check that the notes were: "(1) all of the same denomination, (2) all of the same series, (3) all genuine, (4) altered or raised, and (5) all lower halves."[25] Mistakes could have disastrous financial consequences not only for the government, but for the individual workers as well, since they were required to compensate for losses.[26] The task also demanded speed, and women who worked too slowly risked losing their jobs. Kate McElliote's supervisor nearly dismissed her in 1865 because she had proven "idle and indifferent" in the performance of her duties. Her record showed that in a thirty-day period she had counted only 13,700 coupons, while others had "easily" done 36,000.[27] The women who worked at such jobs were, as well, usually relegated to offices that offered the least comfortable surroundings. Rooms in the Bureau of Printing and Engraving where female currency counters worked, for example, offered few amenities. Women sat at long tables and sometimes complained of insufficient light or ventilation.[28] (See Figure.)

While clipping and counting currency were extremely routine sex-segregated jobs, they offered women a foot in the door. It did not take long for officials to realize that female clerks could adequately and cheaply perform other clerical duties, and within a few years women had assumed various positions in the Post Office, Treasury, and Interior Departments. But unlike the counting divisions, these offices had not necessarily taken on new responsibilities, although they had often confronted a startling expansion in their existing work. Supervisors within such offices could not simply assign women to new work and neatly segregate them from male coworkers. They either had to let women perform the same work as men, or reorganize and subdivide the work within their offices so that men and women carried out different jobs. Women's integration within Washington offices occurred, in fact, in both ways. As a result, women's work within the federal bureaucracy became almost as varied as the work of male employees.

In those few offices where the work had already been narrowly subdivided, women appeared the ideal candidates to perform routine clerical chores that some men were already carrying out. The Patent Office provides a good example. In 1869 that office created a copying division composed entirely of female employees. Such women worked at extremely routine, subdivided labor, each transcribing between 21,000 and 108,000 words per month, depending on the skill of the worker.[29] It was not, however, the presence of women that had caused the Patent Office to rationalize the work. As early as the 1840s the Patent Office had hired temporary male clerks to make copies of office documents and paid them piece rates. By 1863 the office had abandoned this practice, for in that

Women Counting Currency in the Bureau of Printing and Engraving
(*Library of Congress*)

year all such men were listed in the official register of federal employees as permanent, salaried clerks at *per annum* salaries of $1200 to $1400.[30] Evidence suggests that as the work load in the Patent Office increased, supervisors moved these men to more substantive and better paid work, and instead hired women, also at piece rates, to make copies.[31]

Unlike those of the Treasury Department, however, female Patent Office employees were required, at first, to perform their copying tasks at home. A few women were employed on this basis as early as 1854, but not until the 1860s did any substantial number of women take work home from the Patent Office.[32] In 1869, when the Patent Office employed sixty-five such women, the Commissioner initiated a change in office policy. He noted that "in order to secure proper discipline and efficient work," it had become "obvious that this force must labor within the Office." He therefore hired fifty-nine female employees at the rate of $700 per year and placed them in six rooms in the Patent Office building. The Commissioner discovered that these fifty-nine women within the office accomplished more work than the sixty-five who labored at home, and soon assigned them "additional work...from other divisions." The result, he reported, was that "the force of male clerks was correspondingly reduced."[33] Officials thus did not subdivide labor in the Patent Office specifically to suit female employees, for some male clerks performed exclusively routine copying before federal bureaucrats ever thought to hire women. Supervisors nevertheless found it easy to assign women to the large and increasing amount of copying that was burdening federal offices in the post-Civil War years.

In other offices the presence of women did encourage government officials to reorganize the work, often subdividing the tasks and creating certain routinized jobs specifically for female employees. As early as 1866, just five years after women entered the bureaucracy, the chief of one division in the Treasury Department wrote that he wished to "relieve gentlemen employed in the division upon work which could be performed by ladies whose pay would be but little over one half the amount paid to gentlemen, that the latter might be transferred to other duties." He noted that in such a reorganization he would use women as proofreaders, a job they could do with little supervision, thereby reducing expenses in the office by $9000 annually.[34] In 1875 the Secretary of the Interior gave his official endorsement to informal schemes that had already subdivided and sexually segregated some offices within his agency. He suggested that "the number of employees in classes one and two [earning $1200 and $1400 per year respectively] might be reduced and the ordinary copying might be done by persons receiving an annual salary of nine hundred dollars per annum"—in other words, women.[35]

The women who took these jobs were given a new label—"copyists." Regardless of the nature of their duties, all salaried men who clerked in antebellum offices had been called "clerks." But soon after women entered the offices, two groups of employees appeared on government lists: "clerks" and "copyists." The use of this new term to designate female employees implied the existence of a separate category of work. And supervisors did, as we have seen, assign women to the routine copying tasks that were mounting as the size and scope of the bureaucracy expanded in the 1860s and 1870s. But many other officials chose to take advantage of new low-paid female copyists without reorganizing their offices or worrying about whether job titles matched job descriptions.

These supervisors simply moved low-paid female "copyists" into work that was also being performed by high-paid male clerks. In 1877, Laura Meehan, for example, was working as a $900 copyist in the Second Comptroller's Office. That year she applied for a promotion and explained that eleven years earlier, when she had first been appointed, she "was assigned to the desk of a clerk in charge of the Letter Book of the office, without any increase compensation, while the male clerk who had discharged the duties of the desk immediately before [her] assignment received a salary of sixteen hundred dollars per annum."[36] In some offices women like Meehan stepped into work that had previously been assigned to men, in others men and women sat side by side performing the same work—for different pay. In 1870, Mary Raymond had been working for five years as a $900 clerk in the Bureau of Internal Revenue. Her boss maintained, "[S]he is now, and ever since she has been in my section, has been employed upon work which requires all the ability of an accurate bookkeeper, and she performs it to my utmost satisfaction....An eighteen hundred dollar clerk of the section is employed upon work of the same character as hers, and it is no disparagement to him to say that her work is equal, at least, to his, both in amount and in difficulty and importance."[37]

Far from routinizing or simplifying jobs, some offices gave women greater responsibility than the men they replaced. May Estelle Cole became a $900 copyist in the Internal Revenue Bureau in 1865 and remained there until being detailed to the Light House Board six years later. In 1872 her supervisor, writing on her behalf, reported that since her detail *"she had...kept up her work in both offices."* Cole's job in the Internal Revenue Bureau had been in a section where, he maintained, "in addition to the special work of her desk,...she has assisted [her supervisor] in opening and marking for distribution the office mail, in proofreading, in making general indexes to collections of circulars, instructions, etc., and in writing letters pertaining to the work of the section....*This work had previously been done by $1600 and $1800 clerks.* In my own office her work has been chiefly to register our mail (previously done by a $1200 clerk) and to assist in my large correspondence. How large it is, you know—a thousand to twelve hundred letters a month; and I assure you that the only *effective* assistance I ever had—the only assistance that has been a comfort and not a plague—has been from Miss Cole."[38]

The chief of the Bureau of Statistics found it unnecessary to reorganize his office when he assigned work to Nancy Bishop in the mid-1870s. Her description of her monthly duties reveals the diverse nature of her job: "Has charge of correspondence, having to register and distribute between two and three thousand letters and statements of an official or general nature, and to file the letters. Has charge of 'Transportation and Appraisement,' a somewhat complicated set of books, always previously kept by a clerk of 'class two' [earning $1400 per year]." Besides these clerical and bookkeeping tasks, Bishop also had to compile tables and prepare quarterly statements based on the books she kept. Her other chores included taking "charge of the postal arrangements, having to weigh and compute the postage on all foreign and domestic matter, and to make a monthly report of the number and kinds of stamps used. In addition to the above, other work of a miscellaneous character is performed, such as compiling a statement of various kinds, occasionally writing letters dictated by the Chief of the Bureau."[39] When Bishop wrote this letter, her salary had just been reduced from $1200 to $900, although her duties had remained unchanged.

Federal officials even occasionally employed female clerks in those jobs that required technical or professional skills—positions requiring a high degree of expertise, intelligence, and the ability to make decisions. In 1865 the Second Comptroller of the Treasury found how easy it was to slip women into even the most demanding male jobs, and noted what a great success the employment of women had been in his office. "A number of the ladies employed, of mature age and considerable experience, have been found fully competent to examine accounts and settle claims of the heirs of deceased officers and soldiers. They report as large a number of accounts adjusted as their male co-laborers engaged in the same class of work, and they have been found, almost without exception, assiduous in the discharge of their several duties, and uniformly observant of the rules and regulations of the department. The increase in the number of those employed will sufficiently measure the increase in the business of the office." The employment of women, he noted, not only was a "matter of economy," but also opened "a field of respectable employment from which women have heretofore been excluded, and...[established] a precedent of great public benefit."[40]

Officials continued, through the late decades of the century, to assign women to substantive work within the departments. Mary Van Vranken worked for more than twenty-five years in the Office of Internal Revenue, and by 1894 had progressed to an $1800 clerkship. Her job required that she write "briefs of all offers in compromise submitted to the office and [conduct] a large part of the correspondence relating to them." She won praise for her "facility in reducing the most intricate and voluminous case to a clear and concise statement of the law and facts bearing on a just settlement thereof."[41] In 1896 a General Land Office official described Jennie Peyton's responsibilities as those requiring "the reasoning of a fine judicial mind." He asserted that "[in] addition to the timber trespass cases for suit in court and the conduct of necessary investigations incident thereto, Miss Peyton has charge of all matters pertaining to the granting of public timber permits, which has reached its present and perfected condition almost entirely under [her] management; and she has been entrusted from time to time with the formulation of instructions, regulations and circulars, and the preparing of bills relating to public timber matters for submission to Congress with reports thereon, involving much original research."[42]

Women situated in these kinds of jobs often labored in small, sexually integrated offices. And these were most likely to be the best appointed rooms. The dozen or so men and women who clerked in Mr. Smith's room in the Treasury Department in the early 1890s, for example, enjoyed the benefits of commodious surroundings—carpeted floors and chandeliers—not available to the women who counted currency. (See Figure.) What is most important, however, is the range of jobs and offices that women entered in these late nineteenth-century government departments. Female clerks moved into a variety of places within the federal agencies, clerking in both highly rationalized and undifferentiated positions, and carving out a place for themselves within the work world of the new middle class.

Recent studies of the feminization of clerical work in the early twentieth century suggest that the entrance of women was closely tied to the reorganization of work. The growth of the tertiary sector of the economy during the late nineteenth century created a mountain of records to be kept

Mr. Smith's Room, Treasury Department (*Library of Congress*)

and heightened demand for clerical labor. To deal with the ever-expanding volume of paperwork and to increase productivity, businessmen and managers began to subdivide, routinize, and mechanize office jobs. Such changes promised not only greater office efficiency, but made it easier to hire less skilled workers and decrease the cost of labor. Historians and sociologists have argued that native white women represented the ideal labor force to fill such needs. They were sufficiently educated to perform the necessary tasks, and, given limited employment opportunities elsewhere, willingly accepted lower pay than male workers received. Female clerks, often young women interested only in short-term employment, did not worry about clerical positions becoming dead-end jobs rather than avenues of career advancement.[43]

The employment of women in the federal work force validates some, but not all, of these propositions. Women entered government offices in a period when the Washington bureaucracy was expanding. Some departments had recently acquired a large amount of "new" work—often routine and repetitive—which became immediately typed as "women's" work. Such was the case within the note-counting divisions of the Treasury Department. Other offices, like the Patent Office, had already routinized certain aspects of male labor and found it convenient to place women in these positions. Still other officials chose specifically to reorganize the work within their bureaus so that low-paid women would be responsible for newly subdivided, routine tasks. But the introduction of women did not necessarily accompany, nor was it always swiftly followed by, subdivision and rationalization of clerical work. Throughout the nineteenth century, numerous female clerks were incorporated into the federal work force in an entirely different manner. Women simply moved into offices, picked up pens, and carried out identical duties as male clerks. Such jobs ranged from varied clerical positions to jobs that required legal, accounting, or technical abilities. In these offices, supervisors downgraded women's title and salary, but maintained the work load and responsibility.

WOMEN'S ACCESS TO SUCH a wide range of jobs rested largely upon the manner in which the executive departments were run during the Gilded Age. It is essential, then, to look more closely at the federal bureaucracy in order to explain not only why women's work took the shape it did, but the relationship between the work of male and female employees in late nineteenth-century Washington offices. Both the changes that occurred in the federal bureaucracy—and, as importantly, those that did not—influenced the kind of work middle-class men and women performed in this new, white-collar work world.

In the post-Civil War decades, as during the antebellum years, the running of cabinet-level departments was left, almost entirely, to the secretaries who headed them. Indeed, until 1883 there was no established body within the executive branch to set or to enforce government-wide personnel regulations. Other than following the standard pay scale, giving Union veterans preferences for jobs, and keeping within congressionally approved budgets, secretaries were free to administer their agencies in the way they saw fit. The passage of the Civil Service Act in 1883 brought some critical changes to the hiring procedures of the several agencies, and standardized hours and leave time throughout the executive departments, as well. The next chapter will discuss the new civil service system in greater detail, but what is important here is the minimal impact the system had on the everyday workings of the agencies. The Civil Service Commission, formed as a result of the 1883 Pendleton Act, did not interfere with how employees, once hired, were utilized. Such matters remained within the hands of the secretary who, in turn, gave his underlings broad power to delegate jobs, as well as to recommend promotions and dismissals.

As the century progressed, Congress, concerned with increasing efficiency and reducing the costs of the executive agencies, displayed a growing interest in the internal affairs of the departments. In 1887, Senator F. M. Cockrell's Select Senate Committee conducted an extensive investigation of the departments in Washington, D.C. The voluminous report issued by this committee offers a glimpse into the workings of the bureaucracy a quarter of a century after the Civil War and disclosed just what had changed, and what had not, within Washington offices since the antebellum years.

The report of the Cockrell committee revealed that departments were still divided into bureaus, as they had been a generation earlier. But there had been a considerable change in the way bureaus were structured. By 1887 most bureaus had been separated into a varying number of divisions. Seven divisions, for example, composed the Second Comptroller's Office, a bureau in the Treasury Department, while the Patent Office had as many as forty-three distinct divisions. Divisions were entrusted with either substantive or functional responsibilities. The Patent Office contained twenty-nine substantive divisions, each charged with examining patent applications for different types of inventions. The remaining fourteen divisions assumed specific functional duties, such as the copying division, the drafting division, and the mail room division.[44]

The separation of bureaus into divisions reflected the growth in the size and complexity of the federal bureaucracy. Most antebellum offices had been small enough so that "divisions" were not necessary. Instead a few clerks would simply take responsibility for certain aspects of the work in an office.[45] But by the end of the century many offices were too large to allow such an informal mode of organizing the work.

More important, however, than the creation of divisions to handle the increasing amount of work was the fact that some of those divisions were devoted solely to functional duties. This method of organizing the offices suggests that the bureaucracy was beginning to rationalize labor in ways that routinized and removed the intellectual content from the work performed by federal clerks. In offices like the copying division of the Patent Office, the money-counting divisions of the Treasurer's Office, and the recording division of the Sixth Auditor's office, narrowly subdivided work assignments and rigidly structured work routines prevailed. In the latter, for example, fourteen clerks were responsible for "assorting, numbering, and filing in packages all domestic money orders and postal notes." These employees did not "in any way assist" the clerks engaged in other work in the office, nor did the other clerks ever help to sort money orders.[46]

What the Cockrell report makes clear, however, is that this kind of extremely subdivided labor had, by 1887, been instituted in only a minority of divisions. The large number of government offices that carried out substantive work had, instead, created a three-part organizational work pattern that left the labor only moderately rationalized and that allowed clerks to continue to perform varied, undifferentiated tasks. The first and last steps in the process included primarily clerical duties: preparing all incoming work, and making records of all work accomplished. The former required registering and summarizing (or "briefing") incoming documents, while the latter often necessitated writing letters and making letter-press or handwritten copies for permanent office record. In some offices one clerk took responsibility for all these duties, but other offices divided such tasks among several clerks, designating one person a "corresponding clerk," another an "indexing clerk," and a third in charge of the letters received book.

After receiving and before sending material, offices performed substantive work—whether auditing an account, examining a pension claim,
or preparing a decision in a contested land case. Such duties continued
to demand technical or professional knowledge and often required that
clerks make important decisions. Thus, even in the late 1880s the term
"clerk" still remained, in many instances, a misnomer, for numerous government clerks continued to carry out technical, legal, and administrative
as well as clerical duties. Supervisors in different divisions apportioned
these tasks in various manners. Sometimes one clerk performed the entire
job, as in the auditing offices of the Treasury Department. Other supervisors delegated such tasks to two clerks, one of whom checked the work
of the other.[47] Within one division of the General Land Office, numerous
clerks divided substantive work according to specific subjects: two clerks
examined contested cases, nine handled cases concerned with one party,
two took responsibility for amendments, two worked on applications for
hearings, and one served as the examiner of appeals.[48]

The gender breakdown within this three-part organizational structure
varied. In most offices it was men who continued to perform the substantive jobs, although, as we saw, supervisors occasionally put women to work
at these tasks. Thus, John Johnson, a $1600 clerk in the office of the Au-
ditor for the War Department, was in 1897 "engaged in the examination
and settlement of Quartermaster's accounts."[49] And F. P. McClean performed work in the Patent Office in 1885 which involved, he explained,
"[taking] charge of the class of metallurgy and...arrang[ing] and sys-
tematiz[ing] the technical work of this class as shown by my system of process briefs now employed."[50] Gorham Hopkins, a clerk within the Law
Division of the Pension office in 1888, was responsible for "reviewing evidence and action of the Bureau and writing report and pension claims
appealed to the Hon. Secretary of the Interior."[51] Female clerks were
more likely to assume the clerical chores of briefing, indexing, and copying, although women were certainly not the only ones to take these jobs.
Indeed, throughout the late nineteenth century the varied clerical tasks
required within these substantive divisions were performed by both male
and female clerks—albeit usually at different salaries.

While this three-part organizational structure was new to the postbellum years, the diversity of job assignments within the offices reflected the
persistence of a fluid, often undifferentiated work process that had
characterized government employment at midcentury. In its 1887 investigation, the Cockrell Committee specifically requested each division head
to report "the maximum and minimum amount of business transacted
and disposed of by the employe doing the most and the employe doing
the least" amount of work.[52] Over and again supervisors responded that
such information could not be collected. Although certain clerks were
often assigned specific tasks, such assignments were rarely followed
rigidly. One supervisor explained that even the work of those employees
assigned primarily to copying duties could not be compared since these
clerks were also "expected to perform, and do perform, any miscellane-

ous work, such as compiling statistics, preparing blanks, sending off circulars and books, and any other similar duties required of them."[53] The nature of the work, as well as the manner of delegating jobs, made comparison between clerks difficult. The Fifth Auditor explained that "the adjustment of one account" in his office could "involve the services of one clerk from ten to twelve days, while in others twenty accounts can be disposed of in one day with equal facility."[54]

Whether these federal employees performed substantive or clerical duties, their work was still too varied to allow officials to quantify or compare performance. Moreover, supervisors within individual offices retained, throughout the century, the power to assign employees to duties without interference from high-level officials. Many such supervisors chose to shift clerks from one task to another, rather than setting them in permanent positions to do discrete jobs. In these offices, employees needed to understand the workings of the entire office, for they were frequently called upon to assist a fellow clerk or to do miscellaneous jobs that would help keep the work from falling into arrears.

Thus, despite the early beginnings of more rationalized methods of work organization, what remains most striking about the federal workplace during the late nineteenth century was how loosely structured it remained. At the end of the century—as during the middle—no government-wide policy dictated how personnel would be used or how offices would be run. Instead, low-level supervisors determined work routines and delegated jobs, assigning to both men and women a variety of diverse tasks within the office.

THIS FLEXIBILITY OF government employment policy and the decentralized nature of the federal bureaucracy held decided benefits for women, allowing them access to a wide range of federal clerical jobs. For men, however, the absence of clearly enunciated government-wide regulations spelled possible danger. Just as officials were free to appoint women to a variety of positions, so were they free to place men in low-status jobs. Indeed, by the 1880s it appeared that the policy of employing low-paid women in responsible jobs was producing adverse consequences for male clerks. Those men who in the immediate postbellum decades had commanded high salaries for performing jobs that demanded only clerical responsibilities were finding their status undermined by the presence of women who did the same work for considerably less pay. Where all male clerks had once been designated as "clerks" and paid at least $1200 per year, during the last two decades of the century men were being hired as "copyists" at salaries beginning as low as $720 or $900 per year. Such men were not only assuming a label associated with women's work, but were also settling for women's pay.

Although no records reveal the actual supply of potential male clerks in the two post-Civil War decades, there is evidence that in the 1860s and 1870s most male clerks would have declined to work for "female" wages.

In 1870, Senator William Stewart of Nevada warned that raising women's pay to the same level as men's would end opportunities for female clerks in government employ: "There is not a head of a Department nor a head of a bureau who would not rather have a male clerk in the bureau than a female clerk doing precisely the same work; and the effect [of equalizing wages] will be to drive the females from the Department and substitute for them male clerks."[55] Such statements suggest that, at least in 1870, men did not compete with women for jobs paying less than $1200, and that the federal hiring process was conducted in two distinct labor markets—one consisting of low-paid women and the other of high-paid men. Moreover, many officials apparently felt that male clerks *should* command higher salaries than women. U.S. Treasurer Spinner noted in 1870 that some deserving women in his office who presently earned a maximum of $1000 ought to be granted increases in salary. He urged, however, that men be appointed only to positions paying $1200 per year or more.[56]

The evolution of federal employment complicated or blurred this initial pay differential. By the mid-1880s either the supply of potential, low-paid male workers or the perceptions of employers had begun to change—or both. The annual reports of the Civil Service Commission tallied the number of men and women who passed examinations for federal jobs. These data offer a crude index to labor supply in the years after 1884: the figures point to a more than adequate number of qualified male applicants. For most of these years the Civil Service Commission registered at least twice as many "male eligibles" (men receiving a passing score on the examinations) as there were positions to be filled. In fact, throughout this period between 25 and 40 percent of the men competing for positions did so in a category that would qualify them only for those jobs paying $900 per year or less. (See Table 4.1.) Even men applying for first-class ($1200-per-year) clerkships in many cases accepted lower paid positions.[57]

The decline in men's salaries was gradual, but nevertheless persistent over the last decades of the nineteenth century. The percentage of men in the Treasury Department earning salaries below $1000 per year in-

TABLE 4.1
Male Applicants for Copyist and Clerk Positions, 1885–93

Year	Copyist ($900)	Clerk ($1200)	Total
Jan. 1885 – Dec.1885	34%	66%	595
Jan. 1886 – June 1887	33%	67%	1741
July 1887 – June 1888	40%	60%	932
July 1888 – June 1889	28%	72%	951
July 1889 – June 1890	28%	72%	879
July 1890 – June 1891	27%	73%	1560
July 1891 – June 1892	25%	75%	1139
July 1892 – June 1893	31%	70%	747

Sources: Computed from U.S., Civil Service Commission, *Annual Report,* 1884–1894.

creased from only 11 percent in 1871 to 25 percent at the turn of the century. Salaries within the Interior Department conformed to a similar pattern. (See Tables 4.2 and 4.3.[58]) Thus, by the 1890s, many men who wanted to become federal clerical workers had to settle for salaries that thirty years earlier the government would have dared offer only to women.

Falling salaries for men were accompanied by rising salaries for women. Between 1871 and 1881 the percentage of women in the Treasury Department occupying positions paying more than $900 per year grew from 4 to 20 percent, and by 1901 as many as 57 percent of female Treasury clerks drew salaries of $1000 or more. (See Table 4.2.) Women who worked in the Interior Department also reaped the benefits of better pay. (See Table 4.3.) The expanding number of women earning better wages reflected not the government's conscious decision to appoint women to high-paid jobs, but the possibility, given the flexibility of federal policy, for female clerks to move from low-status work to positions involving greater responsibilities and commanding higher salaries. The additional number of men earning low incomes represented the other side of the coin: just as supervisors were willing to allow women to perform what had previously been "men's" jobs and eventually to promote them to men's pay, they appeared increasingly able, as the century progressed, to assign "women's" positions to male clerks.

In fact, the work of many male and female clerks became interchangeable during the postbellum decades, with male clerks sometimes moving back into jobs that women had recently vacated. In 1879, for example, when Mrs. Boughton resigned her $900 copyist job in the Pension Office, her supervisor noted that "the husband of Mrs. Boughton has effected this resignation with the view of taking her place at the same salary."[59] During the following decade Andrew L. Jackson, a $900 copyist in the Patent Office, sent a memo: "To any one wishing to transfer to the Pension Office from the Patent Office, I would be glad to exchange places with him or her. Salary $900." Jackson succeeded in swapping places with a female copyist.[60]

The men who moved into positions that had been vacated by women found, however, that the status of those jobs had been altered in a fundamental way. Women's presence had lowered the salaries attached to many jobs, and men who assumed those positions often had difficulty securing their traditionally higher male wages. William Nestler's case is a good example. Nestler began his stint in the federal departments by working as a substitute for an absent female copyist at the rate of $720 per year. The position was only temporary, and a few weeks before his term was set to expire he wrote to the Secretary of the Interior requesting that he be placed on the permanent role at a higher salary. Nestler explained that at the time he accepted the position he had passed a civil service examination that qualified him for a $1000 position. He had only accepted the low-paid copyist job "with the idea that merit would soon advance" him.

TABLE 4.2
Salaries of Clerical Employees in the Treasury Department

Salary (per annum)	Women					Men				
	1863	1871	1881	1891	1901	1863	1871	1881	1891	1901
$2000–2900	0	0	0	0	0	3%	4%	8%	9%	9%
$1800	0	0	0	0	0	3%	15%	13%	13%	13%
$1600	0	0	0	2%	4%	16%	21%	19%	16%	16%
$1400	0	1%	2%	8%	13%	30%	26%	27%	20%	15%
$1200	0	3%	10%	27%	25%	40%	22%	16%	13%	14%
$1000	0	0	8%	17%	15%	0	0	4%	4%	8%
$900	0	93%	72%	29%	24%	0%	0	1%	5%	6%
$800–840	0	0%	0	3%	3%	1%	3%	2%	4%	4%
$700–780	0	3%	0%	4%	8%	2%	8%	4%	6%	5%
$600–660	100%	0%	7%	10%	8%	5%	0%	6%	9%	10%
	100%	100%	100%	100%	100%	100%	100%	100%	100%	100%
Number	130	647	569	705	797	836	1663	1441	1420	1592

Sources: U.S., Department of the Interior, *Register of All Officers . . . of the United States, 1863;* U.S., Department of the Interior, *Register of the United States, 1871;* U.S., Department of the Interior, *Official Register of the United States, 1881;* vol. 1; U.S., Department of the Interior, *Official Register of the United States, 1891;* vol.1; U.S., Department of the Interior, *Official Register of the United States, 1901;* vol.1.

TABLE 4.3
Salaries of Clerical Employees in the Interior Department

Salary (per annum)	Women				Men			
	1863	1881	1891	1901	1863	1881	1891	1901
$2000–2900	0	0	0	0	5%	6%	9%	9%
$1800	0	0	0	0	8%	8%	11%	11%
$1600	0	0	1%	1%	17%	12%	11%	11%
$1400	0	1%	12%	15%	29%	16%	20%	18%
$1200	0	7%	35%	35%	31%	28%	19%	18%
$1000	0	15%	18%	18%	0	11%	14%	12%
$900	0	60%	21%	21%	1%	7%	7%	9%
$800–840	0	2%	0%	2%	1%	2%	2%	3%
$700–780	0	9%	7%	4%	3%	5%	2%	3%
$600–660	0	5%	6%	4%	7%	6%	4%	5%
	0	100%	100%	100%	100%	100%	100%	100%
Number		288	863	792	369	1177	2036	1977

Sources: U.S., Department of the Interior, *Register of All Officers . . . of the United States, 1863;* U.S., Department of the Interior, *Register of the United States, 1881,* vol. 1; U.S., Department of the Interior, *Register of the United States, 1891,* vol. 1; U.S., Department of the Interior, *Register of the United States, 1901,* vol. 1.
Note: I was unable to analyze wage scales for the Interior Department for the year 1871 since the register did not list "Miss" or "Mrs." next to the names and listed only first initials, rather than first names. It was thus not possible to distinguish male from female employees.

The work he performed for his reduced salary, "charge of the Books [in the Assignment Division]," had, he explained, in the past been performed "for a number of years...by a $1400 clerk."[61] But what is important in this case is that the person who held Nestler's position immediately prior to his entrance into the department was a women who had earned only $720, the same salary offered to Nestler.

William Nestler was not alone. By the last two decades of the century some male clerks who performed even the substantive work of the departments were being paid only low copyist wages. In 1880 the Commissioner of Pensions recommended the promotion of three men on his rolls. Two were "very excellent clerks," earning only $720 per year, who were "employed as Examiners of claims and ought in justice to be promoted to the grade of other clerks employed upon the same work." He therefore urged their promotion to $900—a salary still considerably below what any pension claims examiner would have commanded a decade before. Two other "excellent" claims examiners, clerks earning $900, he recommended for promotion to $1000 positions, as well as suggesting that a $720-per-year male employee, an "accomplished stenographer and correspondent," be promoted to $900 because his work was of a "far higher grade than that of any copyist employed in the Office." The Commissioner explained that he felt "these promotions are necessary to bring their salaries upon an average with that of other clerks employed at the same work and of similar efficiency."[62] Such discrepancies between salary and duties were not new to the post-Civil War decades, for even during the antebellum years, as we saw, numerous men complained of being paid less than others who performed the same jobs. But in the years after the Civil War, as men began to be hired at "women's wages," the discrepancy between work performed and pay received often became more pronounced. As much as a $500 salary gap might exist between men whose work was substantially the same.

By the last two decades of the century an increasing number of middle-class men seemed willing to accept these lower status and lower paid positions within federal offices. The high rate of small business failures and the upheaval within the professions—exacerbated by repeated depressions—had brought many such men to the point of desperation. While certainly not happy with the choices offered to them, male clerks like William Nestler settled for low-paid jobs with the hope of advancing to higher salaried positions. Others thought that they could parlay experiences gained within federal employment into more lucrative ventures in the private sector. Regardless of these possibilities, for a middle-class man to take on "women's work" must have, indeed, been a bitter pill to swallow. That more and more such men did so testifies, again, to the harsh economic problems middle-class men faced in the late decades of the nineteenth century.

FOR MOST of the nineteenth century, clerical workers used two tools in their work—their brains and their pens. But during the last two decades of the century, new office technology added an important dimension to office life and made machines an integral part of the clerk's world. By the 1880s, typewriters had become standard equipment in many private and government offices, and in the following twenty years, telephones and even primitive counting machines began to appear. Managers, businessmen, and government officials were faced with deciding how best to integrate this new technology into their offices. Should men or women operate the machines? Would clerks who worked these new machines do so exclusively or combine such work with other, non-mechanized clerical functions? In the case of government, the answers were not at all obvious, and different supervisors opted for varied solutions. As a result, mechanization had diverse effects upon the organization of work within the federal bureaucracy—in certain offices producing highly rationalized, sexually segregated work environments, and in other offices combining with already established, diversified work routines.

Women and typewriters appeared in offices within the private sector at about the same time, and historians—noting that typing became almost immediately an exclusively female job—have debated the importance of the typewriter in bringing women into the clerical labor force. Margery Davies has suggested that since the typewriter was a new machine, not yet "sex-typed as masculine," it made it easy to assign women to these jobs. Davies maintains that as such, the typewriter facilitated, but certainly did not cause, the feminization of clerical labor.[63] More recently Carole Srole has claimed that women's predominance as typists followed quite naturally upon their prevalence as copyists. As the job of copying became mechanized, the same workers—women—took over the new machines.[64]

Government offices mechanized differently. Typewriting machines first appeared in Washington in the early 1880s, and for the next twenty years both men and women used them. In 1892 the Civil Service Commission reported that 164 men and 209 women had taken the examination for typewriting. As late as 1904, women received only 21 percent of the appointments as government typists.[65]

It was not immediately apparent how these new machines, and the people who operated them, would be integrated into federal departments. In some offices men and women skilled at typewriting found themselves doing nothing else and therefore at a disadvantage. In 1893 the Commissioner of the General Land Office reported that he employed about twenty "typewriters" (persons) in his office and explained that they "are confined, exclusively to the work of typewriting, and therefore have no facilities for making themselves familiar with, and efficient in general duties of the office....These typewriters, as a rule, are a very intelligent and faithful class of clerk, engaged in important and indispensable work of the office, and some of them have for years been employed at a salary of [only] $600 per year....While they are limited to a special class of work they can have no hope for promotion by competitive examination with other clerks whose assignments necessarily bring them in daily contact with the general duties of the office."[66] The Commissioner did not specify if these employees were male or female, but asked that they be allowed a special examination that would afford them an opportunity for promotion. The Chief Examiner denied the request, maintaining that it would single out typists and give them an unfair advantage over other clerks. In arguing against allowing the special examination, he revealed that both sexes were included within this group of low-paid workers: "Would the fact that the typewriter has at least a theoretical knowledge of the general purpose of the bureau wherein employed be regarded as an argument against *his* or *her* efficiency?...[It] certainly is [the typist's] own fault if they allow their intellectual horizons to be bounded by the limits of their typewriting machines."[67] The Commissioner of the General Land Office did not succeed in securing promotion for these employees, but his remarks suggest his concern for those clerks whose jobs isolated them from opportunities in the office and also indicate that in his bureau such extremely subdivided labor was the exception rather than the rule.

In other offices mechanization occurred without the subdivision of labor and the decline of salaries. Clerks were not always confined to their typewriters, but sometimes added typing to their other responsibilities, thereby increasing their usefulness and their status. And this was true for both men and women. Ellen Cushman, a clerk in the Patent Office in 1884, was "specially selected for her quick and ready intelligence in the performance of general clerical work, and particularly [for] her skill as a stenographer and proficiency in the use of the typewriter." Her supervisor remarked, "Her labors in this latter respect are additional to those undertaken by her predecessors and have been of the utmost satisfaction to me in the press of business that has lately existed in this division."[68] Frank L. Warne was appointed as a $900 copyist in the Office of Indian Affairs in early 1890. Ten months later the chief of his division recommended his promotion to a $1200 position on the following grounds: "During the time he has been employed in this office he has discharged his duties in a satisfactory manner. He is a rapid and accurate typewriter, who industriously applies himself to the work entrusted to him, is also a stenographer, and besides this is an intelligent and well educated gentleman."[69] In the same office C. A. Cotterrill, already a $1200 clerk, was promoted to a $1400 position because of his excellent stenography and typewriting, while three other male clerks, earning from $1000 to $1200 per year, not only typed, but reported claims as well.[70]

The introduction of the typewriter thus had little immediate impact upon the organization of work or the sexual division of labor within government offices. In some offices the manner in which officials chose to use these new machines created subdivided work assignments, declining opportunities, and lower paid positions for both male and female clerks. In others, male and female "typewriters" continued to perform a variety of tasks and to receive salaries that were commensurate with those paid to other clerks.

Other office machines had a different impact upon the work experiences of clerks who operated them. In 1890 the federal government experimented with new machines designed specifically to count and tabulate the census. The introduction of more sophisticated census inquiries and the growth of the U.S. population had magnified the job of tallying the 1880 census, causing delays in the publication of the final returns. The tedious and time-consuming effort of hand-counting these figures prompted officials to test Herman Hollerith's punching and tabulating machines for the work in 1890.

Two different machines, each run by different clerks, were required to implement Hollerith's system. First, a clerk punched the data from the census sheet to a card, with each card representing a separate individual to be counted. The keyboard of the punching machines contained twelve rows of twenty holes, each hole with a label corresponding to an item on the census return. According to a contemporary description, "At first glance, perhaps the keyboard looks complicated but it is scientifically grouped, and...it is very readily learned."[71] The clerk manually moved the single punch over the keyboard until each piece of information for that individual had been recorded. An average worker punched between 500 and 700 cards in a six-and-a-half-hour day.[72] (See Figure.)

A different clerk then fed a stack of punched cards into a tabulating machine that kept a running, electronic count of each category. An observer offered his impression of the tabulating division: "As one enters the ear catches the sound of crisp bell ringing, for all the world like that of sleighing. The music comes from the Hollerith machines, on each of which a bell...rings every time a card is counted, while its failure to ring indicates that there is something wrong with the card, or that it has not been slipped in properly."[73] (See Figure.) An average tabulator handled about 7,000 cards per day, with very efficient clerks processing as many as 11,000.[74]

The Census Office first experimented with these machines in the rough count of the 1890 population, a six-week job at which both men and women worked. At the end of this period, Superintendent of the Census Robert Porter reported that women had worked 50 percent faster than

Hollerith Punching Machine (*Smithsonian Institution, photo number 64551*)

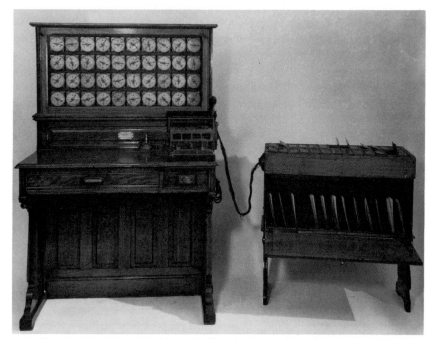

Hollerith Tabulating Machine (*Smithsonian Institution, photo number 64563*)

men. In working on the electric tabulating machines, he believed, "women were better adapted for this particular work than men. They proved more expeditious in handling the [census] schedules, more at home in adjusting the delicate mechanisms of the electrical machines and apparently more anxious to make a good record." He found the same to be true with regard to the punching machines. "It has been found that women are more expert at this work than men. Not long ago my attention was called to the fact that two women, receiving $50 a month each, were punching twice as many cards as men working with them, getting much higher pay." The head of the Census Office therefore decided that henceforth women would do all such work in his office.[75]

Supervisors, indeed, moved more women into machine-tending jobs, but Porter's directives did not compel officials to restructure their offices, and as a result punching and tabulating never, in the nineteenth century, became entirely sex-segregated work. The 1891 official register of federal employees listed 137 male and 527 female "computers" in the Census Office, all employed at $720 per year.[76] The records make it clear not only that men worked at the punching machines, but that some disliked the work enough to protest their assignments. One such male clerk, Thomas Ogle, explained that he had "faithfully and conscientiously" performed his work at these machines, even though it was "often distasteful." The head of the division, however, assessed Ogle's performance differently. He noted that Ogle was only able to punch from 330 to 398 cards per day, a total that was "away below average. Women [were] doing 1000 [per] day."[77] In the same month J. H. LaGrange protested at being assigned to one of the "fast becoming famous" punching machines, and asked to be moved to other work.[78]

The affinity that the superintendent of the census believed he had discovered between women and machines was not, however, what brought women into the Census Office. Officials hired women to work in the Census Office in 1880, a full decade before punching and tabulating machines were invented. It is difficult to know exactly how work was organized for the counting of the 1880 census, for the official register of federal employees named 225 women and 171 men as "copyists and computers" at salaries ranging from $600 to $900 per year.[79] Evidence indicates, however, that by 1880, officials were already beginning to use women to tally census returns. In 1883, Alice Chapman requested a transfer from computing to other duties. A friend, writing on her behalf, asked that Chapman be allowed to perform tasks that did not require tallying figures: "Her head is in an awful condition and even in sleep she cannot prevent computing."[80] Even without the benefit of machines, officials had routinized and rationalized this labor, and put women into these jobs. Thus, while mechanization changed the nature of some work within the Census Office and contributed to the sex stereotyping of certain jobs, it proved only one component in a process that had begun in that office ten years prior to the introduction of new technology. Moreover, women and men—albeit in unequal proportions—continued to labor at even those mechanized jobs that had become most highly rationalized.

OVER THE LAST FOUR DECADES of the nineteenth century the federal government was the site for the creation of a new type of middle-class work. Within Washington departments, and, indeed, increasingly in offices within the private sector, middle-class men and women would find themselves working together, using new types of office machines, and sometimes subjected to work schemes that rationalized and subdivided their labor. Such a world differed dramatically from the workplaces— businesses, offices, classrooms, and homes—where middle-class men and women had labored at midcentury.

The introduction of women into federal departments represented the most obvious innovation. It was, however, not only their presence, but the nature of the work that many such women performed that created within the federal bureaucracy an altogether new type of middle-class work environment. Had all female clerks been immediately and irrevocably relegated to simplified, sex-segregated jobs, they would have maintained a distance from the men in the office. But the women who sat down in government offices, picked up their pens, and successfully carried out duties identical to those of the man at the next desk, necessarily came into daily and direct contact with their male coworkers—something that raised a host of new situations for nineteenth-century, middle-class ladies and gentlemen. Women's demonstrated ability to take on men's work proved particularly problematic since it meant that that under a variety of circumstances male and female clerks competed for positions and promotions. The Victorian codes of behavior that governed relations between middle-class men and women had offered little advice on proper behavior in a sexually integrated office, much less on career competition between the sexes. Thus, as later chapters will demonstrate, the structure of work routines would have important implications for the kinds of business and personal relations that these middle-class workers began to establish within the new white-collar workplace.

The fact that some women's and men's jobs had become interchangeable—in title, salary, and responsibility—may have had ramifications that spread beyond the boundaries of the office. Women who assumed a vast array of office responsibilities once entrusted only to men were, by their very actions, invalidating one of the central tenets of the domestic ideology. Nineteenth-century educators, physicians, ministers, and popular writers had agreed that a woman's intellectual, moral, and physical make-up left her unable to withstand the everyday pressures associated with the male world of work. The middle-class ladies who labored successfully in government jobs may well have made the men with whom they worked wonder about the validity of such prevailing wisdom.

The ease with which women assumed men's work had important consequences, as well, for career opportunities of both male and female employees. For men, there was the loss of certain prerogatives. The high salaries and high status that had once been attached to their jobs began to decline, and male clerks began to accept titles and wages that had once been offered only to female employees. For some of the luckier women clerks, the successful handling of "men's" work brought promotions to better paid positions. But even those women who continued to do men's work for women's pay enjoyed, at the very least, the advantage of working at diverse and sometimes challenging jobs rather than at routine, repetitive chores.

The permeable boundary between men's and women's work resulted not from an enlightened, egalitarian policy on the part of federal officials. In fact, as the next chapter will make clear, neither government regulations nor the men who enforced them favored women's interests. It was, rather, the absence of a highly centralized, rigidly administered federal employment policy that worked to the benefit of female employees. Without regulations or even strict guidelines, supervisors often took the path of least resistance, many apparently realizing that allowing women to perform a variety of jobs was considerably simpler than—and still as economical as—reorganizing the entire office, dividing the labor, and segregating female workers. Women thus profited from the decentralized manner in which a still inchoate nineteenth-century federal bureaucracy functioned.

But to claim that the story of men's and women's work within the Washington departments was only a tale of middle-class workers challenged by diversified, demanding jobs would, of course, be a gross error. For during the last four decades of the nineteenth century the government began to subdivide clerical labor, mechanize certain jobs, and rationalize office routines. It is difficult to determine how many federal workers were so situated, since there are no lists that reveal the actual jobs of all government clerks. With caution, we can, however, use salary groupings to obtain a rough estimate of what percentage of federal clerks worked at routinized and what percent did diversified tasks. Remembering that pay did not necessarily reflect the responsibilities or demands of a job, it is still safe to assume that most of the men earning $1400 or more were not performing mindless, repetitive, oversimplified jobs. In 1891, 58 percent of the male clerks working in the Treasury Department and 51 percent of those in the permanent offices of the Interior Department fell into this category. (See Tables 4.2 and 4.3.) Estimating the percentage for women is more difficult. Since the majority of women earned $1000 or less—regardless of the nature of their work—the correlation between salary and job complexity was lower. At the very least, however, women who had earned promotion to places paying $1200 or more had, in all likelihood, proven their capabilities at more than the most mundane tasks. Using such figures, we can conservatively estimate that a minimum of 37 percent of the women clerking in the Treasury Department and 48 percent of those in the permanent offices of the Interior Department in 1891 worked at jobs other than routinized, simplified jobs.[81] (See Tables 4.2 and 4.3.)

How such findings are interpreted depends largely upon whether we view this glass as half-full or half-empty. The majority of male clerks still, at the end of the century, held diversified jobs, although the decline in men's salaries suggests that the number of men who were so situated may have been dropping. The one-third to one-half of female employees who held responsible positions reveals considerable opportunity for women, indicating that clerical work—at least in the government—offered more to women than dead-end jobs. Given a wide margin for error, this still, however, left enough government employees consigned to routinized, repetitive tasks so that contemporary observers and journalists commented upon how "very monotonous" government work was, "consisting of the same set routine every day."[82] Even those clerks who escaped relegation to routinized jobs no doubt realized that many of their fellow workers held positions that made them, in the words of another journalist, "as automatic as their pens and as narrow as their rooms."[83] Indeed, mechanized jobs and rationalized, divided labor were becoming part of the terrain within the work world of the new middle class. And both male and female clerks must have understood that the possibility always existed that they, too, might one day wind up performing extremely "monotonous" labor.

It is, of course, important to ask whether the relatively diversified nature of government work distinguished federal employment from other types of clerical labor. Unfortunately, a definitive answer will have to await more detailed studies of the evolution of clerical employment within large, private corporations of the early twentieth century. It seems possible, however, that public officials, not driven by the profit motive, may have felt less urgency about reducing labor costs and therefore been less pressured to institute extremely rationalized work routines.

Indeed, the hours which these federal clerks were required to work and the liberal leave time allowed them testify, as well, to a considerably more relaxed environment than most profit-making firms would have allowed. During the two post-Civil War decades, no government-wide policy dictated the hours of labor for Washington clerks. Instead, the heads of specific agencies determined how long their employees would work, and custom dictated a short working day. Most agencies opened at 9:00 a.m. and closed at either three or four o'clock in the afternoon, allowing employees half an hour break for lunch. Depending upon the season, clerks worked either five and one-half or six and one-half hours per day, with many offices closing early during the summer and opening late during the winter.[84] In 1883, Congress standardized the work day for all agencies. Henceforth, Washington departments opened at 9:00 a.m. and closed at 4:00 p.m., six days a week, with clerks lunching from noon until 12:30. Most government employees in Washington, D.C., worked only forty-two hours a week.

Government clerks were privileged not only in the relatively short hours they labored, but in the considerable amount of leave time they were allowed. Federal policy on leaves of absence, like policy on hours of labor, remained entirely within the jurisdiction of specific agency heads during most of the two decades after the Civil War. Officials usually followed the custom that allowed clerical employees thirty consecutive days' annual paid leave, but clerks who claimed illness and produced a doctor's certificate were permitted an additional thirty days—often with pay. Congress codified these informal practices in 1883, and thereafter a department head could grant thirty days' annual leave in any one year. The act specified, however, that more than thirty days could be authorized in case of sickness. Not until 1893 did Congress limit the amount of sick leave to thirty days per year, although it even qualified this restriction by permitting extra sick days "in exceptional and meritorious cases."[85]

A forty-hour week, regular paid vacations and sick leave would become part of white-collar work in the private sector during the twentieth century. But it would take many decades before middle-class men and women who clerked in private firms would receive the kinds of benefits that these nineteenth-century federal employees enjoyed. Moreover, the acquiring of such benefits was often accompanied by other, less propitious changes. For as clerical workers in large, private companies came to enjoy shorter hours and more vacations, they also found themselves increasingly relegated to routinized and mechanized jobs.

But the ultimate rationalization of clerical labor was still, in the nineteenth century, far from a forgone conclusion. We must be careful not to try to understand the past by reading backward from a present characterized by highly mechanized offices in which predominantly female clerks carry out routine, repetitive jobs. The changes wrought in government offices in the years after the Civil War did not initiate a steady, consistent, and inexorable reduction of all clerks to pencil pushers, typists, and keypunchers. Indeed, what the federal example shows is for how long a variety of work arrangements—some rationalized, mechanized, and feminized and others diversified and sexually integrated—coexisted. Not until the second decade of the twentieth century would William Leffingwell begin to suggest that Taylor's principles of scientific management be applied to office work. To see the history of clerical work in the nineteenth century as one of unremitting decline would be to misunderstand the work experiences of large numbers of nineteenth-century middle-class men and women. The slow and haphazard institution of centralized, rigidly enforced regulations governing job assignments for federal clerks left many male and female members of this new middle class able, throughout the nineteenth century, to take pride in the breadth of their duties and the responsibility of their jobs.

CHAPTER FIVE

Getting a Job, Keeping a Job, Winning a Promotion

How to obtain a position, how to hold on to that position, and how to advance within the office—for federal clerks these issues were fully as important as, yet often unrelated to, the mastering of necessary clerical skills. Working within the federal government required considerably more than learning a new job. These men and women also had to become adept at maneuvering within a large, unpredictable, and changing organization. At the time of the Civil War, government offices functioned, in many ways, according to informal, personal, irregular rules. As the number of clerks within the department grew dramatically over the next four decades, increasing efforts were made to institute more rational, formal methods of hiring, promoting, and evaluating government workers. But the process was not a steady and gradual climb toward bureaucracy. Rather, a mixture of the idiosyncratic and the rational, the informal and the bureaucratic, persisted within Washington agencies and presented federal workers with a variety of problems as they made their way into and around the federal workplace. The men and women who clerked in government offices found themselves within an organization that was functioning simultaneously as an informal, decentralized institution and an increasingly structured bureaucracy.

Government clerks were among the first middle-class workers to labor in an organization that was experiencing such changes. As large corporations hired increasing numbers of white-collar clerks in the years after 1890, however, more and more men and women would find themselves in similar situations. Examining how federal clerks fared in this environment reveals what happened to white-collar employees as the places in which they worked became more formal and bureaucratic. It also allows us to see how such changes in the workplace affected men and women differently. The case of the federal government suggests that these middle-class workers did not always profit from increasing bureaucratization, despite the promise of order and fairness that it at least implicitly offered. Moreover, men and women often benefited or suffered from different aspects of the informal or bureaucratic procedures. As they applied for jobs, tried to secure those positions, and competed for promotions, federal workers—both male and female—learned the numerous tactics necessary to survive and prosper within an organization that was on its way toward becoming a formal bureaucracy.

DURING THE FIRST TWO post-Civil War decades the process of acquiring federal clerkships depended not upon rigid entrance qualifications, but upon much more informal, personal, and political criteria. Who an applicant knew counted at least as much as—indeed, probably more than—the skills he or she could demonstrate. Inevitably, party politics played a critical role within the federal job market, and job-seekers quickly learned that clerkships in Washington could not be procured without first successfully manipulating the patronage system. Before applicants could hope to win federal appointments, they had to establish their political credentials and to find influential people to support them.

By the opening of the Civil War, the patronage system, begun under the administration of Andrew Jackson, controlled appointments to the federal service. Each state or territory was allotted its "quota" of government positions, the number of places being determined by the state's representation in Congress. When a vacancy occurred in a state's quota, members of the congressional delegation would recommend an applicant to fill the position.[1] Those who hoped to procure federal jobs had to win the endorsement and active support of members of Congress from their local district. The process, called "acquiring influence," often demanded considerable effort. The number of applicants always exceeded the number of places, and senators and representatives often disagreed over which candidate to support. Applicants were thus frequently required to enlist the aid of others in acquiring congressional backing.

Would-be clerks turned to federal officials, important office-holders within state government, and well-placed members of the business community to request assistance in securing congressional endorsements and government jobs. Those who knew influential men personally were able most easily to secure positions. Austine Snead received help from Senator Guthrie, a friend of her mother's, while James Brown called upon the congressman from his district, someone who had lived in his home town and had known him, he said, "since my birth."[2]

Most applicants, lacking a direct Washington connection, turned to other means of obtaining the necessary patronage. The next best thing to knowing an influential person, was knowing someone who knew him, and numerous men and women tried to exploit such possibilities. Many asked acquaintances from their home town—a rich businessman, the head of the local veteran's organization, or an official connected with the "right" political party—for help in gaining entrée to powerful Washington figures. The files of federal applicants are filled with letters from such patrons requesting that a congressman or senator endorse their friend or acquaintance for a position in Washington.

Some job-seekers, especially those who resided in the District of Columbia, were very resourceful in finding connections. Washingon was a city that afforded various opportunities for contact with the important people living there. Phebe Carter, for example, received assistance from numerous influential men who boarded at her mother's "distinguished" Capitol Hill boarding house. Postmaster General John Wanamaker explained his interest in finding a position for Rose Lee, the daughter of a "very efficient and clever" conductor on the B and O Railroad: "Mr. Lee...sees me every time I go on the train about the appointment of his daughter to a place in the Patent Office." Wanamaker had already written one letter on Miss Lee's behalf, but, he continued, "so far no appointment has been made and the old man is still after me."[3] Thomas Foster—not unlike a hero from a Horatio Alger tale—turned a chance encounter into a powerful patronage asset. During the winter of 1866, Foster happened upon a package of papers that belonged to Senator William Sprague. The senator was so relieved to have his papers returned that he willingly endorsed Foster's application for a position in the Treasury Department. Sprague explained, "This young man proved his worth by returning to me a package that I lost." He asked if it was "a possible thing to reward honesty and to prove [his] gratitude" by securing for Foster a position. The Secretary of the Treasury concurred and Foster received the job.[4]

Many applicants, however, had little direct or indirect access to sources of power, and these men and women often had to appeal to strangers— usually congressmen and government officials—asking for endorsements and jobs. Since congressmen were most likely to offer their influence on behalf of the best and most loyal party members, those who sought government jobs spent considerable time detailing their political backgrounds. Of course, in this era of limited suffrage, establishing political credentials entailed a different process for male and female candidates.

Men straightforwardly expressed their political sympathies. Victor Barnes, for example, applied for a position in 1861 and noted, "In consequence of the active interest [I] manifested in the Republican causes, during the late Presidential campaign, [I] was compelled to leave the county to avoid personal violence...I have been an anti-slavery Methodist ever since the Church divided on that question sixteen years ago; and a Republican, in principle for five years. Previous to that time, I was a Whig of the Henry Clay school. All my sympathies and interests are fully identified with the Republican party...." On the basis of such credentials Barnes hoped to win an appointment to a place then occupied by a Democrat from his home district.[5] Countless male applicants made similar appeals throughout the nineteenth century. The political party to which they avowed loyalty changed, of course, depending upon the administration in power, but the basic message remained the same: party loyalty qualified them for the endorsements and the positions they sought.

Male applicants could point not only to their principles, but to their behavior within the political arena. Men could swear their fidelity to the party in the past *and* promise active support in the future. Male clerks who lived and worked in Washington still journeyed "home" at election time to cast their ballots and work for the party. In districts where elections were close, congressmen could assure themselves not only of the votes, but of the active assistance of the clerks whom they had placed in office. On occasion, in fact, male applicants found that their vote-getting abilities afforded them considerable power in the quest for patronage and jobs. Take, for example, the rather checkered career of John E. Smithers. Smithers had begun to work in the Interior Department in 1880 and had won some acclaim as an accomplished accountant. But in the middle of the decade his work began to fall off because of his tendency to indulge too heavily in drink, and in 1888 he resigned in lieu of dismissal. Despite such a blemish on his record, Senator Higgins recommended him for a job in the Census Office two years later. A letter from another influential party member explained Higgins's endorsement: "[W]e need him [Smithers] in the present close contest, for a vote may secure a congressman and put our state fully in the line of progress. Our election is only a week off today, and Mr. S. is generally on the election board in my district. By his correctness of tallying last election he detected a fraud that would have lost us a county officer. We shall lose his vote and work if this matter fails for he will not brook the disgrace in his home community of standing discharged from office." Assurances were offered that Smithers had reformed—having abstained from alchoholic beverages for three months—and the job was his.[6] While Smithers's position on the election board certainly guaranteed him an unusual amount of political clout, his case nevertheless reveals that male applicants had something they could offer to congressmen in return for the promise of "influence."

Female applicants could wield no such power. A woman had no political persona: she could not vote, she could not hold office. Thus, establishing political credentials proved problematic. The political arena was, in the nineteenth century, designated a masculine realm into which women should not dare to venture, yet women who wanted government jobs needed to muster political patronage. Most often, female job-seekers established their political affiliations by citing the political credentials of their families.

Women talked of coming from a "good Democratic" or "loyal Republican" family. They noted that their fathers or brothers had voted and worked for the party. Often the best way that a woman could demonstrate her own patriotism was by explaining that she had lost a husband, father, or son in the war. Mrs. H. E. Nixon, for example, wrote that her husband had "sacrificed a flourishing business, health, and life itself" for the Union cause.[7] Lillie Deeble had "no parents living but they were Republicans," while Sarah J. Smith belonged "to one of the most respectable families of Allegeny County—and in the past actively identified with the Democratic party."[8]

Women's apolitical position in nineteenth-century America put them at a definite disadvantage in the scramble for direct political influence and government jobs. Women could not promise to vote for the party or to stump for the candidate. Female applicants frequently had to use indirect—and often unreliable—methods of acquiring political influence. When Annie Kurtz applied for a job in the Interior Department in 1881, the person writing on her behalf explained that her uncle was a bishop of the Methodist Episcopal Church and he remarked, "as the Republican Party draws more support from Methodists, perhaps, than any other religious organization, and as the Bishop is not likely to ask any political favor, I venture to suggest that it would be a deserved compliment to him...to have this small favor bestowed upon his niece."[9] Such a tenuous claim to political connections failed to win Kurtz the position she sought.

Women faced other problems unique to their sex in the federal job market. Some congressmen simply opposed the hiring of female clerks, while others preferred to save their quota for voting, male party members. Mrs. M. E. Tuttle, a legal resident of Connecticut, needed the endorsement of a senator from that state before she could procure a position in the Census Office in 1890. The men working on her behalf hailed from other states, but they asked Senator Orville Platt to approve her application. Platt refused, saying that if she were "charged" to his district, she would take "the place of some good man who desires, and whom I desire shall have an appointment from that district."[10] Basically powerless within the political arena, women often found the process of acquiring influence a difficult one.

Female applicants did, however, possess one "commodity" which they could offer in exchange for the support of influential men—themselves. And no doubt some men demanded sexual favors as the price for helping women obtain federal jobs. The first annual report of the Civil Service Commission made a veiled allusion to this problem. It noted that female job-seekers would benefit particularly from the new merit system since henceforth the "need for political influence or for importunate solicitation, especially disagreeable to women," would be abolished.[11] An 1876 article in a Washington newspaper, however, confronted the issue more directly. The story related the plight of a young woman who had worked for only two months in the Bureau of Printing and Engraving before losing her job. Finding herself in terrible financial straits, every day deeper in debt, she made repeated trips to the House of Representatives searching for someone to help her secure another position. Reportedly one member of Congress offered the following propositions: "Well, *you do me a favor* and I will do a favor for you. No one will ever know it but you and

I, and I will put you in a postion to get $75 per month." Horrified, the young woman reminded him, "God would know it, and I should know it," and she ran from the room "hardly able to keep back [her] tears." This story struck an especially responsive chord in Charlotte Cross, a female clerk in the Treasury Department, who clipped the article and sent it to the Assistant Secretary of the Treasury with the following message: "Reading the enclosed, my sympathy and charity alike go out toward this young woman. I know what it means and I want to help her. If you can find out who she is and find her still needing employment, will you assign her to work in your Dept. to receive *one half* of my salary *from this date* till such time as you may have a vacancy for her?" Cross ended her letter: "God help and protect poor women trying to be useful and honest."[12]

It is, of course, impossible to know how often women encountered such problems, but stories of sexual danger for female job-seekers appeared frequently in the writings of newspaper correspondents and novelists familiar with the Washington scene. In the early 1880s, Mrs. E. N. Chapin, one of many Washington correspondents, related the story of Mrs. John Smith to the readers of the Iowa *State Register*. Mrs. Smith, a widow, had journeyed to Washington to inquire about her late husband's pension. Finding the proceedings delayed, and with two children to support, Mrs. Smith approached a senator and requested assistance in obtaining a position in the departments. Apparently the senator responded with an offensive proposition, at which the "plucky" Mrs. Smith "seized the immense inkstand from the table, and dashing its contents against his fine coat and shirt front she made for the door like an angry deer, only to find it locked." The ink-stained senator, regaining his composure, informed Mrs. Smith that he was only testing "to see if [she was] a proper person to put into so responsible a position," and immediately authorized her appointment to the Treasury Department.[13] Whether the tales were triumphant like Mrs. Smith's or more aggrieved like Charlotte Cross's, they suggest that sexual danger presented a real threat to some female applicants.

Even when such situations did not threaten to compromise their honor, many genteel, middle-class nineteenth-centry women found the necessity of approaching strangers a particularly trying ordeal. Mrs. Minnie Voute, for example, wrote directly to the head of the Census Office to ask for a job in 1880. She explained that she had decided to write, rather than to call upon him in person, because it was "so very embarrassing to have to pass through the adjoining room." She pleaded her case: "General you must know how very hard it is for a lady of any delicacy of feeling to be obliged to come to you or any gentleman and state her case asking for bread for self and little ones. I have been very differently situated, never expecting to come to this; it has been my privilege to assist others from my own purse and today I have to ask strangers to assist me in procuring work."[14] Victorian society had sheltered and protected respectable ladies from strange and possibly unscrupulous men. For such women to approach congressmen or government officials—unaccompanied and without proper introduction—constituted not merely a breach of etiquette, but a fearful encounter with an unfamiliar male world.[15]

The process of acquiring federal jobs in nineteenth-century America thus held dangers and problems for women that it did not for men. Mustering political credentials proved difficult, while approaching strangers presented at the least embarrassment and at the worst sexual peril for proper Victorian ladies. There was, however, one aspect of this informal, job-procuring process that women could turn to their benefit. While men could detail their political contributions—past, present, and future, women could graphically depict their need. Indeed, being "needy" was another way to win a job in government, especially—but not necessarily—if that need stemmed from patriotic sacrifices.

Female applicants frequently offered complete, emotion-laden descriptions of the enormous family and financial problems that prompted their entrée into the federal job market. Job-seekers told stories of young children and elderly parents to be supported, of hardships faced, of comforts once possessed but now gone, of the shame of accepting charity, and of the fear of poverty. While the facts offered were no doubt true, the nature of women's presentations were frequently designed to emphasize their unselfishness, neediness, dependence, and helplessness. When Nannie Lancaster asked the Superintendent of the Census for a job in 1889, she used these words: "[I]f you owned a sister who was better than all the people in the world and half of them in the Bible, and you saw her dying, not by the traditional inches, but by square feet, because she needed help that you couldn't give her, why you would ask a favor too—you couldn't help yourself! I don't know how to put it cleverly, because this letter is making me so nervous I can hardly hold my pen, but indeed, indeed, when my sister wants things that I know her health demands, and I can't give them to her why, it hurts just like somebody had put a rope around my neck and was pulling it— hard!"[16] Relaying such information may not have been easy for women, but it was congruent with proper female behavior. Nineteenth-century mores made it entirely acceptable for women to appear helpless, dependent, and needy.

Most male applicants did not feel so free to use such tactics. While men did, in their letters of application, discuss their often tenuous financial positions, they usually did not assume the role of the supplicant. Instead, men might explain that they were between jobs or financially embarrassed for the moment, and that they had families to support. Occasionally a male applicant would admit, as did Maurice Wolfe, that he was "greatly in need of some employment." In Wolfe's case it was, he feared, "only one step between my present position and 'over the hills to the Poorhouse.'"[17] But more common were expressions like "unfortunate in business" used to describe applicant John Ross, or explanations like Timothy Sullivan's: "I am a man of family, and as my funds have become exhausted, I find myself in a peculiarly embarrassed condition and therefore appeal for a favorable and prompt consideration of my application."[18]

Certain male applicants, however, did plead for assistance in letters replete with detailed, often emotional, descriptions of financial, family, and personal hardships. But such letters were usually written either by very old, very young, or physically disabled men—men who found themselves as helpless and dependent as women. Seventeen-year-old William Steadman, for example, wrote in 1880 asking for a position as a messenger: "[I]n consequence of the war I was deprived of a good Father. The death of my mother followed a few years after of grief. I am an orphan, entirely dependent on my own self; I am out of everything; (and almost out of heart); My father left all to fight for his country...but alas! like many others, never returned...I now appeal to your kindness of heart to help a boy along."[19] Men who were crippled or disabled sometimes entreated federal officials in the same ways that did women and young men. Although he had lost his leg after rather than during the war, Pennock J. Cole explained, "[N]evertheless I am a leg out and have a wife and five children depending on me for support, and have for the past 13 months been depending on charity (on account of my accident)...Comrade I need a friend that will help me and I beg of you a sittuation [*sic*] if not a clerkship, anything within your gift will be acceptable and duly appreciated by me. Trusting you will sympathise with me and relieve my forlorn condition...."[20] The very old, often equally desperate, were also willing to humble themselves. Louis Ganbin, aged and rheumatic, wrote describing his family's great need—that they were all living on the $33-per-month wages of his son. Out of these wages, he said, "we have to pay rent, buy fuel and provisions and his clothes. The cold weather is coming, and our fuel will be very expensive."[21]

There could be no doubt that appealing to an official's sympathy sometimes succeeded in winning jobs. And while men were usually loathe to offer specific descriptions of their difficulties, their female relatives were not always so proud. Upon occasion a man's application would suggest only financial embarrassment, but a separate letter from his wife or mother might elaborate upon the sad details. When William Clapp applied for work in 1880, for example, his letter referred to "the necessity of [his] obtaining employment, and [his] great anxiety concerning this matter." He proceeded then to list the influential men who backed him and to assure the Superintendent of the Census that he would cheerfully accept even a salary as low as $600 per year. Clapp received the job, but had held it for less than a year when he was dismissed in a reduction of the force of the office. Clapp began, almost immediately, to try to win reinstatement, and this time his mother took up her pen on his behalf. The tone and content of her letter differed considerably from his. She did not hesitate to mention that she, her husband, and their two invalid daughters depended upon this son for support. Moreover, she explained that her husband was seventy-five years old as well as "feeble...and very sick."[22]

Most men did not willingly or comfortably appeal for sympathy. In fact, the whole process of job-seeking within the federal government, with its required courting of influential men, proved troublesome for some male applicants. Joseph Cooke stated the problem more eloquently and more directly than did other men when, disgusted after four promises of work and four disappointments, he complained to the Secretary of the Interior "[T]hey have treated me meanly, badly, cruelly. I have been trotting back and forth to 9th St. since November last to obtain reinstatement, but in vain. I appear no nearer the goal than when I began." Bitterly he told the secretary, "They seem not to know when they trifle with a man's manhood."[23] If female "delicacy" made it difficult to approach strangers, male "manliness" made it difficult to supplicate. Indeed, a Thomas Nast cartoon depicting male office-seekers in women's dress gave visual expression to the kind of humiliation that men like Joseph Cooke felt as they attempted to obtain federal positions. (See Figure.)

Cartoon by Thomas Nast, "What the Position of a President of the United States Really Is" (Morton Keller, *The Art and Politics of Thomas Nast* (New York, 1968), 237.)

For some men and women, procuring a job followed quickly on the heels of obtaining influence, but for others the process could be protracted and difficult. Once the assistance of influential men had been secured, the next step in the job-hunting process involved repeated appeals—written and personal— to the appointing powers. Applicants and their patrons pressed their cases in letters and in personal visits to relevant cabinet members and officers of the various agencies. While the process was the same for male and for female applicants, gender could be a significant determinant of the outcome.

Many federal officials discriminated against female applicants, arbitrarily restricting the number of places they could occupy. Technically, the head of a department controlled the labor force within his agency and decided where women could be hired. In practice, however, agency heads often followed the recommendations of lower-level officials who supervised various offices within the department. Such supervisors could exercise considerable authority and often determined the character of the work force. In 1863 the Register of the Treasury requested that the Assistant Secretary of Treasury not send him any more "ladies," since, he wrote, "I have now no employment for them." He must have felt that Secretary of Treasury Salmon Chase would disapprove of such a policy for he cautioned that "this is of course not written to be shown to the Secretary."[24]

In most instances officials found no reason to hide their views, for cabinet officers often endorsed and even initiated discriminatory hiring practices. Secretary of Interior Kirkwood's response to Mary Balch, the well-educated daughter of a Presbyterian minister, only thinly veiled his anti-female policy. When she applied for a clerkship in the Pension Office in 1881, Kirkwood informed her that "knowledge of the law was indispensable to those persons appointed to" such positions. Undaunted, Balch noted how "easily" such a problem could be remedied: "I am more than willing to spend my nights studying law and my days working for our glorious government." Kirkwood nevertheless refused her the position.[25] When Mrs. M. C. Knowles applied for a similar job in the same year she received a more straightforward response: "I have to inform you that appointments soon to be made in the Pension Office are exclusively in the higher grade of Clerkships, selection of ladies being reserved for further consideration."[26]

Gender was only one of many components that affected the job-hunting procedure. For both male and female applicants, success or failure in the federal job market also hinged on a variety of other contingencies: the nature of their influence, the state of the fiscal appropriations, the number of positions then available, and luck. Some applicants obtained their positions quickly and painlessly; others waited months, watching their cash reserves dwindle and their debts mount.

When it came to hiring procedures, then, the federal government functioned according to informal, rather than rational, bureaucratic standards. While the idiosyncracies of the political patronage system were unique to the federal workplace, the notion of patronage—in the broadest sense of the term—was not in the least foreign to job-seekers in a variety of nineteenth-century situations. In the immediate post-Civil War decades, remember, most American businesses remained small, owner-operated establishments. And in such organizations, family and personal connections frequently determined who would be hired. Even the one industry that pioneered in introducing modern, bureaucratic management techniques during these years—the railroad—relied upon less than "rational" criteria in recruiting employees. Railroad companies left the hiring of workers to low-level supervisors, and consequently the best way to get a job on the railroad was through the connections of a family member or close friend. When these tactics failed, applicants sometimes resorted to bribery or, in other instances, to methods similar to the ones used by applicants to the federal service—the enlistment of aid from an influential politician.[27] Would-be federal office holders thus inhabited a world where patronage provided a much traveled route to business or professional positions.

IN 1883, CONGRESS PASSED the Pendleton Civil Service Act and took a giant step away from this personal, informal system and toward a more rational, bureaucratic means of staffing the federal departments. Various, often disparate, voices had since the mid-1860s campaigned for reform of the government along civil service lines. In his recent study of state-building in America, Stephen Skowronek has identified three important pockets of reform activity.[28] Perhaps the most visible of the civil service reformers was a group of professionals—lawyers, academics, and clergy—who hoped that civil service reform would remove American government from the hands of corrupt and crude party pols and reconstitute it in the hands of a meritorious, intellectual, patrician elite. Men like Dorman Eaton and George Curtis envisioned a merit system similar to the one instituted in England in 1870. These reformers organized and headed civil service reform leagues across the country, wrote pamphlets, helped to draft legislation, and rallied support for their cause.

A second group of civil service reformers was interested less in the restructuring and moral regeneration of American institutions than in increasing the efficiency of the executive agencies. A small number of government officials backed by urban merchants, traders, and bankers supported civil service as a drive for retrenchment—reducing the "excess baggage of wartime government" and streamlining business within the agencies. The urban businessmen who joined civil service reform groups had found that undependable federal services—specifically inefficiency in post offices and customs offices—threatened their profits. Such men, interested in the "business side of reform," perceived another benefit in the merit system—it seemed one way of protecting government from the unholy and corrupting influences of monopoly-minded, new industrial capitalists.

Civil service reform also took some strength, ironically enough, from political leaders who saw in it a way of preserving their own power or quieting disputes within the party. President Grant, for example, established a short-lived Civil Service Commission in 1871. He was motivated not, however, by a strong commitment to reform, but by political pragmatism. Civil service reform was one of the causes espoused by the defecting Liberal Republicans, and Grant's support óf reform helped to neutralize their impact on the election of 1872.

The assassination of President Garfield in 1881 by a disappointed office seeker helped bring to a head more than a decade of debate on civil service reform. Recently organized civil service reform leagues used Garfield's assassination in a nation-wide propaganda campaign directed against those opposed to the merit system. The final passage of the Pendleton Bill in 1883 came, however, as a result of the efforts of both idealistic, high-minded reformers and pragmatic party politicians. In the 1882 midterm election, the Republican party lost control of the House and, foreseeing a presidential loss in 1884, reversed its stand on civil service. Hoping to take credit for instituting the merit system and, more importantly, to protect loyal party members already in office, the Republicans first succeeded in making certain amendments to Pendleton's bill and then closed ranks behind it. On January 16, 1883, the bill became law.[29]

The purpose of the new law was to remove partisan politics from the federal service. To this end the Pendleton Act forbade soliciting political contributions from government employees. It also established a three-member bipartisan commission that would write regulations and oversee the administration of the new system.[30] Henceforth all positions classified within the civil service could be filled only by competitive examination. The Civil Service Commission held such examinations, graded all papers, and ranked all applicants, thereby creating a list of "eligibles"—a pool from which employees could be selected. The top three names on the list then went to whatever office had requested a clerk, and the head of that office chose one of the three to fill the position.

The procedures were designed to make merit the primary qualification for entrance into federal employment, but various loopholes diminished the system's effectiveness. Numerous positions within the Washington agencies remained "unclassified"—outside the jurisdiction of the civil service regulations. The entire staff hired to count and tabulate the census in 1890—2,150 employees—for example, remained outside the protection of the Civil Service Commission.[31] During most of the nineteenth century the Civil Service also excluded from its jurisdiction all temporary employees, as well as those workers who held "laborer's" positions paying $600 per year. Although theoretically such employees only performed manual labor, in practice many worked as clerks. In 1893 the Secretary of the Interior reported that the civil service system still excluded about one-quarter of the 4,600 people employed in the Interior Department's Washington offices.[32]

For applicants seeking access to unclassified jobs, the patronage system continued to operate as it had for those men and women who had applied for positions in the immediate post-Civil War decades. But once a majority of positions had been classified within the civil service, congressmen had fewer federal positions at their disposal with which to pay political debts. Consequently, the competition for influence necessary to procure unclassified clerkships increased. The Census Office, with its thousands of exempted positions, served as a major outlet for dispensing patronage. The Superintendent of the Census recorded the "accounts" of senators and representatives in a ledger, noting how many positions each could control and when each had reached his quota.[33] To keep better track of the ever-dwindling number of patronage positions within all the federal agencies, Congress ordered the Civil Service Commission to publish, after each change in administrations, lists that enumerated those positions falling within and outside the jurisdiction of the civil service rules. In carrying out such orders the Commission found itself, according to one historian, "functioning as a reluctant broker in what might be called the patronage 'exchange.' "[34] There remained throughout the nineteenth century, then, many positions in Washington offices that still were acquired through the old patronage system.

Even within classified jobs, the Civil Service Commission allowed for two "legitimate" deviations from the rule of merit in selection of federal employees. First, geography was permitted to supersede excellence. The Pendleton Act held that appointments to jobs in Washington Departments be apportioned among the states and territories according to their population and representation in Congress. In fulfilling this obligation the Civil Service Commission certified eligibles from states that had not met their "quota." Therefore, applicants who had achieved high scores on the competitive examination, but who came from places that had already filled or exceeded their allotted number of federal clerkships, were often passed over in favor of less qualified candidates from other states.[35]

The second deviation from the rule of merit concerned gender. A merit system, if strictly enforced and fairly administered, could have had truly radical implications for women's employment. The Civil Service Commission proudly and accurately maintained that "civil service law makes no distinction on account of sex," and that "examinations under it are open alike to men and women."[36] Despite such rhetoric, the egalitarian potential within the civil service system was never realized because, from the beginning, women were denied an equal chance at civil service jobs.

Women were, indeed, allowed to compete in all examinations, but they were not ranked with male applicants or appointed to the same positions. The Pendleton Act in no way diminished the power of a federal official to request the type (gender) of employee he desired for the job. Thus, while touting the benefits the new law would have for women, the Civil Service Commission still had to admit that it possessed no authority to increase the number of "female" positions: "The law in force before the passage of the civil service act gave the heads of Departments authority to decide when women are required or can be accepted. Both the civil service act and the rules leave that authority unimpaired."[37] The heads of agencies continued to request women for "female" job—positions labeled "copyist" that paid $900 per year.

The minimal effect of the Civil Service law on equalizing employment opportunities was not, however, immediately clear, and some women apparently expected the new system to afford them access to better paid places. In 1884, female applicants requested permission to take the examination for the position of pension examiner, a high-paid male job. A member of the Civil Service Commission queried the Secretary of the Interior whether "if such women successfully pass the examination, they can be appointed to such places." The Secretary responded with a curt "No."[38]

The annual reports of the Civil Service Commission reveal what stiff competition prospective federal employees faced in the pursuit of government jobs. Federal clerkships in the nation's capital were highly coveted and difficult to secure, and the number of applicants always exceeded the number of available positions by a wide margin. Between 1883 and 1894, qualified applicants outnumbered jobs by as many as four to one. (See Table 5.1.) But for women, the chances of successfully achieving a government clerkship were even lower. Women received far fewer than their proportional share of appointments. Between 1884 and 1894, for example, women accounted for between 28 and 43 percent of those passing civil service examinations, but they received only 7 to 25 percent of the appointments. (See Table 5.2.) The Commission recognized and periodically commented upon the great "excess" of female applicants, noting not only the large number of women who applied, but how comparatively few obtained positions. It maintained correctly, however, that such imbalance resulted not from the civil service system, but because the

TABLE 5.1
Examinations and Appointments of Men and Women for Classified Civil Service Positions, Washington, D.C., 1883–94

Year	Number passing clerk and/or copyist examinations	Number appointed to positions	Percentage of those passing that received appointments
July 1883–Jan. 1884	459	53	12%
Jan. 1884–Dec. 1885	1,338	438	33%
Jan. 1885–Dec. 1886	826	234	28%
Jan. 1886–June 1887	2,598	547	21%
July 1887–June 1888	1,551	352	23%
July 1888–June 1889	1,630	338	21%
July 1889–June 1890	1,521	416	27%
July 1890–June 1891	2,634	986	37%
July 1891–June 1892	1,997	356	18%
July 1892–June 1893	1,212	296	24%
July 1893–June 1894	1,388	273	20%

Sources: U.S., Civil Service Commission, *Annual Reports,* 1884–94.[39]

TABLE 5.2

Classified Civil Service Examinations and Appointments, Washington, D.C.,
1884–94

Year	Sex of applicants who passed clerk and/or copyist exams			Sex of applicants appointed to civil service positions		
	Women	Men	Number	Women	Men	Number
Jan. 1884 – Dec. 1885	28%	72%	1,338	11%	89%	438
Jan. 1885 – Dec. 1886	28%	72%	826	13%	87%	234
Jan. 1886 – June 1887	33%	67%	2,598	17%	83%	547
July 1887 – June 1888	40%	60%	1,551	14%	86%	352
July 1888 – June 1889	42%	58%	1,630	22%	78%	338
July 1889 – June 1890	42%	58%	1,521	13%	87%	416
July 1890 – June 1891	41%	59%	2,634	16%	84%	986
July 1891 – June 1892	43%	57%	1,997	25%	75%	356
July 1892 – June 1893	38%	62%	1,212	24%	76%	296
July 1893 – June 1894	31%	69%	1,388	7%	93%	273

Sources: U.S., Civil Service Commission, *Annual Reports,* 1884–94.[40]

Commission was required, by law, to "certify persons of the sex named by the appointing officer."[41]

Besides these two "legitimate" exceptions to the rule of merit, the nineteenth century witnessed a good bit of illegal deviation from the regulations of the civil service. Although ostensibly only merit counted, some applicants still attempted to use influence in their quest for clerkships. It is difficult to know how many tried or succeeded in abusing the system, but the letters of male and female applicants suggest that many still perceived patronage as an asset in the pursuit of government jobs. For example, in 1887, Frederick Carson wrote to the Secretary of the Interior to ask reinstatement within the Interior Department. He had several times before considered bringing his case before the Secretary, but he noted, "as often as I would go to Washington, D.C. and visit the Interior Dept. Bldg. I would lose confidence at the sight of so many more strongly backed by 'influence' than myself, unsuccessful in their attempts."[42] And when Ida Edson lost her job in the Census Office in 1891, she began to search for a permanent place elsewhere within the Washington bureaucracy: "I am hoping I can get a...position in one of the other departments. One of my friends will write Senator Paddock on my behalf; another Senator Manderson. Influence seems to be necessary."[43] Legal or not, both Carson and Edson still saw the influence system operating within the departments.

Most applicants knew, however, that the Civil Service Law prohibited the use of political influence for securing classified clerkships.[44] These men and women began their quest for federal employment not by searching for patrons, but by sitting for an examination. Although some federal agencies had required examinations of prospective employees since 1853, such tests differed from those dispensed after passage of the Pendleton Act. Most early examinations were non-competitive or "pass" examinations—initiated as a simple qualifying requirement, not a rigorous test of merit. Moreover, no government-wide standard had regulated the nature of such exams or the testing procedures; rather each agency had administered its own test.[45] According to historian Leonard White, the "nature and quality of such examinations...varied according to the attitudes of Secretaries and bureau chiefs. Each department head was allowed to fix his own standards within the broad range of the act of 1853; Schurz in Interior used competitive examinations, while Sherman in Treasury did little."[46]

The Civil Service Commission created by the 1883 Pendleton Act initiated two distinct examinations for prospective federal clerks—the limited (copyist) and the general (clerk) exam. The former tested only penmanship, spelling, and arithmetic. Applicants who competed in such exams—the majority of whom were women—qualified only for positions paying a maximum salary of $900. Candidates who desired higher paid clerkships sat for the general examinations where they demonstrated their skills in grammar, syntax, and more difficult arithmetic problems, as well as knowledge of history, geography, and government. A potential clerk might be asked, for example, to give the date and circumstances of the Louisiana Purchase, describe and name the several departments within the executive branch of the U.S. Government, and outline the differing functions of the two houses of Congress—all questions that the Civil Service Commission felt could be answered by a person with a good common school education."[47] Both men and women competed in these tests, but since agency heads requested only male applicants for high-paid positions, the Civil Service Commission could not appoint even those women who had excelled on the examination. Many women did, of course, acquire jobs that paid $1000 or more and that demanded, in fact, skills identical to those performed by men. But such women did so by working their way up the ladder, since virtually all female applicants were hired initially at salaries ranging from $600 to $900 annually.

In 1894 the Commission combined the two categories and offered one clerk/copyist examination that tested applicants in all the categories previously covered by both exams: orthography, copying, penmanship, arithmetic (including fundamental rules, fractions, percentage, interest, and discount), elements of bookkeeping and accounts, elements of the English language, letter-writing, geography, history, and government. The new, clerk/copyist examination set the same standards for all applicants—male and female. Even then, however, it did not facilitate women's access to high-paid jobs. Although female applicants often demonstrated that they were as skilled and competent as male job-seekers, agencies continued to request women for low-ranking positions only.

Despite the legitimate and illegitimate deviations from the rule of merit, the new civil service system offered definite advantages to applicants within the federal job market. No longer plagued by the necessity of cornering influential men and scrounging for political patronage, potential office-holders could, after 1884, study diligently, compete on the exam, and win appointment without the fear that political prejudice or personal favoritism would ruin their chances for success. And, no doubt, for some applicants the system worked just as it was intended. A young, well-educated man like Robert H. Read found that the civil service system expedited his entry into a good position within the Patent Office. Read had graduated from public school at the age of fifteen and then entered Lehigh University, from which he received a baccalaureate three years later. After graduation, he worked for six months as an associate editor of a small newspaper and then began to teach high school. At the end of one year, Read decided to enter the federal job market. He competed in an exam held to fill twenty-five positions in the Pension Office and performed splendidly. Of the four hundred competitors, Read ranked twelfth and duly received his appointment. After working in the Pension Office for only ten months, Read decided to compete in another exam for a higher paid job within the Patent Office. And once again, he met with success. Of the more than one hundred who sat for the exam, Read ranked fifth. Four people got the jobs, he amongst them.[48]

For those applicants whose education was neither so extensive nor so recent, however, examinations could prove a considerable obstacle in the quest for government jobs. Even the non-competitive exams administered in the Census Office in 1890 made many applicants—both male and female—"nervous" and "flustered." William Alexander, for example, wrote to the head of the Census Office explaining the problems he had had during the examination: "I was under the impression that the time allowed for each exercise or question was very limited, and I paid more attention to speed than to style or accuracy. I was excited and my hand trembled so that I could scarcely write, and I did not do myself justice."[49] Alexander's fears were not all that different from Eleanor Bryan's. Bryan had completed her education at the age of eighteen, an education which included both public schooling and some training in a private academy. After spending four years attending to "home duties," she applied for a federal clerkship. Despite her strong education, the examination intimidated her: "I do not think the Examination is a test of any real ability, but it certainly is a test of nerves. I was at the time of the examination laboring under most intense excitement. I do not know whether I made the required percentage or not."[50]

Older applicants, especially, found the prospect of an examination troubling. Women such as Mittah Newel blamed the "many long years" since they had attended school for their trepidations.[51] Sixty-five-year-old Elizah S. Wicklin offered a more detailed explanation for his fears. He explained that although he could "write an Essay in Industrial Production, or a Text Book on Physics and Mechanical Philosophy," he felt he had "little chance in a school examination. Time develops new methods. In practical life men narrow down to a few lines of study. Only young men from schools and professional teachers are prepared for an educational test."[52] Indeed, some applicants might have found their confrontation with the civil service examination their first experience with written tests, for not until the second half of the nineteenth century did American schools begin to employ written examinations to measure learning or intelligence. Oral examinations had previously been the custom, and these had been none too rigorous. According to historian Daniel Calhoun, it was often difficult to know whether "a given performance was a serious examination or simply an exhibition staged to please visitors."[53] Products of an educational system that had demanded only oral recitation, some would-be federal clerks viewed the civil service examinations as an especially large and fearful obstacle on the road to government positions.

Potential clerks chose various means of dealing with the problems posed by entrance exams. The least brave expressed their willingness to forgo federal employ rather than submit to the ordeal of an exam. Harriet Harrington, fearing that failure would result, she explained, "in mortification to my friends who recommended me, as well as to myself," solicited advice from her senator and stated that if he so counseled, she would "give it up."[54] Other applicants, however, tried to secure unclassified jobs—usually lower-paid positions as "laborers" that were not within the jurisdiction of the Civil Service Commission and hence exempt from competitive examination. Although the practice was illegal and expressly forbidden by civil service regulations, in many offices both male and female "laborers" performed clerical tasks similar to those of employees earning considerably higher salaries.[55] This practice not only offered timid applicants a means of circumventing the civil service examination, it also offered numerous federal offices a way to reduce labor costs.

Occasionally, men and women, fearful of sitting for the examination, resorted to cheating. Maggie Loftus admitted that upon accompanying her sister to the place for her examination, she found her sister "so nervous and sick," she said, "that I on an impulse took the Examination [for her], this I did without thought of violating any rule of the Civil Service or any intent to deceive or defraud."[56] William P. Smith apparently had the friend with whom he was rooming, James L. Johnson, take the civil service exam for him. He explained that Johnson, already a clerk in the Treasury Department, had had a few years of college and might therefore achieve a higher score. Moreover, Smith maintained that he "understood it was done frequently."[57] Despite Smith's claim, there is little evidence that cheating occurred frequently. More likely a few of the most brazen—or most desperate—applicants turned to this tactic as they contemplated the obstacle posed by civil service examinations.

Much has been written about the creation of this civil service system—why it was done, who endorsed it, its consequences for party politics.[58] But there has been little discussion of how civil service affected civil servants. There can be little doubt that sitting for a civil service examination presented would-be government workers with a considerably more rational and bureaucratic approach to job-hunting than did the cornering of influential men and the pursuit of political patronage. But the move from an informal, personal system based upon patronage to a rational, bureaucratic system based upon merit was not necessarily a clear-cut improvement for all middle-class applicants seeking federal jobs. Under the new system job-seekers both gained something and lost something. They gained freedom from the demands of party politics and of "importunate solicitations"; they lost the help of friends and patrons in the job-seeking process. For many nineteenth-century Americans, this meant exchanging job-procuring procedures with which they were familiar for ones that were new and untested. Those without the necessary intellectual or educational resources might have preferred to rely upon the assistance available through the patronage system. But a disciplined job-seeker who was willing and able to study, compete, and excell found the avenues to government jobs no longer littered with political roadblocks.

The middle-class men and women who applied for government positions after 1883 were among the first Americans to encounter such procedures in their pursuit of jobs. Not until the twentieth century did growing private corporations begin to institute personnel management departments that rationally recruited and trained a suitable labor force.[59] There was, however, a similarity between the experience of civil service applicants and those of aspiring professionals in the late nineteenth century. For intelligence and expertise, measured through standardized competitive examinations, became the necessary qualifications for work in the government at the same time that professional associations began to require similar criteria from would-be doctors, lawyers, and academics.[60] While the body of knowledge demanded of professionals and government workers differed markedly, the similarities between the two forms of recruitment may have seemed important to the middle-class men entering government departments. Many of these men had felt uneasy and defensive about their move into government jobs, fearing that as federal employees they had relinquished their independence and with it their place in the middle class. But by succeeding within the new civil service system, government workers could lay claim to middle-class status on the basis of new qualifications—the kind of standardized measures of competence being demanded of a growing number of professionals. The civil service system thus offered such men a means to reestablish their place within a middle class where expertise rather than self-employment was becoming the benchmark of middle-class status. And in the process the federal government helped to redefine the parameters of middle-class work by making the men and women employed in the Washington bureaucracy accountable to these new standards and criteria.

Those who succeeded could feel qualified by dint of their capabilities, not merely because of their connections or luck. As a result, the new, more bureaucratic civil service system invested self-reliance, an old virtue, with new meaning in the middle-class formula for success. "To be one's own helper, and not to look to others for support," was, according to success writers like William Mathews, "the secret of all individual growth and vigor, the master-key that unlocks all difficulties in every profession or calling."[61] Such advice, addressed throughout the nineteenth-century to

young men, had offered a message that was somewhat at odds with experiences of those numerous middle-class men who had discovered other
"keys"— specifically family, personal, and political connections—to professional and business opportunities in the commercial and early industrial economy of the mid-nineteenth century. The institution of rational,
bureaucratic methods of hiring first in government, and later within private corporations, altered the relationship between individual effort and
success in the job market. In removing patronage from the job-procure-
ment process, it brought these applicants face to face with their own
capabilities and shortcomings. For with merit the criterion of success, applicants hoping to obtain federal positions could now feel that the power
to succeed lay entirely within their own hands.

Provided, of course, such applicants were male. Women, however, had
to submit to the rigors of the new system without being allowed all of its
rewards. No matter how often women competed or how well they performed on examinations, they were not placed in jobs strictly on the basis
of their merits. For women, then, the message was mixed. Self-reliance
had, after all, never been perceived as a female virtue. Nineteenth-century women had been told to behave like the clinging vine, not the sturdy
oak. The woman who wanted to succeed in the federal job market in the
years after 1883 nevertheless had to learn to make her own way, without
the aid of family or friends. While self-reliance never held out the same
promise for women that it did for men, it nevertheless became a critical
qualification for middle-class ladies contemplating positions within a
white-collar world.

WORKING WITHIN A LARGE, increasingly bureaucratic structure had implications not only for the way in which middle-class people found jobs,
but for their employment patterns within those jobs. Nineteenth-century
men who worked in traditionally middle-class endeavors, as we saw in
Chapter One, moved frequently from job to job, and even from one
career to another. Nineteenth-century middle-class women who labored
for wages usually worked for only a few years as school teachers before
marrying and setting up their own households. Working for the government, however, held out the potential of long-term employment. And,
indeed, more than half of federal employees appear to have abandoned
peripatetic middle-class work styles when they entered federal offices.
Forty-seven percent of the women and two-thirds of the men who were
working in the Treasury Department in 1871, for example, remained
within the Department at least ten years, with as many as one-fifth to one-
third working for more than two decades. (See Table 5.3.) The data
suggest that government clerks were beginning to establish new work
habits—ones that encouraged long-term employment. The hope for security and regular paychecks may have begun to lure middle-class men
who had once sought fame and fortune in business and middle-class

TABLE 5.3
Length of Service of Treasury
Department Clerks Employed in
1871

Years	Men	Women
Less than 5	10	19
5–9	23	34
10–20	31	27
More than 20	35	20
	100%	100%
Number	343	272

Source: Computed from data taken from Application Files of the Treasury Department (Record Group 56), National Archives Building, Washington, D.C.[62]

women who had previously foreseen themselves only within domestic pursuits. Indeed, in this instance as in others, federal employment seemed to initiate an important change which helped to reshape the contours of middle-class labor. Stability was slowly becoming a part of the middle-class work experience.

The irony, however, is that if asked, most federal workers would probably have responded that they did not feel particularly secure in their government positions. For while the aggregate statistics reveal remarkable persistence, much about the day-to-day conditions within Washington offices contributed to government employees' insecurity and widespread fear that they might suddenly find themselves unemployed. Such fears were by no means unfounded, for both fiscal constraints and political considerations cost large numbers of government workers their jobs. The half of the labor force that remained for a decade must have been acutely aware of the other half—the men and women who entered and left Washington offices with some regularity. Indeed, all government workers understood that adequate and even excellent performance offered little protection against the various sources of insecurity within government offices.

Shifts in the federal budget frequently led to the removal of government employees or salary reductions for those who remained. When Congress decreased the appropriation for an office, clerks—both male and female—lost their jobs. Wholesale reorganizations of certain departments often followed congressional investigations into waste and inefficiency in the departments, and usually such changes resulted in clerks being turned out. A major restructuring of the Treasury Department in 1876, for example, brought dismissals to large numbers of clerks. Indeed, the files are filled with letters from Treasury Department clerks requesting reinstatement in the years after 1876. These fiscal crises and bureau rearrangements happened often enough throughout the late nineteenth century to present government employees with a recurring source of anxiety. Emma Della Seta described her employment history in an 1879 letter of application to the Interior Department: "I am not without experience as a clerk, having served for nearly two years in the Treasury and Interior Departments....Although the tenure of office in the two above mentioned [places] was not extended, it was owing entirely to the changes and fluctuations in office life so much dreaded by those dependent upon it for a livelihood and existence."[63]

In some instances the structure of the federal workplace itself served to increase the insecurities felt by many government clerks. Numerous offices relied upon temporary workers who were employed at times of increased work and then let go when the normal work load resumed. In the late 1860s, for example, the Treasury Department hired a large number of temporary female clerks to help bring the work in the Register's office up to date. When the task was completed, the head of that office notified the Secretary of the Treasury that seventy women in his office "could be dispensed without detriment to the public service." He anticipated, however, that within a month new work might require additional laborers and recommended that "all of the female clerks reported...as no longer necessary necessary...be granted leave of absence without pay until such time as their services may be required in this or some other Bureau of the Treasury Department."[64] In some offices both men and women were treated as members of a surplus labor force. Every ten years the government employed large and increasing numbers of men and (beginning in 1880) women to count and tally the census. These clerks held jobs lasting from a few months to a few years. When all the census data had been tallied, the clerks were dismissed.

As in other nineteenth-century work situations, supervisors responded to financial problems not only by laying off workers, but by lowering wages. While both men and women suffered in these cutbacks, women— often ranking lowest in seniority—were especially vulnerable. In 1880, U.S. Treasurer Gilfillan demoted two women in his office, one from $1600 to $1400 and one from $1200 to $1000, in order to bring his budget within appropriations for the fiscal year. He explained that he had chosen these clerks because "they [were] the persons last promoted to those grades on that roll."[65]

Financial and budgetary changes accounted, however, for only part of the job instability within Washington offices. Much of the rest could be laid to politics. Political patronage influenced job tenure as well as job procurement, and clerks who had obtained their appointments from a Republican administration stood to lose if Democrats gained control of the White House. Given that the presidency switched back and forth between Republicans and Democrats every four years between 1880 and 1896, government clerks were kept repeatedly on their guard. Changes within the party could also bode ill for federal employees. Many suspected of being "tinged with Johnsonism," for example, lost their jobs when Grant was elected in 1868. Indeed, politics swept as many clerks out of office as did budgetary reductions.

Government workers could not even feel secure in the four years between presidential elections, since changes in the political complexion of congressional delegations also affected the make-up of the federal workplace. An employee's ability to remain in office often rested upon how much pressure his or her "influence" continued to bring upon the department. Clerks who wanted to keep their jobs would be sure to remind their patrons when budgetary or political crises threatened and when a few words on their behalf seemed in order. Consequently, letters from congressmen and senators periodically flooded the departments, urging the retention of clerks. The unlucky employees whose congressmen failed to win reelection found themselves without protection and therefore vulnerable to dismissal.

The uncertainties endemic to government work affected both male and female clerks. Just as women's connection—however indirect—to a political party brought them into government, it also could cause their dismissal. Female clerks quickly learned which precautions were necessary to secure their positions. In 1876, Lucy Chandler, a $1200 clerk in the Treasury Department, began to fear that she would lose her place in the upcoming reorganization. She explained, "As the representative from my district has been a democrat the past two years, I have been holding my place with considerable insecurity; and now in this emergency [budgetary cutback] I must look for one who can by a word or two make me perfectly safe." That person was her senator, but since she was "not personally acquainted" with him, she wrote instead to John Sherman, describing her problem and requesting his assistance. Would Sherman, she wondered, "be willing to ask [the Senator] for a strong letter addressed to the Secretary asking my retention in office? I am one of his constitutents and had I a vote, should most assuredly cast it for him."[66] Chandler weathered this crisis, but others did not. Kate Ways, a widow with a young son, "neglected to fortify herself," and when the money in her office ran short, the supervisor selected her, along with others, for dismissal.[67]

If, as applicants, some women could only make indirect claims to political allegiance, once they became employees they began to identify personally with "their" political party. Female clerks spoke of themselves as Republicans and Democrats, despite the fact that they, of course, could neither vote nor hold office. Nanci Cox, for example, wrote to the Secretary of the Interior in 1892 asking that she be allowed to retain her position in the Census Office for a few more months. After describing her financial need and her good work record, she ended: "I am a Republican, and believe you will give me the benefit of a few months in office remaining for Republicans."[68] Only a few protested that as women they could hold no political allegiance, for most realized that without such affiliations it would be difficult to hold onto their jobs within government offices.

The notion of a woman assuming a political identity was still novel in nineteenth-century America, and some contemporaries expressed sur-

prise that female employees would be subjected to the same political requirements as their male coworkers. A Georgia businessman notified Secretary of Interior Hoke Smith in 1893 that his friend, Agnes Allison, had
lost her position in the Census office "for the reason that she enjoys a
Republican appointment." While expecting that "all men not under Civil
Service law [would] be bounced," he expressed surprise that such a policy
would apply "to women who had no politics."[69] Female clerks did, however, have "politics." In fact, they may have been some of the first women
in nineteenth-century America for whom political allegiance took on an
immediate, personal meaning. When political parties exchanged power
or when congressmen lost elections, female clerks who belonged to the
wrong political party faced demotion or dismissal. Such women were
moved aside to make room for applicants with the right political connections. Gender proved little protection against the political vagaries of federal office holding.

The relationship between politics and job security persisted throughout the nineteenth century. The Pendleton Civil Service Act of 1883
brought marked change to the process of obtaining a government job,
but did absolutely nothing to protect the men and women already in
office. Nineteenth-century civil service reformers—and the Commission
that their efforts helped establish—concentrated primarily upon instituting competitive entrance examinations which they hoped would
monitor the "front door" of the bureaucracy. Although the Pendleton Act
forbade the removal of classified employees for political reasons, the Civil
Service Commission had little power to stop such practices. Not until 1897
did President McKinley issue an order expressly prohibiting dismissals
from the classified service "except for just cause and for reasons given in
writing."[70] Moreover, the numerous employees working in unclassified
positions lacked even the semblance of protection afforded to those in
classified places. Throughout the last half of the nineteenth century, officials continued to dismiss male and female clerks whose only fault lay in
their connection to the wrong political party. As a result, persistency rates
for federal employees in the early twentieth century were much the same
as they had been more than three decades earlier. A 1907 study of the
executive civil service revealed that more than half of all male and female
clerks then employed in the departments had been working there for
more than nine years. Between 24 and 29 percent of the men and women
had been in office from five to nine years, and a quarter or less of these
clerks had been employed for fewer than five years. (See Table 5.4.)

The promise implicit in the civil service system had been that rational
procedures would govern the administration of the Washington departments as well as the recruitment of federal employees. But such was not,
in the nineteenth century, to be the case. Consequently, federal clerks,
once employed, immediately turned their attention to securing those
hard-won jobs. For many this required playing according to two sets of
rules— meeting the formal requirements of a new, more bureaucratic
workplace, as well as manipulating the political and personal strings that

TABLE 5.4
Length of Service of Employees and
Clerks Working in Executive Civil
Service, Washington, D.C., 1907

Years employed	All employees	
	Women	Men
Under 5	31	31
5–9	28	24
10+	41	46
	100%	100%
Number	7,358	17,993

Years employed	Clerks	
	Women	Men
Under 5	18	25
5–9	29	24
10+	53	51
	100%	100%
Number	3,292	7,040

Source: U.S., Department of Commerce and Labor,
Bureau of the Census, *Statistics of Employees, Executive
Civil Service of the United States, 1907,* Bulletin 94 (1908),
73, 103.[71]

had traditionally governed access to much middle-class work. About half
succeeded well enough to secure a minimum of a decade's employment
within federal offices.

MIDDLE-CLASS GOVERNMENT WORKERS, having learned how to obtain
jobs and how to hold onto them, next turned their attention to winning
promotions. In this aspect of office life, as in all others, a mixture of rational and informal criteria determined the fate of federal clerks. Politics,
not surprisingly, played a major role in determining which men and
women would advance within the departments. Those clerks who desired
promotion needed to muster the same kind of influence that had procured them their jobs or protected them from dismissal. Democrats lucky
enough to keep their positions during Republican administrations did not
expect to win promotions, and Republicans knew better than to hope for
advancement when Democrats were in power. Moreover, the institution
of a civil service system in 1883 did not eliminate politics from the promotion process, just as it had not protected clerks from unwarranted dismissals. Although the Pendleton Act had specified that "no person shall
be employed to enter or be promoted in either of the said classes...until
he has passed an examination," nineteenth-century officials made little
effort to institute promotional examinations.[72]

More than politics, however, determined success or failure within the federal workplace. Clerical expertise also counted in the quest for security and advancement within Washington offices. Consequently the middle-class men and women who labored in the federal departments found it essential to establish their credentials as efficient government clerks. Proving one's worth brought an employee face to face with the *ad hoc* and often confusing standards by which supervisors evaluated their underlings.

The manner in which clerks were evaluated depended first upon the nature of the work they performed. Those clerks—both male and female—whose tasks were routine and repetitive were judged by "objective," quantitative measures—the numbers of dollars counted, words copied, pages typed, or cards tabulated. Mr. A. J. Carrier, for example, was dismissed from his copyist position in the Census Office in 1880 on the charge of inefficiency. His supervisor reported that in the previous month "Carrier was continuously employed on 'Rough Work' and his reports show a total of 1763 pages so worked, making a daily average of 63+ pages. In no day of this period was the Division average less than 101 pages, and for the entire time the daily Division average was 117 pages."[73] The men and women who worked on the punching and tabulating machines in the Census Office in 1890 were similarly required to meet a minimum daily average or stand in jeopardy of dismissal.[74] In all these offices it was the job of the immediate supervisor to set the standards, keep account of the work and make recommendations for promotion, demotion, and dismissal. No government-wide standards regulated acceptable levels of clerical output.

The middle-class men and women working in such jobs may well have found themselves subject to a scrutiny that was different in kind from any they had previously experienced, indeed to a kind of close control that resembled what working-class factory operatives suffered in numerous nineteenth-century industries. Many government clerks found themselves able, however, to make the quantitative measurement of their labor work to their benefit. Clerks apparently kept their own records of work performed—records that they could offer as evidence when they felt they had been judged unfairly. James D. Bradley, for example, earned $1200 in his position in the First Auditor's Office during the 1860s. Bradley's duties were quite routine (despite his good salary) and he kept a careful account of his work. Thus, when threatened with dismissal in 1866 he was able to report to the Secretary of the Treasury: "During the present month I have recorded and indexed three hundred and eighty five (385) certificates of accounts and copied and indexed ninety-three (93) letters according to instructions from time to time received from the chief clerk of this office."[75] Bradley's dismissal was cancelled and he managed to hold onto his job for another two years.

Women as well as men tried to influence the evaluation procedures. In 1874, Virginia Dunnavant, fearing that her record had placed her position in jeopardy, explained to the Assistant Secretary of the Treasury, "If I have not been so rapid as some I am always above the average." She admitted making some errors, but claimed, "[Even] the very best counters often make eight, ten, to fifteen, we each know the standing of the others, and I often have not as many by several as some of the best and longest counters."[76] In 1887, Catherine Hoffman, a counter in a different division, received a dismissal notice which cited her "frequent errors." She asked her patron to write to the Secretary of the Treasury informing him that in fact her record revealed only three mistakes, "of which she admits two, claiming one was ascribed to her by mistake." He deduced that her supervisor "had (unintentionally of course) done her an injustice" and upon his request the Secretary reinstated Hoffman to her prior position.[77] Catherine Hoffman had been able to make both the rationalized evaluation procedures and the more informal patronage system work to her advantage. She and others consigned to routine, repetitive tasks found some measure of control and protection against unfair dismissals and demotions in the objective standards by which they were judged. Thus, while immediate supervisors set the standards and made the judgments, the federal hierarchy was responsive to clerks who could prove that they had been evaluated unfairly. Even those jobs which had become highly rationalized still afforded these middle-class workers the ability at least to monitor their status within the office.

In those offices where men and women performed differentiated, complex tasks, the process of evaluation was considerably more problematic. Supervisors could not easily use an objective measure to evaluate clerks who drew up legal documents, examined complicated patent applications, performed difficult accounting procedures, and reviewed pension appeals. Moreover, where each employee held responsibility for a different task, it was impossible to compare the performance of one clerk with another. In these offices the supervisor's assessment of a clerk's ability, attitude, fidelity, and loyalty counted most when time came to decide who would be promoted and who would be dismissed.

Typical was the way Bernard May's supervisor evaluated his three-year record as a clerk in the Second Comptroller's Office in 1869. He noted that May "was always prompt in attendance, diligent and faithful in the discharge of duty, accurate in calculation and reliable in judgement." Moreover, he "required no watching or prompting to duty."[78] When Joseph B. Marvin applied for promotion to the highest-paid clerkship in 1875, his supervisor offered a glowing report: "Constantly entrusted with important and delicate matters I find him vigilant, faithful, laborious, and ever considerate of the best interests of the office. He is also a highly cultivated gentleman, courteous in his bearing and agreeable to strangers having official intercourse with him in the line of his duties....[H]e has few equals and no superiors among the clerks in this Bureau."[79] Elizabeth Rogers won promotion from a $1400 to a $1600 position in 1881 on the basis of her supervisor's claim that "this lady is an expert accountant and has been of great value to this office."[80] The man in charge of Enna Wilson's division in the Second Auditor's Office argued that she was inadequately compensated at $840 per year for "work requiring considerable knowledge, care, and ability; namely the examination of the property accounts" that she performed with "intelligence and industry, as well as accuracy."[81]

Evaluations that depended upon the subjective opinion of individual supervisors posed obvious problems: they offered no check on supervisors who played favorites and provided no means for comparing clerks in different offices. But such a system still held advantages for employees. Although these clerks could not prove their worth by citing the quantity of work they performed, they could still influence the evaluation procedure through the less admirable but perhaps equally effective method of ingratiating themselves with the boss. An informal atmosphere prevailed in many federal offices, with clerks and supervisors lunching together, socializing outside the office, and even borrowing money from each other.[82] In such an environment, federal workers may well have found it possible to influence their superiors when it came time for employee evaluations.

The role of immediate supervisors in determining promotions within their offices made it possible for federal clerks to appeal to the men under whom they worked, detailing personal histories and requesting sympathy and assistance. Most male clerks relied upon some combination of merit, politics, and financial need, usually trying to play their strongest suits, in making their case for advancement within the office. Israel Smith, for example, applied for a promotion within the Third Auditor's Office in 1882. After describing his work history within the department and relating the responsible and important duties that he performed, he continued: "I have a large family to support, and, in reduced financial circumstances, have performed my duties as I have been 'given light to see them.' "[83] Male clerks did not appear at all hesitant about detailing their need for more money. While men usually did not offer emotional descriptions of financial privation, they nevertheless were quite honest about the deficiency of their funds. John French wrote in 1861 asking for a promotion from his $1400 position, saying, "My present pay does not permit me (with my obligations to my father and mother, nearly 80 years of age) to bring my family to Washington; and in my earnest desire for the ability to have my wife and boys with me, I know your kind nature will find all necessary excuse for the intrusion of this note upon your crowded time."[84] Most such letters from clerks were accompanied by the requisite endorsements from political patrons.

Female clerks, on the other hand, less often mentioned their financial need and more frequently relied upon politics and merit to win them promotion. Elizabeth Denham wrote to the Secretary of the Interior in 1881, for example, saying, "For the past three years I have prepared all the record books for the Medical Division of the Pension Office. Have attended punctually and promptly to all my official duties, and when the promotions were distributed I felt very much humiliated to find that for some reason my case had been neglected." She pressed the issue of fairness, noting, "I am the only lady from the Sixth district of Iowa in any of the departments, and if my record as a clerk is equal to the others, I think I should receive the same salary." Denham did not, however, rely only upon the inherent justice of her case. She also wrote to her congressman, asking, "If you will be so kind, as to write a *personal* letter to the Secretary of the Interior and to the Commissioner of Pensions asking my promotion to a twelve hundred dollar clerkship I will forever be your friend. I know if you urge it I will be promoted, and if you have the determination your friends give you credit for you will secure it for me." Trying to win the congressman over, she reminded him, "My brother voted for you, and many of my friends...were your earnest supporters during the campaign last fall."[85] Apparently the freedom female applicants felt to detail their straitened financial circumstances disappeared once they became employed within the Washington department. For as clerks these women were earning what by nineteenth-century standards was an excellent "female" wage—the majority making at least $900 per year.[86] Many of these women, however, shouldered the same kinds of financial burdens as their male coworkers— supporting aged parents, younger siblings, or school-age children. Jane Gemmill, one of the few female clerks who did mention money, noted, "As far as I am concerned $900 a year is a comfortable income; but I find it very difficult to support myself, mother, and a young sister on that sum."[87] Knowing that most women workers managed on considerably less money, female clerks probably felt it wisest to emphasize their qualifications—both political and clerical—rather than their need.

But favoritism and cronyism represented another side of this informal system. Not all officials were known for their integrity or their sympathy, and clerks who displeased their supervisors— whether for legitimate or for frivolous reasons—found themselves at risk. For women this posed special problems. Without government-wide standards and regulations, many officials were free to exercise their anti-female biases. Numerous supervisors recognized the good work that women performed, but were either unwilling to promote them to high-paid positions or would do so only after all the men in the office had been placed.

Many government officials restrained female clerks, offering promotions rightfully due them to male employees instead. Julia Henderson complained to the Secretary of Interior in 1893 that in her fourteen-year career in the Indian Office she had never advanced beyond a $1200 position: "While standing at the head of the $1200 grade in seniority, so frequently have I seen young men pushed over me that I feel disheartened; one young man who only entered the service in June of 1889, and who consequently was my junior by many years, has just received his...promotion [to $1400]."[88] Louise Brown also suffered because of the discriminatory policy of officials in her office. Brown's career began in 1873 when she accepted a $900 copyist job in the Office of Indian Affairs. Within a year she passed an examination that won her promotion to a $1400 clerkship. Such an unprecedented, meteoric rise apparently surprised and displeased some officials, for in 1877 her supervisor reduced her salary to $1200—ostensibly because of "lack of funds available for clerical service" in the office. Two years later the Commissioner of Indian Affairs recommended her further reduction to $1000 although Brown was "then performing the duties of a second class [$1400 per year] clerk and had about that time successfully passed a competitive examination for promotion to that grade." Brown asked her supervisor why her pay had been cut, and he responded: "[It] is the policy of the office that no women receive a salary of more than $1000."[89]

Offices frequently hired women to perform the same jobs as men, but continued to pay them a female wage. Those women who won promotions to high-paid positions of $1200 per year or more had already been performing the duties of such clerks and had proven themselves capable. Nevertheless, acquiring these raises often took years. It was not uncommon for a woman to wait a decade or more for a well-earned promotion. For even when such women could overcome the hesitation of immediate supervisors, they often met with resistance from officials higher up in the hierarchy who, on principle, refused to allow women promotion to high-class clerkships. In 1890, Secretary of Interior John Noble, for example, instructed his appointment clerk to act discreetly in notifying officials in the Department that "recommendations for promotions of women to places of eighteen hundred dollars will not be approved by the Secretary, and that the same are hereby ordered to be disallowed, except in that there shall be special circumstances of extraordinary merit brought to the attention of the Secretary in person, and by him acted upon."[90]

Jennie Peyton was one of those who suffered the injustice of such policies. Peyton had been appointed to a position in the General Land Office in 1879, and had been assigned difficult, complex tasks which she handled admirably. Her expertise brought her rapid promotions, and within five years she had advanced to a $1400 position. While her responsibilities continued to increase over the next decade, her salary remained the same. In the mid-1890s her supervisor tried to get her a raise, explaining that the type of work she performed was some of the most difficult and exacting within the office. To no avail. Then in 1899, another supervisor made a similar plea, saying, "The *character* of the work she is engaged upon, even if performed only in an ordinarily satisfactory way, is entitled to the highest recognition by the employment upon it of a clerk of the highest grade. But when work is presented in a masterful manner, as is hers, it is worthy of special consideration." Three years later the supervisor tried again, extolling "the reasoning of [her] fine judicial mind" and decrying the fact that over the last eighteen years she had failed to receive another promotion "for the reason that she is a woman."[91] It is clear that the resistance to Jennie Peyton's promotion came not from her immediate supervisor, but from the top of the agency. In such circumstances female clerks in numerous offices were denied opportunity for advancement.

AS THE FEDERAL DEPARTMENTS grew larger in the last two decades of the century, more high-level officials expressed dissatisfaction with the variety and subjectivity of evaluation procedures and began to search for more objective means of rating federal employees. Beginning in the late 1870s and appearing more frequently in the 1880s and 1890s, various offices instituted schemes designed to systematize the process by which all federal clerks—even those performing diverse, complex tasks—were rated. The impetus for such plans came from various sources. A growing concern with reforming the civil service encouraged some officials to consider more uniform performance standards. Moreover, Congress, which was repeatedly asked to appropriate larger sums for hiring federal clerks, began to demand assurance that these new employees were performing efficiently.[92]

Carl Schurz, noted civil service reformer and Secretary of the Interior from 1877 to 1881, experimented with one of the first systems intended to evaluate quantitatively the complex, diverse work of Pension Office clerks. In 1879 he instituted a plan which, he claimed, could "ascertain with almost mathematical certainty the proportion of work done by each clerk...in point of quantity as well as quality."[93] The new scheme designated the number of pension claims which clerks of each class should examine each day—1.87 for third-class ($1600-per-year) clerks, 1.47 for second-class ($1400-per-year) clerks. Those who fell below the standard could expect salary reductions, while those who exceeded the average could qualify for promotions.[94]

Schurz's plan foundered almost immediately, because it incorrectly assumed that all Pension Office clerks performed similar work and that this work could be measured objectively. The Commissioner of Pension informed the Secretary that in fact he had rated employees "only so far as the nature of their employment would permit," and warned that there were "a great many others whose work cannot be measured with such figures."[95] The number of cases examined each day was not an accurate gauge of how efficiently a pension clerk had worked, as a report from the head of one division illustrated: "One examiner...writes 361 letters, in each of which the status of the case is given, and 195 circular letters, and as a result he is credited with 43 cases submitted, while another with 130 letters and 870 circular letters gets credit for only 8 cases; and yet while the record shows each to be industrious the results in each case are widely different—and can be explained only by saying that the difficulties in the way of obtaining satisfactory testimony were greater in one case than in the other."[96]

There were numerous, similar schemes introduced in various offices—sometimes within an entire department, sometimes only within a bureau—over the next two decades. The only ones that succeeded were in offices where clerks performed routine work that could be easily subjected to quantitative measurement. In environments where employees carried out a variety of diverse tasks, the very nature of the work, combined with the ever-present problem of subjective judgments of supervisors, mitigated against success.[97]

In 1891, President Harrison took the initiative in attacking the problem of employee evaluations. He requested that the secretary of each federal department "consider whether a record might not be kept in each bureau of all those elements that are covered by the terms 'faithfulness' and 'efficiency,' and a rating made showing the relative merits of the clerks of each class, this rating to be regarded as a test of merit in making promotions."[98] Supervisors were instructed to keep daily accounts of each office worker, giving him or her a score (from zero to seven) on performance in seven different areas: punctuality, attendance, industry, accuracy, aptitude, conduct, and ability.[99]

As an attempt to centralize evaluation procedures throughout the Washington departments, this plan represented a departure from earlier policy. Previously the rating of clerks had remained within the jurisdiction of an individual agency or bureau, and sometimes numerous plans operated simultaneously within a given department. But in 1891 high-level officials appeared concerned with setting government-wide standards. The new program differed from earlier ones, however, in an even more important way: it required that supervisors write daily reports of their clerks. An official who kept a daily log needed to watch employees much more closely than one who wrote a report only once a month. Indeed, such a plan seemed designed specifically to monitor and control the work force, forcing supervisors to be more cognizant of the behavior of their employees.

Had this scheme succeeded, it would have subjected all middle-class workers within federal agencies to an intense level of scrutiny. It became clear almost immediately, however, that this kind of an evaluation program would not work. The Interior Department official in charge of the program decried the lack of "uniformity...in the system of marking" and recommended that supervisors try to "secure [more] *systematic* and *uniform* records."[100] The plan failed because the diversified nature of federal clerical work defied attempts to systematize evaluation procedures. In 1894, when the chief in one division of the Patent Office explained the great difficulty of rating clerks who worked on different tasks, his words echoed numerous responses to similar efforts over the past decade: "It is only where several clerks are engaged upon the same kind of work and their reports compared, that a correct idea of merit can be obtained." He held, moreover, that supervisors' daily reports did not offer an objective measure of employee performance: "Reports in which the chiefs of the various divisions have been allowed to grade clerks according to their estimates have been found by experience to be useless. This is true for many reasons—even admitting that such reports are conscientiously made, there are so many chiefs of divisions, and there are so many different ways of marking the merit of clerks, some chiefs marking all of them very much higher than they deserve and others marking on a lower scale, that confusion and inaccuracy are a necessary result."[101]

The failure of Harrison's plan left officials free to try, again, to experiment with a variety of other schemes. The chief of one division within the Patent Office, recognizing the difficulty in obtaining "objective" evaluations from supervisors, reverted instead to a system that placed considerable control within the hands of the individual clerk. In this office, he noted, "it was thought best that [clerks] be required to hand in a daily report showing, first, the time engaged at work; second, the amount of work accomplished." Such reports would "simply [state] the facts...without any estimate being put upon a clerk's merit by the chief of a division, leaving this to be done by the Commissioner of Patents."[102] Although daily accountings of work performed were still required, the clerks themselves assumed responsibility for making such reports. In most offices, however, this task remained within the purview of the supervisor.

As late as 1901 a newspaper article cited new efforts of the Secretary of the Treasury to establish a more equitable method of evaluating clerks. This story prompted one anonymous clerk to write complaining of the subjectivity and favoritism that still prevailed in the federal workplace: "I am sorry to say that every Chief has his favorites in his division and he has it in his power to keep any clerk down that he may not fancy or like. He can order him kept on a low class of work and prevent him doing better work of a higher grade so that the clerk cannot get an opportunity to be promoted. Any chief can on the other hand place his friends on a high class of work, saying it is their ability, etc. In many cases you will find, you could but look inside some Divisions, the smaller salaried clerks doing more and better work than those drawing higher salaries, this will apply to clerks of both sexes."[103] At the turn of the century, officials were still wrestling with the problem of how best to rate the work performed by government clerks.

The repeated failure to arrive at more objective means of evaluating federal workers lay not in specific defects of various schemes, but in the impossibility of the undertaking. For until the work itself was rationalized, there would be no way for officials to arrive at quantitative systems of rating the workers. The persistence of varied, differentiated work routines within government offices thus proved critically important for federal workers. It allowed them not only access to diversified, challenging work, but an important measure of control and autonomy within the workplace. Clerks could be judged on the number of words copied or cards punched, but not on the number of pension cases decided, patent applications reviewed, or treasury accounts audited. Indeed, this was the lesson that business executives within the private sector began to learn as their white-collar work forces grew in the early twentieth century. Private companies responded by attempting to make office work more like factory work. Books and articles written in the years after 1910 by men like William Leffingwell and Lee Galloway began to advocate scientific management of offices along the same lines that Frederick Taylor had proposed for factories. These plans invariably began with subdividing the labor and reducing it to its simplest components. According to such schemes, the simplification of work would allow hiring of the least-skilled and lowest-paid workers. And once the labor had been so routinized, supervisors could establish standards of worker output and maintain the desired levels either through positive or negative incentives. In the process, control of the work would be removed from the hands of clerks and placed in the hands of owners or office managers. Like Taylor, Leffingwell and other proponents of scientific office management seemed motivated as much by a desire to control workers as to promote efficiency.[104]

This overriding concern for control of clerks is strikingly absent from the nineteenth-century federal workplace. Most government officials sought to make their employees accountable for work performed and to keep offices running smoothly, but did not appear bent on destroying the autonomy of workers. Supervisors exercised their considerable discretionary power in a variety of ways—some of which benefited their employees and others of which proved a detriment. For example, even after an official federal work day had been set, individual supervisors retained the authority to limit or extend the number of hours their employees worked. Some officials shortened the work day, especially during the hot summer months. But others responded to increasing work loads within their offices by requesting that employees put in extra time. Government clerks knew full well that refusal to comply with such "requests" could cost them their jobs. One female employee charged that her supervisor compelled her and other clerks to work evenings and "in some cases Sundays, to keep up their records, with fear of dismissal ever before them."[105]

Not only could officials alter the length of the work day, they also had the power to decide how strictly existing regulations on hours and leave time would be enforced. Some bosses were sticklers, noting exactly the time when employees arrived at work and reporting clerks who reached their desks as few as two minutes late. In 1886 the chief of one division in the Internal Revenue Office noted that a woman in his office had lost eleven and one half minutes in the past year by arriving late at the department on five different occasions.[106] Neither was this kind of close scrutiny reserved for female employees. During the winter of 1886 an elderly male clerk in the Architect's Office of the Treasury Department was reported for being tardy on numerous occasions, although he had arrived for work fewer than five minutes after nine o'clock.[107] But other supervisors were considerably less vigilant about recording the hours when their employees entered and left the office. Officials in one division of the Pension Bureau, for example, instituted a system early in 1893 whereby clerks kept their own "time report." A female clerk explained that "the correctness of said report [was] certified on honor."[108] Similar kinds of variations governed the manner in which supervisors enforced regulations concerning leaves of absence. Some officials were sympathetic toward clerks with serious or chronic health problems allowing them considerable sick leave. Others—far less obliging—fired, demoted, or docked pay from clerks with repeated absences.[109]

While these practices varied from one office to the next, what is clear is that the absence of rigidly enforced government-wide regulations allowed individual supervisors considerable power in administering their offices. For the most part these officials did not use the shop floor as a model for structuring work within their bureaus. Rather, supervisors continued to allow clerks to perform the kinds of jobs that afforded freedom from close scrutiny, and to bend the rules on hours and leave time in ways that often benefited their workers. Why this was the case remains open to speculation. The fact that this was a public bureaucracy, and therefore not subject to the same kinds of cost-cutting requirements as a private, profit-making firm, could very well have made supervisors less concerned about extracting the maximum amount of work from their employees. But much about the informality that persisted within federal offices suggests that the class background and gender composition of the nineteenth-century federal work force may also have helped to prevent the establishment of an extremely controlled work environment.

Government clerks and their supervisors both came from middle-class backgrounds. Moreover, approximately two-thirds of federal clerks were middle-class men who shared a gender as well as a class identity with their superiors. Nineteenth-century government officials may well have felt that middle-class gentlemen like themselves, and even some middle-class ladies, could perform adequately without the imposition of rigidly monitored regulations and rationalized work routines. By comparison, the white-collar work force that became the object of scientific management schemes of the 1910s and 1920s was becoming increasingly working-class and increasingly female.[110]

Indeed, the similarity in class background between nineteenth-century government clerks and supervisors contributed to the informal, personal methods of administration that prevailed within many aspects of office life. For even as the government became a large and increasingly complex bureaucracy, it continued to operate in ways that were reminiscent of small, informal, and even family-run businesses. Formal rules and regulations were often bypassed or ignored in favor of more personal, unofficial methods of administration. Perhaps nowhere is this more apparent than in the variety of ways that clerks were able to make their individual needs felt. Federal officials repeatedly bent the rules, allowed special considerations, and responded to the specific problems of individual clerks within the departments.

The willingness with which clerks asked special favors of their employer suggests that they expected to be treated as individuals with personal and specific needs, rather than as cogs within a large and impersonal bureaucratic machine. Department files are full of letters from male and female workers petitioning for extra leave time when they were sick, requesting substitutes when they could not attend to their duties, and asking for second chances when they had made mistakes. Supervisors usually considered such requests on the basis of their merits, and many were granted. Francis Page, for example, a clerk in the Pension Office in 1880, was arrested for drunken behavior on the street. The Commissioner of Pensions promptly asked for his resignation, and Page complied. But then Page requested clemency from the Commissioner, pledging, "[I]f this request be granted, I will never again, so long as I remain in the Department, indulge in the use of intoxicating liquor of any kind." He reminded the Commissioner that he had lost his arm fighting during the war, and noted, "I have a large family depending upon me for support, and I am entirely without means, other than the pension and the salary I receive as a clerk. If this salary is taken away from me, it will most certainly result in suffering for my family." On the basis of this plea and of Page's efficient record within the office, the Commissioner granted his request and gave him another chance.[111]

Upon numerous occasions officials showed their willingness to invoke the spirit rather than the letter of the law on behalf of their clerks. Bertha Frye worked as a $600-per-year skilled laborer in the Census Office in 1890. Despite her pay and her title, she performed clerical duties analogous to those done by higher paid clerks. Before she could earn promotion to a copyist's title and salary, however, she had to pass the non-competitive examination required of all clerks in the Census Office. Fry sat for the examination, but scored only 62 percent, more than ten points below the necessary score of 75 percent. The Superintendent of the Census wrote to Secretary of Interior John Noble on her behalf, noting that the "Section Chiefs under whom Miss Fry has been employed report that she is doing the same work as other clerks who are receiving a salary of sixty dollars per month, and the Chief of the Division under which she is employed reports her rating as to efficiency as excellent." He requested that she be promoted "in view of her merit and experience." The Secretary of Interior concurred, but warned that this ruling should not be construed "as nullifying the requirement that a promotion in the grades mentioned must be made only after the employee has passed an examination therefore."[112] Bertha Fry's case did not, however, represent a sole exception to the rule, since the Secretary allowed similar dispensations to Geralda Potter, Miranda Farrar, Mary Flenniken, and others.[113]

Government clerks found supervisors willing to meet a variety of their personal needs and problems. Employees were allowed to resign rather than be dismissed, so that their records would remain unsullied; old workers who were no longer efficient were transferred to less demanding tasks rather than fired; and seriously ill clerks were given extended sick leave. Moreover, officials allowed these dispensations to both male and female employees.[114]

Certainly not all clerks found their bosses so understanding. Often the character of the response depended upon the specific official in charge, and some remained unsympathetic and unwilling to assist their employees. Nevertheless, the decentralized and loosely structured nature of the federal bureaucracy allowed supervisors considerable leeway to manage offices in ways that met the individual needs of numerous government clerks. Although clerks sometimes complained of favoritism and too-subjective assessments, there is no evidence that they wanted federal officials to institute more rational methods of administering the agencies.

In contrast, the only other substantial number of nineteenth-century workers to labor within a developing bureaucracy—railroad employees—responded differently to the mixture of rational and informal management techniques that prevailed within their industry. Railroads, like government agencies, allowed immediate supervisors a good bit of discretionary power in hiring, evaluating, and disciplining workers. But the men who worked on the railroads found the subjective and arbitrary actions of their foremen intolerable, and by the end of the nineteenth century were demanding that companies institute more bureaucratic standards, routines, and grievance procedures. [115] The middle-class men and women who clerked in Washington offices apparently were willing to trade problems of subjective and even unfair supervisors for the benefits derived from the absence of rigidly enforced government-wide regulations.

THUS, THE EXECUTIVE DEPARTMENTS of the federal government underwent a slow and often haphazard process of bureaucratization in the last four decades of the nineteenth century. If we define bureaucracy as a formal, hierarchical organization managed by salaried officials according to impersonal, enforced, written rules, then the post-Civil War federal government still had a ways to go before achieving this end. Throughout the late nineteenth century the overlay of the political patronage system, the considerable power afforded low-level supervisors, and the diverse nature of federal clerical work continued to inject much of the personal and unofficial into Washington offices. At the same time, continual growth of government offices—especially over the last two decades of the century—prompted officials to experiment with more rationalized methods of administering offices and evaluating workers. And the creation of a civil service system after 1883 contributed measurably to the formalization of certain procedures within the departments. The middle-class clerks who labored in Washington agencies derived both advantages and disadvantages from this mixture of informal and bureaucratic management techniques within federal agencies.

Informality posed obvious problems, for a system that did not respond to "rational" rules and standard regulations often worked unjustly. Indeed, throughout the late nineteenth century, deserving, well-qualified applicants were turned away and hard-working clerks found themselves dismissed for reasons that had nothing to do with their abilities as office workers. As a result, federal clerks worked in an environment that was pervaded by a sense of insecurity—something that, as the next chapter reveals, would have a profound impact on the relations between government employees. Moreover, such a system required applicants and clerks to present themselves—often as supplicants—and ask assistance of the men who wielded political power. Both men and women found this process difficult, because it in some way threatened their gender identity. Women feared being placed in compromising situations that might jeopardize their respectable reputations, while men found that the process impugned their manhood. The informal and subjective system of evaluating clerks presented women with problems specific to their sex. Without standardized criteria and rules, autonomous officials were free to exercise their anti-female biases. Qualified women who had performed their duties admirably often found it impossible to advance because their supervisors simply refused to promote women. And women and men alike were sometimes subjected to the tyranny of petty supervisors who wielded an extraordinary amount of discretionary power.

But increasing bureaucratization did not necessarily solve these problems or improve the lives of all middle-class federal employees. Rather it represented something of a double-edged sword. The institution of a merit civil service system—the most obvious effort to create a more bureaucratic and rational federal workplace—replaced some of the old obstacles federal clerkships with new ones. And many would-be government employees may well have found the old patronage system preferable to the new and unfamiliar requirements of competitive examinations. Nevertheless, the new civil service system also furnished obvious advantages. It opened Washington clerkships to those who could never have hoped to muster the necessary political patronage to win appointments, and relieved applicants of the onerous burden of "acquiring influence." Moreover, competing and succeeding within the system offered middle-class men, at least, a sense that they had proven their expertise—something that was becoming increasingly important for those interested in establishing middle-class credentials in late nineteenth-century America.

For women the gains were far less clear. In continuing to allow gender to supersede excellence, the civil service system failed to deliver on its promise to make merit the sole criterion for entrance into government jobs. As a result, even under the new civil service rules, women were hired to fill only low-status positions within the Washington departments. The institution of a more rationalized hiring system thus did not put an end to the discriminatory practices of the federal government.

When it came to the day-to-day functioning of the departments, the absence of highly centralized, bureaucratic procedures afforded federal clerks some important advantages. Government office workers found that officials not hampered by rigid regulations were frequently able and willing to respond to a myriad of individual needs. Moreover, the power wielded by low-level supervisors to organize work within their divisions often meant that tasks remained largely unrationalized, allowing these middle-class workers relief from routinized jobs and closely controlled work routines.

Female clerks, especially, profited from the decentralized manner in which offices were run. In an environment pervaded by the belief that female workers were less capable than male workers, the dearth of formally enunciated and rigidly enforced regulations held decided advantages for women. Low-level officials frequently took the simplest and most expedient course when delegating tasks within their offices, and often this meant assigning women to "men's" jobs. In such situations women seized the opportunity to prove their worth and to win promotions from low-paid to more remunerative, prestigious positions. These promotions occurred not because of an articulated, enforced policy of egalitarianism, but because of the *ad hoc*, decentralized manner in which many offices functioned. In fact, when high-level officials did make policy pronouncements concerning women, such pronouncements invariably institutionalized prevailing ideas on women's limited worth and served to inhibit rather than to expand women's opportunities. Thus, despite the unfair treatment that many women received at the hands of their immediate supervisors, female clerks probably found their interests better served by a system that allowed low-level officials the leeway to place and promote workers. Bureaucracies are, after all, only as "rational" or "neutral" as the people who create them. And a rational system devised and governed by men with traditional nineteenth-century ideas on female worth might well have been worse than no system at all.

Those middle-class men and women who remained and prospered within the federal government learned to maneuver within both the bureaucratic and informal systems that operated in Washington offices. These clerks found that employment within a developing bureaucracy offered the possibility for a kind of stability and security previously absent from other lines of middle-class work. Long-term employment within a single institution—something foreign to the nineteenth-century middle-class—became a feature of government employment in the Gilded Age that would come to characterize white-collar middle-class work in the twentieth century.

GOVERNMENT CLERKS who remained within the offices for any length of time soon discovered, moreover, that the informality of administrative procedures would spill over and affect relationships between clerks themselves. For a sexually-integrated, middle-class workplace in nineteenth-century America, this presented problems of its own.

PART THREE

A Sexually Integrated, Middle-Class Workplace

CHAPTER SIX

Adapting to a New Style of Middle-Class Work

In 1893 a letter from "One Who Knows" appeared on the desk of the Commissioner of Pensions. The letter charged Minnie Reed, a $1400-per-year clerk in the Pension Office, with "being a mischief-maker," illegally taking three extra days' leave of absence from the office, and acting as a spy for a Republican newspaper. The anonymous accuser further denounced Reed as "crooked" and maintained that she had boasted "that she would hurt our administration all she could."[1] Minnie Reed's case merits examination, since it reveals the complexity of the relationships among federal clerks in late nineteenth-century Washington offices. The conflicts between Reed and other clerks and the manner in which those conflicts were resolved suggest how government employees—both male and female—were beginning to adjust to a variety of new problems posed by working with a sexually integrated, middle-class bureaucracy.

Minnie Reed's first problem was gender. She had been working for a few years within the Special Examiner's division of the Pension Office when she got into a scrap with her male supervisor, a Mr. Clapp, over what she perceived to be his rude and ungentlemanly behavior—he had answered "none of your business" when she asked him a question about the nature of the work. Reed brought the matter to the attention of the Chief of the Division "and this man Clapp was transferred out of the Bureau."[2]

If Reed was victorious in this instance, on another occasion her efforts to curb what she considered unacceptable male behavior backfired. By the early 1890s, Reed was working in a different section of the Pension Office and again found her boss lacking in good manners, but this time the issue was liquor. Reed accused him of being drunk on the job—in a voice loud enough for other clerks to hear: "What I said to Mr. Simms when he questioned my word in an official matter was this: 'That if he would come in here sober, he might be able to remember today what he did yesterday.' " She had apparently had to deal with Simms in this inebriated condition more than once, for she noted, "Frequently between the 4th of March and the date of my transfer he had been at my desk when he was not entirely sober, and on the morning preceding my transfer he was, in my judgment semi-intoxicated." This time it was Reed's boss who triumphed. He made an issue of her "insubordinate" language (perhaps to deflect attention from his drinking habits) and used this charge in a campaign to have her transferred to another office.[3]

Reed's transfer came, apparently, not only because she had called her boss a drunk, but also because she had jumped to the defense of a friend in the office—a Mr. Fred Peck—who had himself just been transferred. Someone in the office had reported hearing Reed exclaim that Peck's transfer was an example of "base ingratitude." It is unclear how the friendship between Reed and Peck began, but it is not difficult to see why she chose to defend him. Peck had once done Reed a favor by stretching the rules on her behalf while he was serving as acting chief of the division. He had allowed her to take three days' leave time in January of one year that she had not yet used up for the previous year. As significant as Reed's and Peck's actions was the fact that someone in the office took it upon himself or herself to relay Reed's insubordinate words to the proper officials.[4]

Most of Reed's problems, indeed, seemed to stem not from conflict with men over gender issues, but from conflict with other clerks—both male and female—over what many perceived to be Reed's aggressive behavior. Testimony taken during the investigation suggests that Reed had less than harmonious relations with many of the clerks around her. One of Reed's so-called friends, a woman named Kate Norwood, testified ("reluctantly" she claimed) that "it is generally understood that she [Reed] makes trouble wherever she goes and for that reason she is frequently transferred from one division to another. This is general office talk about her."[5] Reed admitted that she had been transferred upon numerous occasions, but only twice was this because of "trouble" with people in the office. On other occasions she had requested a transfer so that she could be situated in more comfortable or more commodious surroundings. She explained her most recent transfer: "I was in a very exposed position in the room in the Southern Division, and as I am subject to rheumatism I preferred employment on an upper floor." On an earlier occasion she had asked to be moved because her division was located on "the north side of the building on the second floor...[in] exceedingly crowded quarters."[6] Reed's reputation as a "troublemaker" may well have come from her insistence on finding for herself a comfortable situation in which to work.

Minnie Reed's case reveals some of the tension that characterized relations between federal clerks during these years. During her thirteen-year tenure in office she had to deal with inebriated and ungentlemanly male supervisors, uncomfortable working conditions, and hostile coworkers—both male and female. The environment in which Reed worked was one where employees reported each other to supervisors and testified (albeit "reluctantly") about each other's behavior in the office. Moreover, these offices were places where women and men sometimes came into conflict over proper modes of conduct within the office. Not all relationships in these offices were negative, for Reed did make friends there. She reported that she and another female clerk ate lunch together every day. And certainly Reed's defense of Mr. Peck and his willingness to bend the rules on her behalf speak to the importance of some friendships within the office. Nevertheless, much of Minnie Reed's office history involved conflict both within and across gender boundaries.

Minnie Reed may have been a difficult individual, but her problems were not unique. The partially bureaucratized nature of the federal departments combined with the class and gender composition of the government's work force to create new and often difficult situations for middle-class workers. In manipulating both the persistently informal and the increasingly rationalized aspects of the Washington bureaucracy, government workers confronted not only supervisors and officials, but each other as well. The work-related problems that emerged and the adjustments that these clerks made reveal much about middle-class behavior in one of America's first white-collar bureaucracies. In Washington offices clerks like Minnie Reed and Fred Peck and Kate Norwood and Mr. Simms would converge and conflict, and then fashion new rules of conduct—both written and unwritten—for middle-class workers to follow.

THE POLITICAL PATRONAGE system which operated in Washington departments throughout the late nineteenth century created considerable insecurity for federal workers. Government clerks were constantly on their guard, fearful that an upcoming presidential election, or even the midterm congressional changes, would leave them turned out of office. Promotions as well as appointments depended heavily on political pressure. It was difficult to remain or advance within the bureaucracy without someone exerting "influence." Indeed, the failure of efforts to rationalize evaluation and promotion procedures within the Washington departments left politics as a critical factor in the success of a government worker.

In this insecure, politically charged atmosphere, competition became a staple of office life. And while competition was not new to the middle class, competing within a bureaucracy did, in fact, present new challenges. First, the rewards had changed; advancement up the bureaucratic ladder rather than individual achievement in business or the professions became the measure of success. Second, the cast of characters had changed, for now it included both men and women. In such an environment government clerks quickly realized that one of the ways to secure or advance their positions was by threatening or undermining fellow workers—something that both male and female clerks did with some regularity. While members of both sexes indulged in this unsavory behavior, some subtle differences distinguished the ways in which men and women competed within the office.

Male clerks employed a variety of means to achieve their self-serving goals. One of the favorite methods was to accuse a coworker of harboring the "wrong" political sympathies. Emotions ran especially high during the Civil War years, with men accusing each other of disloyalty. George Worthington, a third-class clerk in the Treasury Department, proved an easy target since he had once been a slave owner. Worthington had apparently freed his slaves during the early 1850s and moved to Washington to enter upon a career as a civil servant. In 1862 he was forced to resign his position when a fellow clerk in his office brought a charge of disloyalty against him—a charge that Worthington protested as "egregiously false in its general tenor and in the most important specification."[7]

The War's end did not bring a halt to political conflict within the office. During the postwar years, men continued to hurl accusations at coworkers. Samuel Goodman, for example, found himself dismissed in 1868 after six years' employment in the Treasury Department. Goodman claimed that his discharge had been "procured by the influence of a Democrat in the same room with myself, a former pet of Andrew Johnson, who desired to make a vacancy in the hopes of securing the promotion."[8] Luckier than some, Goodman won reinstatement one year later and held his clerkship for the next twenty-five years, advancing in that time to Chief of Division.

During the Johnson administration, male clerks in the Treasury Department even went so far as to form a "Johnson Departmental Club," an organization with the express purpose of recommending for dismissal those clerks who did not support the President. Then, when Grant took office, men accused each other of having been members of the dreaded, and now defunct, Johnson Departmental Club. Typical was Robert Patterson who was dismissed in 1868 "on the false representation of some two or three clerks in the same bureau that [he] was a Democrat and belonged to the Johnson Department Club," a charge which he "positively" denied.[9] Even the rumor that L. J. Anderson—a thirty-eight-year veteran of the department—had attended one meeting of the club was enough to cause his salary to be reduced from $1600 to $1200.[10]

Male clerks continued to accuse each other of political wrong-doings throughout the late nineteenth century; only the specifics—dependent upon the political issues then current—varied. As Republicans and Democrats alternated control of the White House every four years between 1880 and 1896, men willingly charged their coworkers with membership in the wrong political party. Examples of bitter, vitriolic conflict between male clerks over such issues abound. The case of A. B. Jamison and Hector McNeill could be replicated many times. Jamison began working in the Treasury Department in 1865, and over the next twenty years

years won numerous promotions until by 1886 he held an $1800-per-year position. Then, midway through the first Cleveland administration, a Democratic official reduced Jamison's salary to $1400. Jamison won reinstatement to his $1800 position when the Republicans resumed power two years later, but during the second Cleveland administration he was again reduced to the lower status clerkship. Apparently, both times another clerk in the office— one Hector McNeill—had been instrumental in having Jamison demoted and had reaped the benefits by being awarded Jamison's high salary. When the Republicans took power again in 1896, Jamison wrote to the Secretary of the Treasury requesting reinstatement to his previous position. He noted that during Cleveland's administration the former Union soldiers in his division had "been discriminated against. All have been reduced and Democrats in other parts of the office given their salaries." Jamison requested that the Republicans now restore these former Union soldiers and demote the Democrats to lower paying jobs: "That was the kind of medicine dished out by Mr. McNeill and his friends to the Union soldiers. We were compelled by conditions surrounding us to submit to the humiliation and loss of salary." For Jamison it had been a particularly painful experience twice to "give up [his] salary for this same gentleman's convenience and profit."[11] Such goings-on were common in government offices. Mr. Greenwell, a clerk in the Interior Department, felt little compunction about "testify[ing] to the political affiliations of his associates," even when he knew that such actions might "result in their connection with the service being severed."[12] Apparently men like McNeill and Greenwell were plentiful in Washington departments.

Male employees even reported each other for offhand remarks or statements made in jest that hinted at disloyalty to the administration. For example, James Dugan's joking remarks that the Commissioner of Pensions seemed to be acting as "deputy" to one of the important pension attorneys in town found its way to the supervisor's ear via the man at the next desk.[13] Male clerks sometimes spied on each other after office hours, watching to see which workers kept company with people known to be enemies of the administration.[14] Activities and words outside the office were not safe from scrutiny of competitive clerks who used whatever evidence they could muster to discredit coworkers and advance their own positions.

These men no doubt had strong political loyalties, but it seems clear that politics served more often as the pretext rather than as the cause of much of the conflict within government offices. Men seemed to use whatever charge—political disloyalty, misconduct, neglect of duty, or inefficiency—was most likely to bring the desired result. The prevalence of political accusations suggests that politics provided one of the most effective weapons in the arsenal.

While many middle-class men might have disliked the hostility and discord within government offices, they had already lived and worked in the public male sphere where competition was a fact of everyday life. Indeed, as one nineteenth-century advice purveyor warned in 1874, "Never before in the world's history was competition in every calling and pursuit so fierce as now."[15] By the post-Civil War years, competing for success and advancement had become part of the definition of middle-class manhood. Anthony Rotundo's recent study of American manhood reveals the importance of what he calls the ideal of the "manly achiever" for middle-class Victorian men. This ideal middle-class man was independent and driven by ambition—a man of "push, of 'go-ahead,' of endless exertion."[16] While such a man sought wealth and status, these goals were perceived as by-products of his work and therefore of secondary importance. Success in business or the professions became the primary standard by which a man measured his worth.[17]

As members of the middle class, male government employees shared the same concerns as other middle-class men—they, too, sought to prove their manliness and their worth by succeeding in the work world. But the federal workplace presented a different kind of arena for the struggle. Here middle-class men competed not against other businessmen for customers or other professionals for clients, but against coworkers for better paid or more secure government clerkships. Government clerks tailored the individualistic, competitive middle-class work ethic to fit a bureaucracy where personal and political, rather than rational, criteria often determined success. Engaging in this kind of office conflict thus served an important function for male clerks. Many had feared that accepting a job in the bureaucracy would be tantamount to relinquishing their independence and, with it, their claim to middle-class status. But engaging in competition—something that defined middle-class "maleness" in nineteenth-century America—allowed these men both to reassert their manliness and to reestablish their status as members of the middle class.

Competitiveness and individualism were not universal middle-class attributes. They applied, in the nineteenth century, only to middle-class men. Middle-class women had been taught a different set of virtues—domesticity, selflessness, and piety. Sheltered within the domestic sphere, women were specifically kept apart from the competition of the public world. The domestic ideology posited, in fact, that women's influence would serve as an antidote to the cutthroat, aggressive values being generated in a burgeoning industrial society. The domestic ideology notwithstanding, middle-class women in government offices were subject to the same pressures as male clerks, and they responded in remarkably similar ways.

Female clerks, like their male counterparts, contended with competition and political intrigue in departmental offices. Since the government attempted to reward widows, orphans, and dependents of Union soldiers with federal jobs, women accused of harboring disloyal sentiments, belonging to the wrong political party, or being "reb sympathizers" risked dismissal. Such accusations against female clerks surfaced fairly frequently. In 1869 an anonymous informant claimed that Lizzie Bachelder, a native of Georgia, had been a secessionist. Bachelder, proclaiming her innocence, charged that certain women in the office "prone to evil rather than good had manufactured" the charges in order to make "their own positions more secure by lessening their numbers." Bachelder held that it was "painful to record such of one's sex," but noted that self-preservation necessitated her attempt to vindicate herself.[18]

Women seemed quick to learn the tactics of office competition—spying and reporting on each other for political or other breaches of conduct. Sometimes conflict erupted between women and their female supervisors. Mary Ruckman complained that her supervisor—a Mrs. Smith— had sent another woman to eavesdrop on the conversation of Ruckman and her coworkers: "Miss Kingsbury lingers around. We have surprised her at the door." The primary conflict in this case, however, was between Smith and Ruckman, and it was a conflict that had apparently begun outside the office. Ruckman recalled that she had boarded at the same house with Smith and hinted that Smith did not always behave like a lady: "I missed several meals rather than compromise myself by conversing with her. Her actions were not ladylike, calling to the waiter in loud tones, snapping her fingers at them, complaining of her food and drawing attention to herself from all in the dining room. She was not allowed to stay here I am told, and from the expression I have seen on her face I know she is determined to be revenged. The next move will be to have me dismissed."[19] The charge of unladylike behavior could be as potent a weapon as the charge of political disloyalty or inefficiency, and Mary Ruckman did not hesitate to use it.

The conflict that was rife within government offices crossed gender lines. The absence of highly rationalized and strictly sex-segregated work routines in Washington departments left women and men frequently working at similar jobs and therefore in competition for positions and promotions. And both women and men found reasons to complain about the unfair treatment they felt they received compared to coworkers of the opposite sex. Men sometimes expressed resentment at the women who broke into their midst and took their jobs. The very first women clerks— those who clipped treasury notes in 1861—displaced men who had recently been put to work at these jobs. One of these men, John Buxman, described his "humiliating position amongst boys and girls." To add insult to injury, he complained, he and other male clerks were soon dismissed "on the plea for want of material while the Ladies were kept employed and the number even increased...."[20] As women assumed a variety of other clerical tasks throughout the departments, they encountered some hostility from the men who resented having to work and compete with lady clerks. Almond Woodward, a clerk in the Census Office in 1890, wrote indicating his anger at having been dismissed. He noted: "When I came home from vacation there were three girls in the office....If it was so necessary to reduce the force, how could Mr. Porter dispense with my services and retain three lady clerks...."[21]

Women also expressed hostility toward male coworkers. Frequently women's anger stemmed from their (usually correct) assumption that men earned higher salaries and received more promotions. Ann Story, for example, was furious at having been denied promotion while numerous young men advanced ahead of her. She repeatedly wrote angry letters to her supervisors asserting that she deserved "the same compensation accorded a man, for the same services, performed with equal ability."[22] Similarly, Fannie Wadleigh protested the injustice of her situation. Wadleigh, a $1600-per-year clerk in the Treasury Department, had earned her high-paying position after ten years with the agency. But in 1876 she received a peremptory dismissal. "The reason assigned to me for this dismissal," she explained angrily, "is that I have been receiving too much salary; some man considered it his right and the Secretary, I was told, has never been in favor of giving any lady more than $900 per annum; consequently all was taken from me." She argued that she had performed her duties diligently and then retorted, "It is my misfortune—and not my fault—that God made me a woman and that Congress has not made me a voter."[23]

While these examples reveal conflict between men and women, the source of such problems lay in economic rather than specifically in gender issues. Both men who lost their jobs to lower paid women, and women who felt underpaid for performing men's work had legitimate grievances. In such cases government clerks expressed their hostility as much at the officials who devised the system as at coworkers of the opposite sex. While gender was not the cause of such conflicts, it nevertheless entered into and complicated the tensions generated by a highly competitive and insecure bureaucracy.

It was these tensions that precipitated most of the overt conflict between men and women—much as they had caused problems between members of the same sex. Male clerks as willingly undercut the status of a female employee as of a male coworker. Those women lucky enough to hold higher paying positions were most likely to face competition from men in the office. When Republicans replaced Democrats in 1888, Emily Neyland, a $1600-per-year clerk with Democratic influence, believed her job in jeopardy. For months she waited for the ax to fall. She wrote that during that time she "lived the life of a toad under a harrow, and bets were made that I would be discharged." Although in the end she kept her job, she did receive a demotion, instigated, she maintained, by a man who "descend[ed] to an unmanly war upon a delicate woman merely because she belonged to a family differing from him in the matter of political faith."[24] Neyland, a well paid and responsible government employee, was not the least averse to representing herself as a "delicate woman" and attempting to use her gender as a defense. But such efforts usually proved fruitless, for Neyland and other women like her received no different treatment from similarly placed men. They were, however, more vulnerable to such attacks. Female clerks holding high-paid jobs had to fear more than the usual political intrigue of the office. These women also were easy targets of men who resented women's ascension to better paying positions and officials who believed that such jobs should be reserved only for men. Their gender did not protect female clerks from the infighting and back-biting, but rather added another burden with which they had to contend in efforts to survive within a competitive, politically oriented bureaucracy.

While both male and female clerks faced and brought similar accusations, there were nevertheless some subtle but important differences between conflicts that involved women and those that involved men. Women were much more likely to have been accused anonymously. When men wrote complaining that someone had charged them with political infidelity, they could most often name their accuser. Women, on the other hand, more often referred to unknown enemies. Typical was Margaret Brown. In 1889, Brown left for a two-week vacation in Atlantic City and returned to find her discharge papers on her desk. According to Brown, some clerks who "wanted to make capital for themselves by representing me as a zealous rebel" had reported that five years earlier Brown had made some disparaging remarks about Grant. One of Brown's backers wrote on her behalf and noted that since her job was covered by civil service regulations it "could not be filled by a favorite or by a political partisan—except by promotion." The implication was that some unknown person in the office had schemed for her place. Brown was lucky enough to win reinstatement, but at a reduced salary of $900 per year.[25]

The miscellaneous correspondence files of the Treasury Department are filled with accusations against both male and female clerks. Those against the men come in two varieties—signed and unsigned. But those letters that brought accusations against female clerks were in most instances anonymous. The contents of many such letters make it clear, however, that the senders were either current or former employees of the office. One former female clerk—apparently the widow of a Union soldier—wrote to the Secretary of the Treasury in 1869 imploring him "to see that justice is done." The anonymous letter was insistent in its demand that disloyal women be dismissed: "It is hard that we who have suffered and lost...our husbands in trying to sustain this Government should now be cast out in the cold to starve with our children and these offices held by such women as Miss Strashly a woman without claims to justify you in giving her this office and from her own admission she has a home in Virginia, and only wants this office to dress and live in this City upon, and also from her own account—a great Seccessionist, with all her brothers fighting in the rebel cause to destroy a Government that she now holds an office under and also boasts that she can hold her office—no matter how many northern widows may be dismissed."[26] Some informants sent long lists of women whom they felt should be removed. One list read in part: "Mrs. A. Johnson—Reb—Mail Room Register's office. Mrs. S. Hutchings—Rank Reb. and never attends to her duties. Sarah C. Johnes—N.Y. Reb—Johnson sympathizer. Mrs. Ella Coey—Reb and bad character—Mail Room."[27] The person who sent this letter was obviously familiar enough with the office to know where the women worked and which ones "attend[ed] to [their] duties." It seems likely that that person was another female employee within the same office. The nature of these anonymous charges against women varied, ranging from one which claimed that Mrs. Steile and her daughter were both employed within the Treasury Department (a violation of the agency's nepotism rules) to another that charged that "Mrs. Hart is without doubt mistress to a man by the name of Flanigan who passes as her brother."[28] Letters like these often bore signatures such as "Watchful" or "Justice" and were no doubt penned by both male and female accusers.

The tendency for women both to accuse and be accused anonymously suggests ways in which these clerks were adapting nineteenth-century middle-class norms to fit the conditions of a sexually integrated federal workplace. Women were clearly subjected to the same pressures as men: both had to muster patronage, keep their political credentials current, take care to appear loyal to the present administration, observe the rules of the department, and deport themselves in a proper fashion. Failure to fulfill these criteria could leave clerks of either sex vulnerable not only to official reprimand but to the searching eyes and ears of competitive, self-interested coworkers. Male and female clerks responded similarly to such pressures by going on the offensive: accusing fellow workers in the hopes of diminishing the number in the office and securing their own positions. Although women acted as competitively as did men, their tendency to hide behind a screen of anonymity indicates that they were not entirely comfortable with such behavior. Female clerks may have feared for their reputations as proper women if they engaged openly in such masculine, unladylike activities. Similarly, while middle-class men treated female coworkers with the same ruthlessness as male coworkers, they too seemed reluctant to be identified as the accusers. Given a dominant ideology that saw men as the protectors of defenseless women, male clerks might have felt it would impugn their manhood to compete with a woman for the same job, much less to intrigue against a lady's position in the office. Anonymity served to preserve these clerks' reputations as "ladies and gentlemen." Thus, government clerks were still cognizant of the rules and expectations of proper middle-class behavior, but they were forced to modify those rules as they jockeyed to preserve or advance their positions within the bureaucracy.

While both male and female clerks accused each other of various political or work-related offenses, women also devised other means of advancing in office. Quarrelling often characterized the relations between women in the office—harsh words and gossip abounded. Some arguments no doubt grew from personality conflicts, but squabbles may also have resulted when some women tried to improve their positions at the expense of their female coworkers. For example, women sometimes tried to alter the physical surroundings of the office. Sarah Huse was one who won the enmity of her fellow clerks because she "claimed the right to manipulate the shades of the window opposite her desk to suit her fancy and very much of the time did so to the great discomfort of those around her....She would move her desk or chair or turn it so that the passage to the window would be blocked by her desk, chair, and screens."[29] Since physical position in the room often bespoke status, Sarah Huse's behavior reflected more than cranky temperament or concern for her own comfort. It represented, rather, an effort to enhance her prestige in the office. When the head of a bureau in the Treasury Department rearranged the desks in his office in 1884 he noted that "it was with the view for the convenience of all in the room, due regard being had to claims of those longest in the service." One woman complained of the position of her desk, and the chief explained that she could not be moved without displacing a woman with greater seniority.[30] Changing the placement of a desk could alter the office hierarchy, and the women who tried to control such circumstances were, in the process, competing with workers around them.

Male clerks apparently did not engage in this kind of behavior; indeed, the records reveal almost no instances of men arguing about the placement of a desk or the opening of a window. Rather, men were more likely to try to advance themselves in office by making direct accusations against other clerks. This difference between male and female behavior reveals ways in which gender influenced the adaptation of middle-class men and women to a bureaucratically organized workplace. Men were more familiar and therefore more comfortable with direct and open office competition. Women, new to the game, may have relied upon more familiar modes of female conflict: gossip or bickering. Female clerks were also probably more sensitive to the physical surroundings. Many may, in fact, have felt that it was their due, as middle-class ladies, to demand a minimum level of comfort.

But even more, these differences suggest the relative power of the two genders within the federal bureaucracy. Men were voters (an important asset in an employment system where political patronage was an avenue of advancement) and were the legitimately perceived holders of high-paid jobs. As such, male clerks no doubt could more effectively advance their positions within the competitive bureaucracy. But women, devoid of personal political power and suspect in the role of high-status clerk, often resorted to playing for smaller stakes and settling for less grandiose rewards.

Despite such variations in conduct, the similarities between women's and men's behavior in the office are important. Both acted aggressively and competitively; both willingly advanced their own standing, even at another worker's expense. According to nineteenth-century standards, these women would have been playing by men's rules. Reputed Victorian wisdom held women to be passive, nuturant, and retiring while men possessed the combativeness and strength to tackle life's challenges. But such "female" virtues had little place within the competitive, cutthroat atmosphere of the federal bureaucracy. When put into this "male" environment and subject to the same pressures as men, Victorian ladies altered their behavior—assuming many male characteristics and modifying traditionally female modes of conduct to serve their new needs as middle-class workers.

The ease, however, with which these middle-class ladies, schooled in the dictates of the domestic ideology, eschewed certain female traits suggests the need to examine more closely the purported separateness of the two sexual spheres. Indeed, men and women were no doubt less different than the purveyors of the domestic ideology made them out to be. Although instructed to remain passive and to restrain from participation in the public world, nineteenth-century women had probably, in fact, become quite familiar with competition and conflict. Not only the marriage market, but the domestic realm itself served as an arena for power struggles. Women, the central figures in nineteenth-century middle-class families, may well have had long experience manipulating power relationships within their homes. Thus, rather than creating new types of female behavior, the demands of office life may have required middle-class women to give public expression to a competitiveness that previously had remained hidden behind a facade of domestic harmony.

CONFLICT WAS the predominant but not the only mode of interaction amongst government clerks. While federal employees engaged in aggressive, competitive behavior, they also formed friendships, helped each other out, and—once in a great while—performed truly self-sacrificing deeds. As employees within the first large white-collar bureaucracy, federal clerks were among the first middle-class men and women to labor in an environment with many other similarly situated workers. The presence of such a concentrated body of government employees offered middle-class workers the potential for cooperative or collective action. The kind of affiliations that these middle-class men and women formed in the office rested, however, primarily upon personal, familial, or political connections. Government clerks made little effort to forge associations that would create a sense of unity or solidarity among federal employees generally. Indeed, the connections formed between government workers reveal how these men and women brought their distinctively middle-class habits and values into this new work environment.

Clerks—both male and female—found that the office fostered friendships. While conversation in some offices produced political quarrels and gossip, in others amicable chatting contributed much to the quality of work life. Women, especially, seemed to find the ability to converse at work important. When some supervisors, trying ostensibly to create a more efficient work environment, attempted to curb the conversation, female clerks resisted. Kate McElliote's supervisor reported her for "constant talking" that, he claimed, disturbed the other ladies in the room and prevented them from working. He tried to remedy the situation by moving her seat, but found that "when she could not talk she would write notes."[31] Similarly, one Patent Office official attempted to stop the "considerable conversation and gossip" going on "among a few [female] clerks" by issuing an order "to the head of the room to report...any clerk who engaged in unnecessary conversation during office hours." The edict so displeased one of the women in the room that she confronted her supervisor and denounced the order, saying "that it was intended to make a slave of her and she would not submit to it."[32]

The official records of the departments reveal almost no evidence of male clerks chatting in office or of officials trying to limit the conversation among their male employees. This may be due, however, less to men's taciturn behavior than to supervisors' willingness to tolerate different standards of office conduct for men and women. For it is clear that men did converse at work. Lester Frank Ward worked as a clerk in the Treasury Department in the late 1860s, and noted in his diary that the clerks in the office had held "religious discussions" and that on the first of April there "was much joking in the office. April fool jokes were played on all sides."[33] Interaction within the office produced friendship among both men and women—friendships that spilled over into after-work activities.

The men within the Washington bureaucracy sometimes engaged in specifically "male" forms of recreation with their office mates. One Pension Office clerk testified before a congressional investigating committee that he had encountered a group of male pension office employees at one of the city's pool halls. These establishments were apparently not places where billiards were played, but rather saloons where men met and placed bets on the ponies—kinds of bookmaking joints that served alcoholic refreshment.[34] At other times male clerks engaged in more respectable forms of entertainment with coworkers. Lester Frank Ward recorded that he and other clerks often listened to congressional speeches and attended lyceum lectures and debates together.[35] In the 1890s, when James Engle won reinstatement to the Pension Office, he hosted a lunch at a nearby restaurant and invited several friends from work. Some of those who attended apparently did so reluctantly, however. Green Raum, Jr., the appointment clerk and son of the Commissioner of Pensions, claimed that he was not friends with Engle, did not even like him, and in fact had originally recommended him for dismissal. When asked why, then, he attended Engle's party, he replied, "I thought it would be better policy to accept the invitation, because he would be offended if I did not."[36]

Women also engaged in out-of-office activities with coworkers. Emily Neyland, a well paid clerk in the General Land Office, took a three months' leave of absence from her job and journeyed to Europe with two female employees from the same office.[37] Emma James met Julia Wilbur while working under her supervision in the Patent Office. A few years later James left the government to become a newspaper correspondent, but maintained that Wilbur "remained in my affectionate regard among the very few departmental ladies whose acquaintance I have found time to retain in my busy professional life."[38]

While friendships within the office certainly improved the work environment for both men and women, they served a more practical function as well. Clerks often relied upon friends to defend or assist them in the numerous conflicts and crises that emerged within the office. In 1867, when the Secretary of the Treasury suggested that some of the least efficient clerks be fired, U.S. Treasurer Francis Spinner objected. He explained that "the persons spoken of are in ill health and have suffered greatly by reason of the rebellion [Civil War]." Moreover, he assured the Secretary that "there is a disposition on the part of the more efficient employees to do overwork in order to save their more unfortunate fellows from misfortune."[39] It is unclear if these specific workers were men or women, but other examples show that this type of assistance was offered and received by both male and female clerks. George Barry claimed that he had done not only his own work, but that of another man who was "in bad health." The extra work meant that Barry had to forgo his annual leave one year.[40] In another office Mrs. S. B. Kennaugh, a currency counter, wrote to the chief of her division explaining that her partner, Mrs. Hoffman, often made errors in counting because of her imperfect eyesight. Rather than request a more efficient partner, Mrs. Kennaugh wrote, "I am aware her health will not permit a more rigid discipline, and having full confidence in her statement, and her disposition and effort to do perfect work, I beg you will treat our misfortune with your usual kindness and consideration."[41] Gender apparently did not prove a barrier to this kind of helpful behavior. Virginia Robinson stated that in addition to her work in the office she had sometimes assisted a male coworker with his jobs when "he was hurried."[42] The sources reveal only occasional instances like these, but those that occurred apparently happened amongst persons of both genders. Male and female clerks may have alleviated some of the pressures and insecurities of federal employment by supporting each other in these small ways. More than likely it was the personalities of specific individuals within offices that determined when and how much assistance of this type was offered and accepted.

More important, perhaps, than help with clerical tasks was the aid clerks offered each other with political or bureaucratic troubles within the office. Both men and women acted on behalf of coworkers whose positions were being threatened by financial cutbacks, ill-tempered supervisors, or competitive fellow clerks. But in these cases the response or behavior of men and women differed, and, moreover, changed as the century neared its end.

During the 1860s and 1870s, men tended to write letters on behalf of their male friends in efforts to assist them with problems. When Benjamin Messer's temporary clerkship ran out in 1865, for example, one of his coworkers sent a letter to the head of the office saying: "I take pleasure in saying I have known Mr. Messer for the last two years and have been engaged much of the time in the same room with him in this office. I know of no man here more industrious and more faithful to his duties." He also assured the auditor that Messer was a good anti-slavery man and added "he has a diligent wife who is unremitting in her attention to the wants of our suffering and sick soldiers."[43] Messer won appointment to a permanent position and held it for twenty years. Similarly, Philip Hopkins seemed to have enjoyed a pleasant relationship with the men in his office, for when he was dismissed in a reduction of the force in 1874, one of his fellow workers wrote—this time to Hopkins himself—expressing the hope "that you may speedily find suitable employment for your feeble health and that you will have the best of success in whatever you may undertake."[44] Hopkins put this letter in his file, hoping it would improve his chances at reinstatement, and found that within a year he was, indeed, reinstated.

Upon occasion an example of truly self-sacrificing friendship between male clerks surfaced in the records. One such instance was the relationship between Major Burch and Mr. Westervelt. The incident began when a fourth-class clerk—William Elder—resigned, thereby creating a vacancy. Where the availability of a high-paid slot often evoked severe competition within government offices, in this case very different behavior ensued. Elder, the man resigning, explained that "Major Burch, disbursing clerk, has long been entitled to promotion, but the case of Mr. Westervelt is so strong and so urgent that Major Burch desires Mr. W's claim to take precedence of his own." Apparently Burch and Westervelt were friends and Burch recognized Westervelt's extremely precarious financial situation.[45]

While friendship alone probably motivated Mr. Burch, in more cases politics lay beneath the assistance that one male clerk offered to another. Political factions or cliques often divided government offices, and hostility between groups could sometimes be balanced by friendship or cooperation within factions. On numerous occasions men used their pens to defend coworkers of like political leanings. For example, when John F. Bentley came under suspicion of disloyalty in 1862, a man in the same office jumped to his defense: "I have worked beside Mr. Bentley ever since you appointed him last July. He is as loyal a man as I know in the country and thoroughly honest."[46] Similarly, Josiah Bellow wrote on behalf of Robert Patterson, a friend who had been discharged after coming under suspicion of being a "Johnson" man. Bellow insisted that he had known Patterson since 1864, had boarded in the same house with him, and had clerked beside him in the same office. Although they no longer boarded together, they still met frequently and Bellow attested to Patterson's radical Republican proclivities and proclaimed him "an enemy of Andrew Johnson and his policy."[47]

These cases reveal individual men helping others who shared political convictions. In other instances men acted collectively to achieve the same goals—to rescue a beleaguered member of their party from attack by the other faction. Twenty-three male clerks within one division of the Second Auditor's Office signed a letter endorsing the political credentials of Josiah Harding and defending him against the accusation of "Johnsonism": "[W]e have been personally and intimately acquainted with Mr. Josiah F. Harding...since his entry herein and we have no hesitation in stating that he is, and has been, a good Republican, true to the party and an earnest advocate of its principles during the period of our acquaintance with him."[48] Similarly George Barry's 1862 dismissal for the charge of "talking secesh" drew a response from twenty-one of his fellow clerks. They wrote to Barry expressing their "deepest regret that [his] connections with [the office had] been severed," and assuring him of their readiness to testify to the zeal, fidelity, and efficiency with which he had carried out his duties. Moreover, they continued, "[A]ll of us, some expressing the feelings of a mature friendship of many years others of the acquaintance of a few months, acknowledge the courtesy and gentlemanly bearing you have always observed toward your brother clerks, and beg you to accept this feeble testimonial from us who have known you so well."[49] In Josiah Harding's case, the letter from his coworkers appeared to do some good, since he succeeded in fending off the assault and keeping his job. George Barry was not so fortunate. He spend five years in retirement from the government before he could win reappointment. The assistance that was proffered and received—whether individually or collectively—no doubt served to alleviate some of the tensions within the office. It did not, however, alter, the fundamentally conflict-ridden nature of office relations. Men used their friends and political allies in efforts to protect themselves from the competition and conflict of government work. The letters that some male clerks wrote on each other's behalf and those letters that indicted or accused coworkers represented opposite sides of the same coin.

Many of the ostensible acts of friendship between male clerks, in fact, masked pragmatic and even self-serving motives. For example, men wrote on occasion petitioning to have one of their number promoted to supervisor. Such letters were prompted by more than a desire to aid a fellow worker. A supervisor wielded considerable power. Not only did he have control over who performed what work, but he also made recommendations for promotions and dismissals. Being able to choose your own supervisor, therefore, was the next best thing to becoming supervisor. This might have been the motive of the eleven clerks who tried to influence the outcome of a power struggle for control of their office in 1875. These men wrote to the Secretary of the Treasury informing him that "one Robert S. Widicombe, a clerk in this office, is making strenuous efforts to obtain the reversal of the recommendation by our Auditor of Mr. F. I. Seybolt to be Chief of the Registering Division." Widicombe's actions, they maintained, were entirely selfish—he wanted to be chief. The clerks affirmed their loyalty to Seybolt, a "faithful officer, as well as a competent one, and a courteous gentleman," and asked that he be kept on as chief of the division.[50]

An 1861 petition from thirty male clerks in the Third Auditor's Office made no attempt to hide the self-serving motives of the petitioners. The men asked that Henry K. Randall, a clerk in the office, be promoted to the newly vacant chief clerkship. They explained that the "usefulness and comfort" of the clerks in the office "are dependent in no small degree upon the disposition, character, and qualifications of their superior officer." Randall, they felt, was a "suitable person for the position."[51]

The same motives that impelled male clerks to work collectively to advance one of their number to supervisory status also induced them to try to remove an unacceptable boss. In 1882, for example, eighteen men within one division of the First Auditor's Office signed a letter complaining about their chief, William B. Gunnison. These clerks revealed not only their hope that collective actions would effect a change, but the characteristics which they found unacceptable in a supervisor: "[H]e is arbitrary and ungentlemanly in his manners toward 'my Men' as he terms the clerks of his Division and has caused tears to flow from the eyes of some of the lady clerks who chanced to be under his control." Moreover, they complained, he was "incompetent, inefficient, manifestly impractical and...[is] justly entitled to the well earned reputation of a 'shirk.' " The men in Gunnison's division apparently also had a personal ax to grind, for their supervisor "engaged in the nefarious practice of loaning money to his fellow clerks at 5% per month."[52] These clerks objected to Gunnison's patronizing manner ("my Men"), his ungentlemanly behavior toward the ladies, and the distasteful manner in which he exercised both official and personal power.

Examples of more altruistic collective actions do appear occasionally in the records, and these are instances where men petition on behalf of someone considerably beneath them within the office hierarchy. For example, in 1853, thirteen clerks from the Office of the Treasurer requested that Henry B. Croggon be promoted from laborer to messenger. They noted that Croggon, although designated a laborer and paid a laborer's wage, had for many years been "discharging the proper duties of messenger...to the entire satisfaction of all concerned."[53] In the same year clerks in another part of the Treasury Department petitioned to have the messenger in that office, George W. Fale, promoted to a clerkship.[54] In neither instance were these attempts successful, for both men had to wait a minimum of four years before receiving their promotions. Nevertheless, the efforts on the part of these petitioners suggest that male clerks occasionally behaved altruistically—at least toward men who presented little threat of competition.

Male clerks seemed much more willing to use their pens to aid or defend coworkers in the third quarter of the century than in the later decades. The federal bureaucracy was flexible and responsive enough during these years for clerks to feel that it was worthwhile to intervene on behalf of friends or political allies. Government employees apparently wrote such letters frequently—too frequently, in fact, for the taste of some federal officials. For in 1875, Secretary of the Interior Zachariah Chandler tried to put a stop to such activities by issuing an order prohibiting "clerks and other employees," under threat of dismissal, "from making written or verbal recommendations for appointment and from giving any information relative to vacancies that may exist or occur in any branch of the Interior Department."[55] And while the order was not entirely effective, the sources reveal few letters from one man recommending or endorsing another in the 1880s and 1890s.[56] In this case, as in others, efforts to make government offices respond to rational procedures rather than to political or personal imperatives limited the kinds of activities in which male clerks engaged, diminishing some of the independence that had traditionally been associated with middle-class male behavior.

At no time during the four post-Civil War decades did men seem particularly disposed to make such efforts on behalf of female coworkers. Although women were clearly involved in the competition of office life and subject to the hazards of office politics, they may not have been included within the dominant political factions of the office and thus probably did not receive the support that alliance with such groups offered to male clerks. Other than the men who protested that William Gunnison "brought tears to the eyes of the ladies" in the office, few examples of men taking up their pens on behalf of women in the office have come to light.

Neither did women write these kinds of letters for members of their own sex. The records reveal almost no examples of women writing to defend the political position of office mates or petitioning officials to ask that one of their number (or some male within the office) be promoted to supervisory position. This does not mean that women failed to intervene on their friends' behalf, but they seemed to have used different methods.

Rather than rely upon formal letters or petitions, women would, upon occasion, defend or assist a coworker in a more personal and often impulsive manner. Frances Cougle's boss wrote to the head of the Pension Office complaining about Cougle's behavior when she learned that a friend, a Mrs. Sloane, was to be temporarily transferred to another office: "Mrs. Cougle opened upon me a torrent of abuse for allowing her friend Mrs. Sloane to go out of the Division." Although the initial outburst was verbal, Cougle was not afraid to put her words in writing. She wrote to the Commissioner of Pensions charging her supervisor, David Gitt, with a variety of offenses, among them transferring her friend "from her comfortable desk to a room unfit for a lady, where there was no work for her...[and where] she remained six weeks not having one week's work until the insult and exposure prostrated her upon a sick bed." Gitt attempted to have Cougle fired for such an outburst. No doubt fearing for her position, she apologized for having "assumed the attitude or appearance of insubordination" and offered assurance that she would never again "be found lacking in the strict observance of all the orders, rules, and regulations of the Office."[57] Emily Brown indulged in similar behavior and found herself in the same kind of trouble. She had protested when her niece was transferred to a different office. While we cannot know her exact words, one man who testified in the case noted that Brown "is brusque, and would naturally take up the cudgels of her niece, and it is possible that she may have said or done something displeasing to McKevitte [her boss]."[58] Carrie Sheads, an employee in the Bureau of Statistics, jumped to the defense of her friend, Miss Crane, by offering to swear, under oath, that the record of absences filed against Crane was "utterly false." Such an oath was tantamount, of course, to calling her supervisor—the person responsible for recording the absences—a liar. In response, Shead's supervisor charged her with insubordination and tried, unsuccessfully, to have her salary reduced from $1200 to $900 per year.[59] Such incidents appear only occasionally in the records, but they reveal that although women rarely wrote formal letters of endorsement for coworkers, they were nevertheless willing to put themselves at considerable risk to help friends whom they felt had been mistreated.

The differences between male and female behavior toward friends in office is worth examining. Why did women not write the same kinds of letters on behalf of their coworkers as did male clerks? Men might have been familiar with the traditional means of endorsing coworkers and more optimistic that their letters would bring the desired results. Women, not used to public, collective action, may not have realized that employees could intervene formally on behalf of coworkers, or might have felt that— given their basically powerless positions within the bureaucracy—such efforts would have been useless. More curious, perhaps, is the lack of caution that accompanied women's efforts to assist friends in the office. A man who wrote a formal, polite letter had little to lose, but a woman who heaped verbal abuse upon a supervisor risked being charged with insubordination and dismissed. In none of the cases cited above did the women actually lose their jobs, but in each case investigations were conducted to determine if the woman should be fired. It is difficult to know if female clerks were braver or more foolish than their male counterparts. What is clear, however, is that these women were certainly not selfless paragons of virtue. The same women who risked their jobs to help friends or kin did not act kindly toward all their coworkers. Although Frances Cougle defended Mrs. Sloane, her boss maintained that she did not get along with the other women in the office, and that he had "to remonstrate on more than one occasion with her, because of her slander of her fellow lady clerks."[60] And Emily Brown who protested on behalf of her niece was also known to be "fussy and quarrelsome with other clerks."[61] Thus, for women as for men, acts of friendship remained embedded within a larger context of conflict-ridden office relationships. Women did, nevertheless, seem willing to defend specific personal friends (or kin) and may occasionally have leapt into the fray before considering the adverse consequences of their actions. It seems likely that such women, believing formal protest was of little avail, relied instead upon a more personal, informal, and risky mode of protest. They may, however, have waited to register such complaints until their frustration level had reached the point where an outburst was likely.

For male and female clerks, friendships and alignments within the office might have reduced some of the tension of office life and therefore improved the work environment. Having friends or political cohorts in your corner could only have made a troubled clerk feel better. Men and women formed friendships and sometimes acted on behalf of their coworkers, but they each used methods with which they were comfortable and familiar. Men wrote formal letters and petitions to try to assist co-workers, although in many instances such efforts combined self-serving with altruistic motives. Women seemed to take a more personal approach and berate supervisors whom they felt had mistreated friends or kin. The actions of both men and women reveal the essentially individualistic nature of the relationships between federal clerks.

Only upon rare occasions did these middle-class workers choose to act in unison to improve their collective lot. Typically government clerks would form *ad hoc*, short-lived groups to address specific grievancs. In 1864, for example, more than three hundred male clerks petitioned the Senate explaining that "in these extraordinary times the salaries paid to them *are insufficient*, especially to such as have dependent families." They requested added pay at least "till the war be over."[62] The workers received support for their cause, for in February 1867, Congress passed a bill awarding federal employees in Washington, D.C., a 20 percent bonus for that fiscal year. Several months later a group of men in the Interior Department formed a Government Clerk's Association to petition the secretary of their agency for his assistance in "secur[ing] continuation of the (Twenty-per-cent) bill by Congress at its approaching session." They thanked the secretary for his "endorsement of the application last year," noting that his "efforts in its behalf are well remembered by all connected with the Interior Department."[63]

The records reveal a few circumstances when women joined together to protest conditions or problems specific to their sex. In 1865, twenty-two "ladies of the Register's Office" petitioned the Secretary of the Treasury for relief "from duty on Saturdays at 3 o'clock." They based their claim upon the special domestic burdens that female workers shouldered along with their official responsibilities: "Those who have families and domestic duties are much inconvenienced by the late hour of dismissal at the close of the week, and will be much benefited as well as gratified, if it will please the Honorable Secretary to grant their request."[64] The women apparently failed in this endeavor, for there is no evidence that they were permitted to leave the offices earlier than their male coworkers.

Twenty years later, women from various examining divisions of the Patent Office sent a petition to the Commissioner of Patents requesting his "favorable consideration of *our equitable claim to an increase in salary.*" They chronicled the history of women's employment as examiners' clerks, noting how in 1872 the then Commissioner of Patents placed one low-paid woman into the position previously held by men who had earned from $1200 to $1400. The reason for this "experiment" was "to test the fitness and ability of a woman to perform such duty, as well as to *save* to the office the difference in salary." They begged the Commissioner to reward their expertise, diligence, and skill by recommending that Congress increase their salaries to $1200. The men who headed the divisions in which these women worked endorsed the petition with their signatures.[65] Regardless of such efforts, this petition, like that of the "ladies of the Register's Office" failed to achieve its goal.

In some instances men and women jointly protested conditions that affected their circumstances or status in the office. In 1872, for example, male and female clerks in one division of the Treasurer's Office protested that "the air is foul and odors so unpleasant that the health of those engaged in said room is placed in peril."[66] And early in 1893, men and women in the General Land Office petitioned the Secretary of the Interior to try to persuade Congress to amend an appropriations bill in order to "avoid the proposed reduction by dismissal of sixty-eight (68) clerks and copyists."[67]

Not until 1900 did federal workers successfully create a permanent employee organization. In that year Treasury Department clerks, fearful of an order that threatened to require the retirement of all "superannuated" employees, organized the United States Civil Service Retirement Association. Different from earlier groups of government clerks, the USCSRA not only attracted large numbers of employees from various Washington agencies but held onto its membership for the next two decades. The USCSRA represented a different kind of response on the part of government workers, and it resulted from increasing efforts by federal officials to institute more rational, bureaucratic methods of office management. As long as the federal government functioned according to personal or political standards, the individualistic methods that clerks employed to advance or protect themselves often proved effective. Increasing rationalizations of departmental procedures, however, threatened that effectiveness. Throughout the late nineteenth century, for example, older clerks had found themselves protected by sympathetic and friendly supervisors who allowed them to retain their positions even after their efficiency had declined. The departmental order requiring the retirement of all seventy-year-old employees substituted a rational procedure for a personal one, and in the process left many older government workers without jobs or income. Individualistic attempts to assist coworkers, influence bosses, or undercut fellow clerks could be of no avail here. The clerks who formed and joined the USCSRA realized that they needed, rather, to work collectively toward legislation that would guarantee retiring federal employees a reasonable pension.[68]

WHILE GOVERNMENT WORKERS sometimes banded together to press for needs beyond those of an individual clerk, faction, or office, formal collective protests still occurred infrequently during the nineteenth century. Much more prevalent were the numerous personal or political efforts by individual clerks or small factions within an office, and these were as likely to involve competition as cooperation. Middle-class workers continued to behave, in other words, in decidedly middle-class ways, even when the environment in which they labored had changed. Indeed, federal clerks faced the tensions within this new, bureaucratic style of employment by attempting to make the middle-class, competitive work ethic function in an altogether different setting. They found that the partially rationalized nature of the federal bureaucracy allowed considerable room for individual efforts at self-aggrandizement. Moreover, the ability to compete, to maneuver, and to advance their own interests became, especially for middle-class men, reassuring reminders that government employees had not relinquished their claim to middle-class status.

The nature of the relations between federal clerks reflected tensions inherent in this new style of middle-class labor—tensions generated not only by class, but by gender as well. Competition between clerks for security, status, and advancement within the bureaucracy precipitated most of the conflict within government offices. This conflict, nevertheless, crossed gender boundaries, and in so doing created a variety of problems for these middle-class men and women. The presence of women in the offices did not measurably alter the competitive, cutthroat environment of the federal workplace. Rather, men came to learn that success in a sexually integrated work environment would require them to treat middle-class women in their offices in the same way that they treated male coworkers, despite the fact that such behavior would be considered improper in the world outside of work. Similarly, women soon realized that if they were to survive as civil servants they had to behave contrary to the rules prescribed by the cult of true womanhood. Indeed, women learned fairly quickly to engage in the aggressive tactics of their male coworkers. They intrigued, they schemed, and they competed with coworkers. With apparent ease many women left behind the dictates of the domestic ideology and adopted male norms. When faced with the real demands of federal employment, women had little difficulty behaving in ways which previously would have been defined as abnormal or deviant.

But gender still continued to play a key role in government offices. Although women learned to behave in certain regards like men, they did not necessarily acquire the same advantages. Women's opportunity and ability to wield influence within the office remained circumscribed by their gender. Moreover, a whole range of activities occurred within Washington departments that were not specifically related to work. The entrance of women into the federal bureaucracy raised a host of issues that had never presented themselves within the office—issues such as etiquette, manners, and sex. Here middle-class ladies were considerably less willing to forgo female norms or to adopt male behavior. The stage was set for a different sort of conflict.

CHAPTER SEVEN

Manners, Morals, and Money

Male and female government clerks, as members of the middle class, had grown up in a world which didactic writers had carefully divided, prescribing separate roles and ascribing separate character traits for men and women. As Victorian America's specific variation on an old theme, the cult of true womanhood sought to limit women's access to positions of public power and keep them restrained primarily to domestic roles. From the pages of ladies' magazines, the pulpits of ministers, and the advice of doctors came warnings of the dangers attending women's removal from the domestic sphere and their mixing into the public male world. Of course, not all nineteenth-century middle-class women spent their entire lives cloistered within parlors and kitchens. Many pushed at the boundaries of women's sphere and broadened their world to include church, reform, and charitable activities. Moreover, the Gilded Age saw women fighting for the vote, entering coeducational universities in the west, and pursuing higher education at female institutions in the east. Nevertheless, in 1861, when women first entered federal offices, there were few women who had placed themselves in an all-male work environment, and few men who had yet to deal with the presence of Victorian ladies on the job. Those middle-class women who did perform paid labor were usually writers or school teachers, and in neither instance did such work bring them into direct contact with large numbers of adult men.[1]

In the immediate post-Civil War years most middle-class women still encountered men—other than relatives—only upon carefully circumscribed occasions. In families, in parlors of respectable friends, at church, and perhaps at lyceum lectures or charitable associations, proper middle-class ladies and gentlemen met and mingled. All of these settings, however, were places where the rules of Victorian propriety prevailed and where women could expect protection from ungentlemanly or unscrupulous men. Women were not required—indeed not allowed—to converse with men to whom they had not been properly introduced. One etiquette manual noted: "If a gentleman is presented to a lady, it should be done only after her permission has been asked and received."[2] Advice literature devoted considerable ink to telling men how they should moderate their behavior in the presence of ladies. Any man, one book warned, who "smokes in any lady's presence without asking her permission [would have] the seal of vulgarity...impressed on him."[3] By the late 1880s some of the prescriptions on uses of tobacco were being relaxed, but men were still required to defer to the sensibilities of their female companions. One writer stated that "ladies no longer affect to be disgusted by the odor of tobacco, even at table," and another noted that a cigar was permissible "when by the seaside, or in the country, or in any but fashionable headquarters, if your fair companion doesn't object."[4] Didactic writers also instructed young men to watch their language and "not make a practice of using slang, and...never use it in the presence of ladies."[5] At least in the ideal, then, interaction between middle-class men and women was carefully regulated and the occasions upon which they did meet were monitored so that women would be spared some of the worst excesses of "male" behavior. Moreover, most of the places where middle-class men and women interacted in Gilded Age America were within a broadly defined "female" sphere—places where rules designed to make women safe and comfortable were observed.

But government offices were clearly men's turf. One had only to look at the spittoons that adorned every office. A diagram of three rooms in the General Land Office in 1882 revealed a spittoon next to each desk.[6] This drawing suggests that male clerks spit with great frequency and that the government preferred the expense of numerous cuspidors to the work time that would be lost as men wandered in search of centrally placed receptacles. Men also smoked in the office, used rough language, and occasionally appeared for work in an intoxicated condition. Mr. Simms (Minnie Reed's supervisor) was not the only federal employee to fall off the wagon during work hours. Michael Higgins was reported by the chief of his division for appearing for duty "under the influence of intoxicants to such an extent as to unfit him for duty for several days" and George Talbot was recommended for dismissal for "using liquor during office hours."[7] Although federal offices represented middle-class work environments, there could be no doubt that they were middle-class *male* work environments.

Enter proper middle-class ladies. What happened as such women began to work together with men in a hitherto male space? Did male and female cultures conflict, and if so, which one proved dominant? We have already seen how the demands of the highly competitive federal bureaucracy forced women to leave behind many of the conventions of female culture and behave in ways which, by nineteenth-century standards, were defined as specifically "male." But there were other components of office life—the more personal aspects—where women made their presence felt. Officials found they would have to deal with new issues and write new rules so that the federal bureaucracy would become a place where women could work comfortably. Moreover, the clerks themselves—used to dealing with members of the opposite sex only in carefully circumscribed settings—would begin to fashion new ways for middle-class men and women to interact within an office. While these changes were not necessarily self-conscious, and while some may, in fact, have created as many problems as they solved, the results were offices where middle-class men and women implicitly challenged nineteenth-century prescriptions and behaved in ways that presaged the emergence of a more modern, twentieth-century work environment.

SOME OF THE PROBLEMS involved manners. The rules of middle-class propriety under which these men and women had been raised did not apply to office life, and no new code of proper office etiquette yet existed. The result was occasional conflict between men and women over the conduct of male clerks in the office. Women sometimes complained because men behaved in an ungentlemanly fashion or used rough language. William Barker, chief of the record division in the Pension Office in 1889, noted that two male clerks, Mr. Ford and Mr. Sidell, "were brought to [his] attention during office hours, whereby they used very harsh language towards each other, ungentlemanly language, so that the ladies had to leave the room...."[8] Whether it was the women or other men who brought this incident to the attention of the supervisor is unclear, but such behavior was nevertheless perceived as problematic in the presence of ladies.

On other occasions women, themselves, protested when men misbehaved. Mary Ruckman objected that the men in her office "idled their time, ate fruit, wrote letters and were very insulting to the ladies."[9] Frances Cougle charged that her immediate supervisor, David Gitt, had made "unmanly insults to respectable women." She cited his remarks to "two ladies of standing and character that it made no difference to him whether a woman was a harlot or a virgin if she came and did her work." Moreover, she complained that he allowed "messenger boys to walk about with their hats on their heads whistling as they pass where ladies are sitting at their desks."[10] Women used to being treated like "ladies" sometimes encountered men within their offices who did not always behave like "gentlemen."

It is impossible to know how prevalent such problems were. The records reveal only occasional complaints on the part of women. The actions of federal officials, however, suggest that curbing male behavior was becoming an increasingly important concern. Indeed, while women were learning to behave in specifically male ways in their competition for office jobs, men were being required to modify their conduct because of the presence of ladies in the departments. For example, supervisors began during the last two decades of the century to recommend the dismissal of men who had come to work in an intoxicated condition. What is curious is that officials made almost no such recommendations during the 1860s and 1870s. It seems unlikely that men did not drink in the immediate post-Civil War years and much more likely that supervisors only began objecting to such behavior in the latter part of the century. Various reasons account for the official crackdown on drinking—a desire to increase the efficiency in the office, and to upgrade the rather tarnished reputation that the bureaucracy had acquired in the public mind. Moreover, increasing temperance activities throughout the country had created a heightened awareness of the problems associated with alcohol. But the presence of women within the office no doubt also contributed to officials' demands for more proper deportment amongst male clerks.

Concern for the comfort of female employees led administrators to require that men alter more than their drinking habits. In 1896 the Secretary of the Interior ordered that henceforth "no smoking will be allowed in the halls of the building occupied by the Interior Department, nor in any rooms occupied by lady employees of the Department."[11] Some of the "female" rules that had heretofore applied only within the Victorian parlor were being transferred to the workplace. By the end of the century, men who worked in what was now a sexually integrated, middle-class work environment needed to make sure that their social conduct within the office would meet some of the standards of Victorian propriety.

Manners and etiquette were, however, relatively easy problems with which to deal; the more difficult issue raised by women's entrance into the federal workplace was sex. The domestic ideology of the early nineteenth century had succeeded in changing an image of women that dated back to the story of Eve: instead of earthy, lusty temptresses, women in Victorian culture became non-sexual and passionless. Indeed, the nineteenth century had mounted an assault upon a long history of female sexuality and had left half the human race allegedly devoid of sexual impulse. The victory was, of course, an uneasy one. For beneath the restrictiveness of Victorian culture lay the fear that women's exposure to the world would not only leave the fair sex vulnerable to sexual assault, but might also awaken an uncontrollable female sexuality. The dual nineteenth-century view of women—mother and prostitute, pure and depraved—hinted at Victorian fears of female sensuality lurking behind true womanhood.[12]

One of the most radical aspects of women's entry into the federal workplace was that it brought middle-class women into contact with strange men without the protection of male family members or the benefits of well-observed and respected codes of behavior. It was possible, of course, for such interactions to produce respectable outcomes—for friendships begun at work to blossom into courtships and matrimony. For example, Mary McKinney asked that her name be changed on the office rolls after she married a fellow clerk in the Census Office in 1890.[13] In 1883, Fannie Simpson resigned her position in the Pension Office to marry Mr. Bender, a clerk in the same office. "Being very tired of my present name I have concluded to go on a 'Bender,' " she wrote. The Commissioner of Pensions regretted having to file such a "vulgar" document with the Secretary of the Interior, but noted, "As it contains her resignation, I am compelled to do so, without any further comment upon its delicacy."[14] Although Simpson's levity was not appreciated by the Commissioner, it makes clear that federal offices were places where men and women could meet, fall in love, and decide to marry. But proximity between male and female clerks could produce other than marital relationships. For Victorians, the exposure of women to strange men in a male environment spelled danger—and that danger was specifically sexual.

And, indeed, sex became an issue almost immediately upon women's entry into government departments. By 1864, only three years after the first women became clerks in the Treasury Department, a special congressional committee was already investigating "certain charges against the Treasury Department" and discovering that some supervisors had tried to extract sexual favors from their female employees. Mano Lulley, the father of one of the victims, testified that his sixteen-year-old daughter had worked in the department for one month when her supervisor demanded that she stay until ten o'clock in the evening: "She worked, I think, six nights, when I refused to allow her to go to the department at night at all. During the time my daughter worked nights, Mr. Gray [her supervisor] made the following proposition to my daughter: That if she (my daughter) would go with him (Gray) to a certain hotel in this city and submit to his (Gray's) wishes, he (Gray) would raise her (my daughter's) salary to $75 per month."[15]

Jennie Germon, one of the first female employees of the National Currency Bureau, told the committee a similar story: "[The supervisor] came to me in the office and asked me to come to his private residence. On the next Saturday night...I went to [his] house...[we] went to a private bedroom, and both occupied the same bed until morning."[16] The difference between Lulley and Germon was that while the former was certainly coerced, the latter might have willingly participated in these activities.

The revelation of sexual improprieties within the Treasury Department confirmed many people's worst fears about introducing women into the bureaucracy. Indeed, Germon's and Lulley's experiences exposed the two dangers that seemed most likely to result from putting women into government offices: first, that the departments would attract unsavory women and encourage sexually free behavior; and second, that those innocent women who did become federal clerks would find themselves seduced by immoral supervisors or corrupted by promiscuous women posing as virtuous ladies.

Writers and journalists seized upon the image of the "treasury courtesan," a product of this early scandal, and kept it before the public mind.

In his 1869 book, *The Sights and Secrets of the National Capital*, John Ellis discussed many of the contemporary concerns about female clerks. Ellis knew of the scandal in the Treasury Department and called it "the original cause of the suspicion attaching to [these women's] position today." He held, however, that to brand an entire class of female clerks as immoral adventuresses would bring "unjust and unfounded" suspicion upon many virtuous women. Ellis declared that "nine times out of ten [a female clerk] is the child of poor parents, or her father may have died under the old flag, and she may be the only hope of a widowed mother for bread, and, to lose her place would be to bring starvation upon loved ones."[17]

While proclaiming the innocence of the majority of women who entered government departments, Ellis nevertheless feared that working in federal offices could cause the downfall of even once respectable young ladies. Becoming a government worker, Ellis argued, subjected a woman to "men who would seek her moral destruction." Unscrupulous supervisors "surround her with flattery, with temptations of every description, and when these fail, threaten her with dismissal from the place in which she earns her bread, if she does not yield." Concluding that too often "women's virtue is made the price of such an appointment," Ellis cautioned women against entering government offices. He warned about the high cost of living in Washington, and called the $600 annual salary then paid to many women "notoriously insufficient" to support them decently, implying that it might drive them to prostitution. Ellis was thus not primarily concerned that federal jobs would attract immoral women, although he admitted the presence of numerous "black sheep" within government departments. Rather, he feared that government employment would corrupt innocent women: "The acceptance of a Government clerkship by a woman is her first step in the road to ruin."[18]

Concerns over the immorality of female federal clerks continued to appear in public writings throughout the late nineteenth century. Columnists in local Washington newspapers as well as correspondents for out-of-town newspapers returned repeatedly to this issue. While most such commentators attempted to replace the image of the "treasury courtesan" with that of the hard-working, needy, respectable lady clerk, they agreed that government employment endangered these women. In 1871, George Allen Townsend, editor of a Washington weekly, wrote a poem called "The Lady of the Treasury" for his newspaper. In it he portrayed a worthy widow, beset by temptations and dangers in the department:

> No prude is she, to seek and pry
> If each one round her be a saint;
> She knows her own soul pure and high
> And nothing else can do her taint;
> She knows that dear temptations vex
> This weak and craving human nature
> And how the mighty spell of sex

> O'ercomes a lonely, loving woman...
> Her intuition teaches that
> The statesman still is but a sinner
> And Mammon drops his key to chat
> As readily as General Spinner.[19]

It was difficult to argue for innocence in a situation that contemporary morality defined as fraught with danger and frustration. Defenders of female clerks refuted the charges of immorality by offering evidence of these women's high social standing and impeccable character, often naming individual women and citing their upstanding family backgrounds.[20] Mary Clemmer Ames, journalist and women's rights advocate, was one of those who vociferously supported female federal clerks. Her views apparently proved influential, for other writers who commented on government offices often cited her observations.[21] In her 1873 book, *Ten Years in Washington*, Ames protested that only in isolated instances did disreputable women still hold positions within the government: "The truth is, that there is not any other company of women workers in the land which number so many ladies of high character, intelligence, culture, and social position." Ames attributed the few remaining instances of immorality to the "unjust modes of appointment," not to the corrupt character of the women. Only through a fair and well-run civil service system, she felt, would women find "redress" from the necessity of seeking assistance and favors from unscrupulous but powerful men.[22]

The taint that blemished the reputation of so many female clerks originated not only from a fear of their vulnerability to lecherous men. Some people simply refused to accept the idea that respectable women would work in government offices; they branded as disreputable all female clerks. An 1871 front-page article in the *Washington Capital* described a campaign of slander directed against General Spinner's "great innovation" of hiring women as clerks. The writer, who used only the signature "H.M.B.," argued that those who opposed "broadening women's industrial life and the independence likely to flow therefrom" had unfairly accused female clerks:

> The unjust and false aspersions set afloat...were the result of persistent opposition from a class who refused to see the good results that must flow from this opportunity for women to meet the issues of life in a pecuniary ease far removed from any employment opened to them elsewhere, for the reason that it proved their prejudices, built upon theories of a proscribed sphere for women, false.[23]

Perhaps H.M.B. had an especially conspiratorial view of the situation, but he or she probably pinpointed one of the causes of these women's bad image: public distrust of the motives and morals of these pioneering women workers. Even the journalists who defended women clerks seemed concerned with the potential danger within government offices and not entirely convinced that all female clerks were blameless. Their frequent protestations that immoral women "no longer" worked in the departments, or that such women formed only a small minority, no doubt reflected their sincere attempt to upgrade the tarnished reputation of female clerks. However, by protesting too much, they may have unintentionally given credence to the notion that women in the departments were not all proper ladies.

The stigma of the "treasury courtesan" continued to plague female federal clerks even into the twentieth century. During the Wilson administration city officials in the nation's capital tried to clean up Washington's notorious red-light district. When a well-known madam was called before the judge and asked how she pleaded, she responded, "Your Honor, everybody knows I run the second-best house in the city....The Treasury runs the best."[24]

The issues raised by this public debate reveal that more was at stake than the presence of a few shady ladies in the departments. These working women posed an enormous challenge to the Victorian middle class because they threatened to invalidate the standards by which middle-class society judged a woman's character. Ellis hinted at this concern when he noted that "the good and the bad are mingled together. Outwardly they are all ladies."[25] Where male and female spheres remained distinct, society could easily distinguish the "good" from the "bad." Respectable ladies exercised great care, especially when outside their homes, churches, or schoolrooms, to follow rules of decorum that guaranteed their reputations as virtuous women. But those women who left their sphere, flouted the rules, and placed themselves in compromising situations, knew that they risked their good names.

As long as the standards governing acceptable behavior remained clear, the public could rest assured that immoral women would not masquerade as proper ladies. But when such rules began to change, the litmus test for respectability became indistinct. All female clerks (innocent or guilty) now behaved in ways that would previously have been defined as improper: they approached and asked favors of strange men, they conversed and formed friendships with men to whom they had not been properly introduced, and they worked at jobs that were previously reserved for men. Society, no longer able to judge a woman's status by her behavior, could not differentiate between respectable women and their immoral counterparts. In such a situation, the "good" found themselves constantly under suspicion.

What was needed for these workers were new rules—new ways of structuring male and female behavior within the office so as to defuse the sexual dangers that seemed ever present. Unfortunately, quick solutions were not easy to come by. The public debate on the sexual hazards in office life offered warnings, but little or no practical advice to the men and women working in the departments. In fact, the public attention given to sexual problems within the office may have made the pressure on federal clerks more severe. The government—looking perhaps to its own reputation—was on its guard to punish any breach of sexual etiquette amongst its employees, thereby proving that Washington offices were not dens of iniquity. These standards were especially strict in the immediate post-Civil War decades and were imposed on both female and male employees.

For women the consequences of sexual misconduct could be dire. Often just the rumor of wrong-doing on the part of a female clerk was sufficient to cause—at the minimum—her dismissal from office. In 1868, Addie Tyrrel wrote asking for a few months' work in the Treasury Department. She felt that she deserved the job since her sister, Jessie, a former employee, had suffered so terribly as a result of her experiences within the office. "You know the persecution we have endured in the Treasury, but you do not know that my fair young sister, Jessie, is a hopeless maniac, made so by the vile slander of the clerks in your Department." While Addie Tyrrel didn't specify the source of Jessie's torment, the severity of the response suggests that the accusations were sexual.[26] Charges of sexual misconduct eight years later against Cornelia Mills did not result in her derangement, but did cause her dismissal from the office. Two men apparently started a rumor that Mills had engaged in sexual acts with the man in whose home she boarded. The rumor was enough to cost Mills her job. But Mills fought back. Determined to vindicate herself and win reinstatement, she had depositions taken that proved her innocence, and finally won her restoration to office.[27]

Female clerks remained suspect throughout the century and had to guard their reputations and their conduct if they were to remain safely in office. There was, however, at least one office within the bureaucracy that, by the 1890s, had begun to relax some of the strictures on women's sexual conduct. In 1892, two women in the Pension Office, Mrs. Foss and Mrs. Friend, were accused of being "immoral women." When asked about how these charges were handled, the Commissioner of Pensions, Green B. Raum, admitted that the women were not dismissed immediately, but were allowed to remain at work until they found other jobs. Moreover, the office decided to let them resign rather than have letters of dismissal placed on their records. Raum explained that since the charges "did not go to their abilities as clerks" he felt it would not hurt to give them a few more weeks to find new positions. Raum maintained that "these women were very respectable women. They are both very intelligent women, and one, I understand, is quite a highly educated woman, and the father of one of them was in the Pension Office for twenty years." He continued, "You know, if a woman goes astray generally it gets out, and if there is much fuss made about it it is all in a flame presently. I found these women in that office when I went there. As far as their official conduct is concerned, why, it is quite satisfactory and one is one of the smartest clerks in the office."[28] There had definitely been some changes. At least within the Pension Office, officials had begun to separate their employees' private from public or professional lives, another indication that more rational and bureaucratic management was beginning to characterize some aspects of federal employment. The hint of immorality was no longer enough to result in these women's immediate and ignominious dismissal from office. This does not mean that all sexual principles were abandoned, for indeed government officials continued to maintain that the highest standards of sexual propriety were demanded of federal employees. The same Commissioner Raum who seemed to take Foss's and Friend's indiscretions so lightly, testified that most of the people in the departments—both male and female—were "of as high characters as you have in the country" and he saw no reason to let the federal bureaucracy serve as a "refuge of fallen women." Moreover, he claimed that if it were in his power he would "remove such persons" that were guilty of immoral conduct.[29] Nevertheless, Raum's actions toward these two women seemed to speak louder than his words. The ever-present and seemingly explicit sexual dangers that had loomed so large upon women's first entrance into the federal bureaucracy may have abated somewhat. Female clerks accused of wrong-doing were not always summarily dismissed. Foss and Friend did, of course, have to leave the office, but they were not ridden out on a rail. At least one bureau within the government had become somewhat less insistent that any woman suspected of immorality be excised like a cancer.

Nineteenth-century prescriptions had always demanded the highest standards of sexual morality from respectable women. But men were allowed more latitude. Although moralists and clergymen tried to exhort men to sexual purity, conventional wisdom held that men were constitutionally deficient when it came to controlling sexual urges. The double sexual standard, in fact, took men's weaknesses into account and treated men's sexual misdeeds lightly. Despite this widespread view, male clerks were not permitted to engage in sexual misconduct with impunity. Officials fired Bernard May in 1875 after police charged him with procuring an abortion for a woman with whom he was involved in an adulterous relationship, and William Walton was accused (by someone who wanted his job) of being a "drunkard and Debauche of the very lowest stripe, openly living with a Negro woman as his wife."[30] The criminal and racial components of May's and Walton's respective behavior no doubt made their "offenses" especially odious to federal officials. But even men charged with simple adultery risked dismissal. Mrs. Catherine de Hart wrote to the Secretary of the Interior in 1880 reminding him that since "my husband and the woman...who caused him to abandon me were both dismissed," she hoped she would be given a position in the office.[31] George W. Black lost his job in 1880 for supposedly having an affair with another clerk's wife. Twenty years after his dismissal he wrote to the Secretary of the Interior claiming that the charges against him were "as false as false can be" and asking that his record be cleared.[32] The lenient actions of Green Raum in the case of Mrs. Foss and Mrs. Friend notwithstanding, many officials apparently refused to tolerate any sexual misconduct—whether it occurred inside or outside of work. Throughout the century, male clerks found themselves in trouble if want of discretion let their sexual misbehavior become known. In the 1890s, men were using accusations of sexual transgressions as another weapon in their competitive wrangling within the office, suggesting that such charges were serious enough to cause trouble and maybe even to warrant a clerk's dismissal.

In most federal offices, in fact, officials seemed to toughen rather than relax the requirements that their employees behave, at all times, like ladies and gentlemen. Government efforts to curb excessive male social behavior—smoking and drinking—as well as vigilant guarding of the sexual standards suggest an attempt to transpose norms of middle-class propriety to the federal workplace. Such efforts to regulate the social and sexual behavior of federal employees and to create a more genteel work environment did not, however, diminish the very real problems that male and female workers faced as they dealt with the sexual dangers and tensions implicit in this new, sexually integrated bureaucracy. Supervisors could punish employees for known breaches in conduct, and administrators could write new regulations, but it was the men and women themselves who would have to face and try to solve the situations that emerged as they met and mingled within the offices of the nation's capital.

For women, it was sexual harassment that posed the most immediate and perhaps most frightening problem. Miss Lulley of the Treasury Department was certainly not the last female federal employee to be offered rewards for sexual favors or threatened with punishment for withholding them. In the mid-1870s, when Ann Douglass was dismissed from her job in the Treasury Department she explained, "To none of my friends... would Secretary [of the Treasury] Manning give a reason for my removal, other than that he had been requested to do so, not even telling by whom." A letter from one of Douglass's friends clarified the situation: "Miss Douglass had incurred the enmity of a man who had sufficient influence with Secretary Manning to cause her discharge, simply because she would not consent to, but refused, an improper proposal."[33] How many women experienced problems similar to those of Lulley and Douglass is unknown. Compared to the hue and cry within the public press, the sources reveal, in fact, relatively few clear cases of sexual harassment in late nineteenth-century federal offices. This cannot, however, be taken as evidence that the practice did not exist. Even today such incidents usually go unreported. It must have been much more difficult for Victorians to discuss such problems—much less to leave written evidence of them for curious historians. There are, however, other clues that female clerks sometimes found themselves sexually harassed. In 1891, Lewis Bogy, a Pension Office clerk, published a novel called *In Office* in which he exposed the sexual dangers for women within government service. The story relates how the lovely and innocent heroine, having procured a $720-per-year job in the Patent Office, journeyed to Washington to begin her career as a government clerk. Her boss, a scoundrel named Lecher Thompson, flattered her, showed her preferential treatment, and offered her a promotion to $1200. When she refused his overtures, however, he made office life miserable for her and attempted to ruin her reputation by circulating a rumor that she had become mistress to a Congressman.[34]

Bogy's book offers two kinds of evidence. First, it is another example of the public preoccupation with sexual dangers attendant upon women's release from the domestic sphere. But since Bogy was himself a clerk, his book suggests a more valid— if somewhat exaggerated and melodramatic—picture of the sexual dangers of office life in the nation's capital. Writing the book was, in fact, a courageous act, and it is unlikely that Bogy did so lightheartedly. Son of a former senator from Missouri, Bogy nevertheless chose to publish his book under his real name, rather than hide behind a pseudonym. And the book hit close enough to home to make government officials angry, for Bogy received his dismissal immediately after the book was published.[35]

Still, none of this offers direct evidence of how frequently women in government offices faced the problem of sexual harassment. That remains, for now, a mystery. It seems safe to assume that some women did have to fend off advances from unscrupulous supervisors and coworkers, but that most female clerks probably did not receive explicit sexual overtures at work.

Sexual relations within the office could work two ways. While sexual harassment implies a power relationship controlled by men, women may not always have been the passive victims of sexual politics within the office. Some women may have used sex as a means of advancing within the office. One anonymous clerk informed a Washington newspaper in the mid-1880s that women in the Pension Office "whose records are not good, were promoted because they were the particular pets and favorites of certain heads of the division."[36] The innuendo was that women became "pets" by having sex with their supervisors. Jennie Germon, remember, had never maintained that she had been coerced by Mr. Clark. In an environment where women were politically powerless and repeatedly subject to discrimination, female clerks might well have decided to use one of the few advantages that their sex afforded them. Again, it is impossible to know how prevalent were such practices. Probably only a small minority of female clerks engaged in this kind of behavior—despite the lurid portrayal of office life in much contemporary literature.

Many more women, no doubt, tried to curry favor in more acceptably feminine ways. Some officials enjoyed having women in the office, provided they behaved like "ladies." Enna Wilson's supervisor tried to obtain for her a promotion from her $840-per-year job in the Treasury Department in 1894. He described the difficult work that she performed, noting how others who labored at similar tasks earned $1200 and $1400. Further, he maintained, "her kind heart and ladylike bearing have won the regard of all who have had the good fortune to be associated with her."[37] In other instances a little flattery or flirtation might have proved a useful tool for a female clerk. In 1892, William Ford, an assistant chief of a division within the Pension Office, maintained that Mr. Barker, the head of the division, "has become notorious in the division as a man fond of talking to the ladies and having them about his desk." According to Ford, Barker's notoriety stemmed from his "talking to ladies and strutting up and down with his Prince Albert coat buttoned up, and with a big bouquet in it, walking around with the ladies." In Ford's estimation, such behavior made Barker look "silly."[38] We can readily imagine Barker preening for the ladies, but it is more difficult to guess what the women around him were thinking. It seems possible, however, that female clerks understood the potential benefits to be derived from flattering their male supervisors.

Barker's behavior and Ford's response to it suggest that the issues concerning sex became, over the last decades of the nineteenth century, increasingly complex. Where once it had been clear just which kinds of behavior were acceptable and which were not, by the end of the century a new, more relaxed style of interaction between male and female clerks presented federal workers with new dilemmas. While some instances of sexual harassment by men and sexual manipulation by women no doubt persisted, there seemed to grow up a large gray area where innuendo, flirtation, and bantering became the norm. These ostensibly innocent forms of behavior could, however, pose problems of their own for both men and women workers—problems as troubling as were sexual harassment and sexual manipulation. A male clerk or supervisor who made explicit sexual overtures toward a female employee knew he was taking some risks, for if discovered he would certainly lose his job. A woman who used sex to advance in office knew that, if discovered, she would lose her job and her reputation as well. But what of those men and women who flirted, dropped hints, and made suggestive but joking remarks? Although the sources are scarce, there is evidence that near the end of the century this kind of behavior had become common in some offices.

In 1892, news of corruption and scandal within the Pension Office erupted in the newspapers, and Congress responded with a major investigation of that bureau. The thousands of pages of testimony that resulted disclosed much about the sexual dimensions of office life and these new, more informal but perhaps still just as troubling interactions between male and female clerks. The Pension Office investigation revealed, first, that all the old problems had certainly not disappeared and that women still feared sexual harassment. What seems new, however, is that behavior between men and women which would have once been regarded as improper was, by the 1890s, often seen as innocent. The line between good natured, "innocent" flirtation and impropriety had become muddied and difficult to determine.

Take, for example, the case of Mrs. Caddie Wright and Mr. William Ford. Wright, described by a newspaper columnist as "a slender young woman of about thirty, a brunette with large dark eyes and a refined face," testified that Ford, her supervisor, had made "disrespectful" and suggestive comments to her one day after work. She told the story this

way: "I had been in the office a month probably more or less...and I was
going home from the office one evening and at the corner of F and Eighth
Streets Mr. Ford was standing. I don't know whether—I can't say whether
he was there to wait for me or not...I couldn't say; and he stepped up to
me and said, 'Mrs. Wright, can I speak to you?' and I said, 'Why yes, sir.'
And he said. 'Can you walk down this street?' and I said, 'Yes, sir.'...And
he immediately began. He said, 'Now, Mrs. Wright, I am a married man
and you have been a married woman,' and he said, 'I want to be your
friend, may I?' and I said, 'Why I don't understand you.' and he said. 'Yes
you do understand me,' and he repeated this several times." By that time
they had approached the corner of the street where a Mr. Donahue,
another section chief within the office, was standing. Upon spying
Donahue, Mrs. Wright testified, "[Ford] turned to me and said 'Don't tell
Donahue what I said to you,' and I bade them both good evening and
went home." The incident did not end here. Wright claimed that since
that evening Ford had treated her in an unfriendly way in the office. He
arranged for her to be detailed to the chief clerk's office, and when he
told her of the new arrangements he spoke to her "in a very ungentlemanly way." The incident troubled Wright enough for her to report it to
her immediate supervisor, a Mr. Landon. She noted, however, that she
would not have complained had it not been for Ford's unfriendly behavior toward her in the months following the incident. She became convinced that "Mr. Ford was inclined to be an enemy." She needed, she said,
"to protect myself."[39]

Ford, a "fine looking" man of about fifty-five or sixty, told a different
story.[40] He proclaimed his innocence, saying that he had just happened
upon Mrs. Wright on the street and called out, " 'Heigho, are you going
this way?' She said, 'Yes!,' I said, 'Well, then we'll walk a lonesome road
together.' This was said playfully and referred to the fact that the block
has no private residences and is not much of a thoroughfare." Ford maintained that he had spent less than two minutes with Wright. Moreover,
when they reached Mr. Donahue at the end of the street, he claimed, "I
repeated my conversation with the lady in [his] presence, and she went
off laughing about it." Ford protested that the incident had been entirely
innocent, and that he did not even know the woman's name. As to the
charge that he had treated her insolently within the office, he responded,
"Subsequently, while I was acting chief of division, the chief clerk sent for
a clerk to be temporarily detailed in his room. I sent Mrs. Wright down.
In rebutting her charge of insolence to her before a number of people, I
have to say that it has always been considered a compliment to be detailed
in the chief clerk's room or anywhere around headquarters, as the best
clerks are invariably selected."[41]

Ford's claim that being detailed was an honor rather than a punishment
would seem to have exonerated him from the charge of mistreating
Wright within the office, but the story becomes even more complex.
Wright revealed how, in fact, she could legitimately have felt as though

Ford was punishing her for her unwillingness to become his "friend." First, she objected to the manner in which her new assignment was made. "I wish to say," she explained, "that Mr. Ford detailed Miss Brinley to the chief clerk's room, and that he took her down and introduced her personally to the chief clerk." Wright, however, was hastily dispatched to the chief clerk with only a messenger as her escort. "I felt very badly, indeed, and cried about it," she said. Second, even though being detailed was usually considered an honor, in Wright's case there were specific circumstances that would have made it more attractive for her to remain where she was: "Miss Barnett was away, and Miss Foster and I were in charge of a certain class of work....At the time it was considered very important work, and it had taken me some little time to learn the work, and Capt. Riply and Mr. Klopfer thought it was strange I should be put off the work, but they said nothing to me about it."[42] Thus, it was not only the manner, but the fact that she was being removed from work which she enjoyed and which obviously gave her some status within the office that made her feel mistreated.

Testifying before a congressional committee proved an ordeal for Caddie Wright, leaving her, according to newspaper accounts, "confined to her home, too much prostrated by the severe nervous strain she has experienced to be able to resume her work in the Pension Office."[43] When newspaper correspondents called at Wright's house requesting an interview, she refused to see them. Wright sent her sister, however, with the following message: "Mrs. Wright...does not wish to add anything further to the account. She shrinks from any publicity as a woman reared as she has been would naturally do. She has felt, however, that the cause of other women in the office demanded that she should tell this story to the committee, painful as it was, and she has acted upon her judgment. I assure you this whole subject is embarrassing and painful to us both...."[44]

It is difficult to know how to interpret this story. Was Ford a master at subtle types of sexual harassment or was Wright exaggerating and jumping to unwarranted conclusions about Ford's intentions? Exasperated with the whole affair, Ford told a newspaper reporter, "Now, we come to this woman's [Wright's] charge, and you can see what a hell of a time a man has in dealing with a lot of women?"[45] What seemed to be happening, however, was that "dealing with women" in the office was becoming both more relaxed and subsequently more complex. By the 1890s women had been in office long enough for familiarity to breed situations that could be perceived as ambiguous.

William Ford was involved in another of these somewhat ambiguous incidents where his too-informal style of treating the ladies caused eyebrows to be raised. The charge was that Ford had thrown his arms around a lady clerk in the office. Ford, in an interview with a New York newspaper, endeavored to clear up the matter. He explained that the incident was merely an "illustration of how when [you] were for months in the same division how you become familiar." All he had done was playfully to throw his arms above the woman's head and say "'If you had been that tall see what would have happened....It is no use; my wife will never die and we cannot get married.'" Ford protested, "[The woman] was a refined lady. If she had been tall enough I would have hugged her. That is what I indicated by the motion of my arms. The lady is a grandmother, sir, and there is a gentleman in the room well acquainted with her husband." Such pleasantries were always done in a "fatherly" way and he insisted, "would have been done in the presence of my wife, and no offense taken at it."[46] Ford's true intentions in his interactions with the women in his office remain unknown, but the congressional committee investigating the Pension Office seemed to take the whole matter rather lightly. There was, the committee concluded, "quite a rivalry between Ford and Maj. Barker in their competition for the admiration of the ladies in the Pension Bureau. Maj. Barker, with his Prince Albert coat and buttonhole bouquet, eventually retired from the field and Mr. Ford holds the fort."[47]

It is the levity in the committee's remarks, as well as the report of Ford's interactions with the women in his department, that suggest a decided change in the relations between men and women within federal office. At the same time that official regulations were requiring men to curb their masculine behavior—drinking and smoking and rough language—and demanding the highest standards of sexual propriety from both male and female workers, the men and women themselves were creating a less formal and more relaxed mode of interaction. Some clerks were beginning to behave in ways that would have once been seen as improper, but that were now being defined as only innocent fun. This informality in gender relations strikes us, in fact, as decidedly modern—the banter, the innuendo, and the "innocent" flirtation. And no doubt it had its benefits, serving perhaps to defuse or at least reduce some of the tensions that both male and female clerks felt as they encountered members of the opposite sex in new and unfamiliar situations. Some female clerks might have found these new modes of interacting useful, for now they could use flirtation and flattery with less fear that their reputations or their virtue would suffer. Male clerks could now enjoy the presence of ladies and the bolstering of egos that such flirtations afforded.

But this new informal style also brought its own problems. The incident between Mrs. Wright and Mr. Ford indicates that the line between playful banter and sexual harassment could be indistinct. In such situations women might have found it more difficult to protect themselves. If a woman received a direct overture from a male supervisor or coworker, she could perhaps approach some honorable man for assistance and protection. But how was one to ask for protection from innocent or "fatherly" flirtation? Indeed, much of the behavior that today we have begun to label as sexual harassment was until recently perceived as nothing but playful and harmless banter. It seems possible that this type of behavior came to characterize the relationships between middle-class male and female workers within late nineteenth-century offices. In an effort to defuse the

sexual dangers and tensions that moralists and writers warned would accompany the creation of a sexually integrated workplace, these male and
female clerks seemed to have created an environment that was less formal
and more relaxed, but still fraught with the potential for sexual exploitation and manipulation.

IF SEX PRESENTED one of the most troubling aspects of office life, then
money was certainly another. Understanding the relationships between
male and female clerks in government departments requires that we
examine financial interactions as well as sexual ones. Government clerks,
although well paid by most nineteenth-century standards, seemed never
to have enough money to meet expenses. This was a problem that
plagued both male and female clerks. Dunning letters from all sorts of
creditors appeared in these people's files, suggesting that one way government workers met money problems was to buy on credit.[48] Another
way was to borrow from almost anyone who would lend, including people
in the office.

Indeed, money-lending seemed to have been an integral part of the informal work culture within federal offices, occurring at all levels within
the government bureaucracy and persisting throughout the four postbellum decades. Cash passed not only between the hands of coworkers, but
up and down the bureaucratic hierarchy, with supervisors both loaning
to and borrowing from underlings. George Wayson, a section chief within
the Pension Office noted in 1892 that it was "very common practice for
one [clerk] to borrow from another." Wayson was particularly free with
his money: "Anybody that came to me and wanted it, if I had it, I would
let him have it....Oh, I have loaned to a number of people. I can't recollect
them all. It is a very common thing here." He apparently borrowed as
freely as he lent: "I have borrowed from all of them, I think." He maintained that clerks within the entire department, not just the Pension Office, were involved in these financial transactions.[49] Despite Wayson's benign characterization of such activities, this kind of money-lending clearly
offered considerable opportunity for abuse. The members of Congress
investigating problems within the Pension Office in 1892 asked the obvious question. Should the chief of a division, someone who has "charge of
a number of persons...[who] are all striving for promotion and looking
to [him] for official favors" be asking such persons for money? William
Ford, one of the supervisors who had borrowed heavily from clerks in his
office, answered, "If I am an honest man I don't think it makes any difference to anyone." According to Ford these were simply "transactions between friend and friend."[50]

Not only did financial transactions within the office cross bureaucratic
boundaries, they also crossed gender boundaries. Female clerks were definitely involved in the monetary exchanges within the office, but it is difficult to determine if they participated as frequently as did the men. The

sources reveal abundant examples of male clerks lending and borrowing but only a few incidents that included women. Female clerks may have only participated in a limited way or may have been more circumspect about publicizing their activities—hence the dearth of evidence. Nevertheless even these few examples of women's participation in money transactions reveal the ways in which some women had, by the 1890s, become integrated into the informal work culture of federal offices.

Women's role in monetary matters within the office differed somewhat from men's. Female clerks only participated as lenders. This is not because women did not need the money, for many female clerks' files contain angry letters from landladies, dressmakers, schoolmistresses, and grocers asking that the women be forced to pay for goods and services they had purchased. Women appear to have bought on credit, but there is no evidence that they borrowed money from either male or female coworkers. Such evidence, of course, may simply not have survived, but it seems possible that women were reluctant to borrow money in the office—at least from the men with whom they worked. After all, the morals of female clerks were already suspect, and accepting money from men—no matter how innocently—might have made the women feel too vulnerable to charges of immorality or to sexual exploitation by the lender.

But women did lend money. If William Ford claimed that most of the financial transactions within the office were "between friend and friend," then he obviously counted some female employees among his friends. He borrowed money from at least two women in his office—Mrs. Newton and Mrs. Sloan. The financial arrangements between Ford and Sloan reveal how women's participation affected money matters in the office and, more broadly, the role gender played as male and female cultures converged in the workplace.

The story is convoluted, with different people offering contradictory testimony. The problem involved Mrs. Sloan's efforts to recover the $30 that William Ford, her supervisor, owed her. Many clerks had difficulty collecting debts, but Sloan found herself at a special disadvantage. A clerk within one division of the Pension Office testified that one day he found Mrs. Sloan "in great distress...[speaking] rather excitedly....[S]he came in and sank into a chair with her head back on the chair and appeared to be about to faint...." He continued, "I remember one thing she said; she seemed to be afraid her character would be affected. I told her her character would not be affected, and she went on to tell about her folks." Ford had apparently become annoyed when Sloan requested her money and had threatened to have her name drawn into the Pension Office investigation then making the headlines: "[S]he said she had asked him for money, and he had said her name would appear in this investigation and in the newspapers."[51]

Mrs. Sloan was, in fact, called to testify, but she offered an entirely different version of the incident. She said that she had sent a male coworker to Ford to collect the money, and that a day or two later Ford paid her.

She denied that Ford had threatened her and denied that she had discussed the incident with any of the men in the office. "I may have said
that I wanted my money but not anything any further than that."[52] Sloan
did admit that Ford was late in repaying the loan, but she became evasive
when the committee questioned her about just how long the note had
been overdue. She maintained that she had been ill at the office at the
time of this incident, but held that the illness had nothing to do with anything William Ford might have said.[53] The difference between these two
testimonies is troublesome. It is possible that Sloan was so intimidated and
frightened by Ford that she refused to say anything to the committee that
might anger him. Moreover, her fear of publicity and the shame attendant upon appearing before a congressional committee may have influenced her to keep her statement short and simple. It is also possible that
certain men in the Pension Office fabricated the story in an attempt to
discredit William Ford. But in any case this incident reveals that although
female clerks may have been involved in a variety of informal office activities, their gender still rendered them vulnerable in numerous—often
subtle—ways.

  If some women participated in "friendly" money-lending, there were
others who apparently engaged in more serious financial transactions in
the office. Clerks unable to borrow money from coworkers or requiring
large sums often turned to professional money-lenders who operated
within the departments. Such transactions usually required a third
party—frequently another clerk—who would arrange and endorse notes.
These middlemen were occasionally women. A man named Latourette
had become infamous within the Pension Office for loaning money to
some clerks while using others as go-betweens. In the Pension Office,
clerks in need of cash could approach Margaret Fithian or James
Donahue, amongst others, who would then borrow the money from
Latourette and lend it to their needy coworkers at usurious rates of interest. The congressional investigating committee uncovered allegations
that these people had charged as much as 10 to 15 percent per month.[54]
But it appears that even these figures might have been well below the rate
sometimes demanded in the office. In 1890 the chief of one division
within the Pension Office succeeded in having Margaret Fithian dismissed because "she loans out money to the unfortunates of this Bureau who
need financial aid at exorbitant rates of interest, in one case charging forty
per cent per month."[55]

  Within three months after her dismissal Fithian was attempting to recover her position in the office. The Commissioner of Pensions wrote to
the Secretary of the Interior on her behalf explaining: "Mrs. Fithian was
formerly a clerk at $1,000 per annum in this bureau and was dis-
missed...on the ground of charging a usurious rate of interest on some
money loaned to fellow clerks. This she does not deny but states that if
she is reinstated there will be no further cause of complaint in any direc-
tion, and in view of her services to disabled Union soldiers during the Re-

bellion, I am inclined to recommend her reinstatement." Although the Commissioner of the Civil Service initially refused to rehire her, explaining that "the Commission is without authority to...[reinstate] any person who has been dismissed for delinquency or misconduct," Fithian procured a position within a few months.[56]

Margaret Fithian apparently did not reform after winning reinstatement, but continued to lend money in the office and may have even engaged in bribery. William Barker testified before the congressional investigating committee that he tried to borrow money from her for his friend, Green Raum, Jr., the appointment clerk in the office (and the son of the Commissioner of Pensions). According to Barker, Fithian "took the note and said 'I will see,' " and then proceeded to approach Raum, Jr., and offer him the money if he promised to promote her.[57]

We can only speculate on what might have induced Fithian to engage in this seamy side of office life. Her background resembled that of other female clerks. She had applied for a position in the Interior Department in 1882, basing her claim for employment on familiar reasons: that her husband was an honorably discharged Union officer, that her only son gave his life for the Union cause, and that their Washington, D.C., home had been used by soldiers during the war. "I then had ample means, now I am poor, and need a place. I have never received a pension or other pecuniary assistance from the Government."[58] Perhaps Margaret Fithian was never a terribly honorable person, or perhaps the desire to regain her once "ample means" was what prompted her to resort to bribery and usury. Her case reveals, however, the extreme limits to which women might go as they became involved in the informal culture of office life. While women like Mrs. Sloan participated marginally in the money-lending transactions within the office and may, in fact, have been burned even by such limited involvement, other women like Mrs. Fithian participated as fully and as ruthlessly as did their male coworkers.

THROWN TOGETHER in offices where the old rules of separate spheres could not apply and where no new rules yet existed, middle-class men and women began the process of adjustment to a new type of proximity. The process involved—surprisingly enough—a minimum of conflict. The sources reveal only occasional instances of overt gender conflict in the offices, although it is possible that the few examples that surfaced were symptomatic of more prevalent but not often recorded problems. There was, nevertheless, much tension attendant upon the mixing of the sexes within the government bureaucracy. The entrance of women into this all-male arena called up fears of sexual danger, questions of proper office etiquette, and doubts about the ability of women to function in the bureaucracy. Bringing women into government jobs meant breaking the barrier that divided the nineteenth-century world into separate spheres. Although women in post-Civil War America had, in fact, progressed far beyond their hearths and homes, they had made most such advances by extending their sphere—almost amoeba-like—and encroaching upon the men's world rather than by marching boldly across boundaries. In fact the rationalization for women's involvement in a variety of civic, charitable, and reform activities during the Gilded Age was that women would be bringing domestic virtues where they were desperately needed. Women's entrance into federal offices was different. Here middle-class ladies were invading male territory, not because such territory required a woman's benign, compassionate, and caring influence, but because federal offices needed cheap labor and middle-class women needed good jobs. As male and female cultures converged within federal offices, the net result was less a victory for either than a melding of the two.

In the process women left behind many of the strictures of the domestic ideology—specifically those that delineated the female gender as passive, submissive, and non-competitive. As the previous chapter discussed, the dictates of government employment and the desire for advancement and security within the federal bureaucracy encouraged female clerks to act in an aggressive, competitive fashion toward fellow workers. In so doing they replicated what, by nineteenth-century standards, was classified as "male" behavior. Middle-class women may, of course, have had considerable experience with a variety of types of conflict and competition within the domestic sphere, but never before had they exercised such impulses in a public arena. Working in federal departments was thus important not only for the opportunities it offered middle-class women, but for the ways in which it altered middle-class female behavior. Moreover, the men who witnessed the competitive wrangling of their female coworkers may well have begun to question the validity of long-held beliefs on the passive nature of the feminine character.

At the same time that women were being changed by the experience of work they were also changing that experience. Before women became government clerks there was little reason to be concerned with the manners or the sexual habits of male employees. Women's presence, however, made officials rethink what proper office conduct should be. The decorum of male clerks—both inside and outside the office—became important to government officials who tried to curb some of the worst excesses of male behavior. In the process supervisors were making gentility—at least in respect to social behavior—one of the requirements of middle-class employment. Women's entrance into the federal bureaucracy brought some of the female sphere into the office, reducing the "maleness" of that environment and making the federal workplace in certain ways more like the domestic sphere.

But federal offices did not become Victorian parlors. These sexually integrated, middle-class workplaces presented situations loaded with new tensions. The separation of spheres that characterized the nineteenth-century middle-class world had, after all, carried with it some crucial assurances: women could feel safe from sexual harassment, and men could feel free from the threat of sexual manipulation at work. But new settings in which middle-class men and women met and worked did not provide such guarantees. The old rules no longer automatically prevailed and new rules had to be devised. Middle-class men and women had to begin to chart new territory in their dealings with each other. In the process behavior that had once been considered improper became proper: not only were middle-class ladies allowed to work within the male sphere, but their interaction with men within the office assumed a more relaxed tone. Middle-class women became an integral part of the informal work culture within the office—loaning money and engaging in "innocent" flirtations. But more relaxed behavior became more complex in its implications, and the parameters of what we now call sexual harassment emerged as part of life within a sexually integrated office. These casual modes of interaction between male and female clerks neither eliminated all problems nor reduced the dangers that Victorian moralists had foreseen, but they did point middle-class men and women toward a twentieth century where an increasing number of situations would require them to leave separate spheres and move into a more sexually integrated world.

CHAPTER EIGHT

Conclusion

Between 1860 and 1900, America witnessed the creation of a new kind of middle-class work, and with it the beginnings of a new, white-collar middle class. Although it would take until the turn of the twentieth century before the shape of this new middle-class work had emerged clearly, some of its most salient characteristics became apparent within post-Civil War federal offices.

First, this work would be salaried. Different from a nineteenth-century middle class composed primarily of professional or entrepreneurial men and domestic women, the new middle class would include salaried workers laboring in a vast array of white-collar occupations. Second, these people would engage in sexually integrated labor. In the nineteenth century, middle-class men rarely encountered women in their workplaces. Indeed, the middle-class work world remained, almost by definition, well beyond the boundaries of the female sphere. Although, certainly, some middle-class nineteenth-century women worked for wages, those who entered the labor force usually remained in occupations such as school teaching that kept them, for the most part, removed from the male world of business. The growth of the white-collar labor force in the twentieth century, however, would make working in sexually integrated environments an everyday activity for large sectors of the American middle class.

Third, the organization of middle-class work would change. The small scale of operations of most businesses in the nineteenth century had meant that middle-class men usually answered only to themselves, or perhaps to a relative from whom they were learning the business. But the members of this new middle class would find themselves laboring in large hierarchical bureaucracies—reporting to a superior in a chain of command and being held accountable to impersonal rules and regulations.

These alterations in the nature of middle-class work brought with them changes in some long-held middle-class aspirations and goals. No one could deny, for example, that advancement up the bureaucratic ladder was a different kind of success than the middle class had traditionally sought. A career in the federal civil service, after all, could promise neither the fortune gained by the legendary Andrew Carnegie, the junior partnership prized in the stories of Horatio Alger, or the domestic bliss proffered in the pages of Sarah Hale's magazine. Members of the middle class began, reluctantly, to fashion new goals—security and the promise of an adequate (if not extravagant) salary—to replace dreams of striking it rich and the hopes for leisured domesticity.

These government workers faced, however, a critical problem: it was not at all apparent whether the physical, social, and ideological dimensions of this new white-collar labor would bring with them the assurance of middle-class status. By engaging in salaried, sexually integrated, bureaucratically organized work, these men and women knew that they might well be jeopardizing their standing within the middle class. In the nineteenth century, remember, a "middle-class employee" was nearly a contradiction in terms. For these middle-class men and women—some of whom had, in their lifetimes, witnessed the transformation of a one-time artisanal community into an industrial, wage-earning working class—working for wages was what characterized how members of the working class made their living. Those men and women who called themselves middle-class took pride in the autonomy (if they were men) and leisure (if they were women) that their class status afforded them. It is no surprise, then, that would-be federal clerks approached government jobs with hesitation. The defensiveness, excuses, and rationalizations that accompanied the application of government job-seekers spoke loudly to such fears.

But such work jeopardized more than class status, for in Victorian America class and gender roles were inextricably bound. Being middle-class and female, for example, carried with it a whole battery of requirements—many of which were predicated as much upon gender as upon class criteria. "Ladies" remained out of the wage-earning labor force not only because they supposedly had men who could support them, but also because they were reputedly too delicate, shy, vulnerable to exploitation, and respectable to expose themselves to the harsh realities of the work world. A woman who assumed a government job thus not only advertised the absence of a man on whom she could depend, but also left herself open to charges of being indelicate, coarse, and cavalier about the dangers that respectable ladies might encounter in the wider male world. For men, too, being middle-class was tied to concepts of manhood that called up visions of independence, achievement, aggressiveness, as well as Christian morality and chivalry.[1] A man who assumed a job that would require him to take orders from others, strike a deferential pose, and curb his desire for wealth not only publicized his sorry financial plight, but suggested that he had relinquished a critical component of his manliness. The assumption of government jobs therefore threatened to endanger not only these men's and women's status within the middle class, but an important part of their identities as men and women.

There was, of course, much about the nature of federal employment that could have served to relieve some of these anxieties. The high wages, generous leave time, year-round employment, and short working hours clearly differentiated government clerks from industrial laborers. Like the pay and hours, the nature of the work federal employees performed offered compensations. All clerks needed to demonstrate their educational qualifications—not only basic literacy, but the ability to write grammatically and legibly. Moreover, the reluctance of government officials to subdivide and rationalize clerical labor meant that many Washington jobs required sophisticated skills. Men and women laboring in government departments often held positions that demanded expertise in accounting, knowledge of the law, and the ability to make decisions and policy recommendations. Clerks working at such tasks maintained not only a sense of their own intelligence and expertise, but control over their work as well. And those government employees consigned to more routine and repetitive tasks could look to the possibility of transfer or promotion to more diversified and challenging jobs.

The relationship between clerks and supervisors also contributed to the middle-class tenor of federal employment. Clerks and supervisors socialized together, borrowed money from each other, and sometimes boarded at the same houses. While not all such relationships were friendly, federal employees could feel that they shared class and culture with those who directed and supervised their work. The possibility for advancement within the bureaucracy and promotion to a supervisory position appeared all the more likely without class barriers separating management from labor. Thus, the basic structure of the work combined with a belief in the potential for upward mobility may have assuaged some of the fears that these men and women experienced as they moved into this new kind of work.

But only some. For the advantageous material conditions of federal employment did not sufficiently guarantee to these workers the middle-class status to which they so tenaciously clung. Despite the benefits that government employment offered, it nevertheless differed in important ways from the work of other nineteenth-century men and women. As a result, government workers seemed to make an almost conscious effort to bring middle-class attitudes and values with them into the Washington workplace. Indeed, it appeared as though federal clerks needed to create work routines and customs that would protect their positions within the middle class before they could enjoy the benefits that this new kind of white-collar work conferred.

Since this process involved gender as well as class criteria, it engaged men and women somewhat differently. The kind of wrangling and infighting rife in government offices and the absence of any sustained, collective effort to solve work-related problems, for example, reveal the individualistic values of nineteenth-century middle-class male culture being transposed to a new, bureaucratic work environment. Clawing one's way up the hierarchy became a substitute for the rugged individualism and extreme competitiveness of the business and professional world. Middle-class women left their mark upon this new white-collar world in a different manner. They brought gentility and respectability to clerical employment. Female clerks helped to transfer some of the norms of the Victorian parlor into the workplace, in the process incorporating important aspects of middle-class female culture into the business world. The trappings of white-collar work—the comfortable environment, the good manners—became critical means of identifying the office as a middle-class environment. It was women who made sure that offices would be places where ladies and gentlemen worked.

For these men and women, then, the relationship between class and occupation was a reciprocal one. The workers brought certain values with them to the workplace—values which bore the mark of the nineteenth-century middle class. The men and women who moved into government departments in the late decades of the nineteenth century tried to invest their work with a middle-class outlook and to shape white-collar labor according to their own middle-class image. And government offices proved a receptive environment. Indeed, the material conditions of federal employment had much to do with the success these men and women achieved in establishing clerical employment as middle-class labor. Trying to turn jobs in nineteenth-century laundries, steel mills, or sweatshops into middle-class work would, no doubt, have been exercises in futility, regardless of how valiant the efforts. But the ability to dress properly, to remain clean on the job, to work short hours, and to earn good pay made it considerably easier to stamp this new kind of work with a middle-class imprint.

Even as these middle-class men and women transformed the federal workplace, it, in turn, was leaving its mark upon them. In order to succeed in government employment, female clerks realized that they needed to act in an aggressive, competitive fashion, despite nineteenth-century norms that counseled shy, passive female behavior. And the women rose to the challenge. They competed aggressively for better paid jobs, sometimes acting callously to undercut the status of fellow workers. Using words that continued to pay homage to traditional norms of middle-class female conduct, these women took on new modes of behavior appropriate to the pursuit of successful careers within government employ. In the process they devised new standards of propriety for middle-class womanhood—ones that took into account the demands of the white-collar work world.

The experience of government work changed the middle-class men who labored in Washington offices as well. Male clerks found that they were required to stop smoking, refrain from the use of alcohol, and curb their language in the office. Ladies were present and men had to behave accordingly. But the women who worked in offices, they discovered, could not be given all of the considerations that traditionally had been accorded to ladies. For these women were coworkers—indeed, even competitors—and, as such, open game. While a man had to display good manners in the office, politeness did not prevent him from scheming to displace a woman whose position he coveted. These middle-class men thus learned not only to substitute advancement up the bureaucratic hierarchy for the more traditional notions of middle-class male success, but also created new rules governing the most effective means of achieving such success. A middle-class male clerk could remain a gentleman even though he treated the ladies in the office as ruthlessly as he treated his male coworkers—provided, of course, that he did so without forgetting his manners.

But sex remained a difficult problem. Women's presence in the white-collar work force had initially raised the specter of extreme sexual danger. Offices were not parlors—no one guarded the door to make sure that only gentlemen approached, no male family members stood ready to offer protection, and no rules existed that regulated behavior for women's comfort and safety. The middle-class women who entered government offices had to risk exposure to possibly unscrupulous men without any of the usual protections. And while the dangers were certainly less severe than many Victorians feared, women's entrance into government work did introduce sex into the office and create new problems for middle-class men and women. Sexual harassment became part of middle-class women's experience, and middle-class men found themselves vulnerable, perhaps for the first time, to sexual manipulation on the job.

These were new situations for middle-class Victorians, and finding solutions was no easy task. Government officials attempted to exact the most rigid standards of sexual propriety from their workers, but the mixing of men and women in the office had made the problems not only more prevalent, but also more subtle. As men and women worked together, informal modes of interaction began to replace the rigid rules that had defined Victorian propriety. It became acceptable, for example, for respectable women to converse and even strike up friendships with men to whom they had not been properly introduced. While such informality no doubt contributed positively to the environment of the office, it nevertheless posed problems of its own. More subtle types of sexual harassment— those with which modern office workers are familiar—began to creep into the everyday interaction between men and women.

The men and women who clerked in government offices in the late decades of the nineteenth century were thus creating, within this narrow interstice between their respective worlds, a new kind of middle-class culture—one that began to dissolve the barriers between the separate spheres of nineteenth-century middle-class America. The culture of the white-collar middle class not only allowed for women and men to take on certain characteristics that had once been reserved for members of the opposite sex, but also to meet and interact with a new kind of informality and familiarity. New tensions, however, accompanied the creation of this sexually integrated world. Sexual politics—present primarily in the domestic arena during the nineteenth century—became a permanent fixture within the middle-class world of work.

IF THESE GOVERNMENT WORKERS were on the cutting edge of the formation of a new white-collar middle class, they nevertheless remained different from their twentieth-century successors in some critical ways. In the decades following 1900, a number of changes occurred in both the nature of the clerical labor force and the substance of much office work. Larger numbers of women entered the occupation, until by 1930, female office workers represented nearly half of all clerical employees.[2] Moreover, the tasks that many clerks performed, the conditions under which they worked, and the salaries which they earned began to resemble those of manual, blue-collar workers. These changes emerged in a two-step process—the working conditions of white-collar workers began to decline as those of blue-collar workers began to improve. Clerical labor became more rigidly subdivided and rationalized in the twentieth century, with clerks responsible for only the most mundane and routine aspects of office work. And those who performed such work found themselves increasingly subjected to controls that were as rigid as those imposed upon assembly-line operators. At the same time, blue-collar workers began to press for and receive better pay, shorter hours, and work-related benefits.[3]

As the white-collar work force grew in the twentieth century, the people who composed it and the occupations that they pursued became much more varied. Sales clerks, typists, mid-level managers all came to share a middle-class label. As a result, the divergence in income, education, and status among white-collar workers increased considerably, while the distance between white-collar employees and other members of the middle-class—elite professionals and businessmen—became even greater. This wide disparity between members of the middle class, combined with the changes in the nature of much clerical work, have led historians, sociologists, and political theorists to question whether many men and women who called themselves middle-class were, in fact, only proletarians in white collars.[4]

Whether the twentieth-century white-collar middle class has been proletarianized is a question that lies beyond the boundaries of this study. But however much the material conditions of their work resembled those of factory laborers, men and women who wore white collars on their shirts or blouses continued to think of themselves as members of the middle class and to derive middle-class status from the white-collar labor in which they engaged. For this they can thank—or perhaps blame—those nineteenth-century men and women who succeeded in conferring middle-class status upon the new kind of work which they encountered within the offices of the federal government.

APPENDIX

Sources and Methods

The primary sources for this study are application files that were maintained by two federal agencies. The Department of the Interior and the Treasury Department were two of the largest government agencies in Washington, D.C., in the last four decades of the nineteenth century. Housed in the National Archives at Washington, D.C., the records kept by these two departments document the lives and work histories of thousands of federal employees.

The files of unsuccessful applicants contain only letters of application from the would-be clerk and letters of recommendation from congressmen, friends, or other sources of "influence." But for those applicants who succeeded in obtaining jobs, these files became the repository for all their future correspondence with the department. Clerks often wrote asking for promotion, describing the nature of their work and why they felt they deserved more money. In other letters employees discussed difficulties within the office, from crowded or uncomfortable surroundings to interpersonal problems with fellow clerks or supervisors. Copies of official notifications of promotions, demotions, or dismissals were also filed within these dossiers. These varied documents reveal much about the intricate, everyday work patterns of clerical workers in government offices.

These files are rich sources for historical research, but because of their size (well over one thousand boxes) and the manner in which they are arranged, they posed some obstacles to systematic exploration. The files of the Treasury Department are in alphabetical order, without regard to chronology. The files of the Interior Department, on the other hand, are arranged chronologically. Thus, letters from men and women who applied for work in the Department of the Interior in a given year can be found within the boxes so designated. The Interior Department did not, however, begin to save application files until 1879, and so it is impossible to study the 1860s and 1870s through these records. For these years it was necessary to turn to the records of the Treasury Department. Since there was little difference in the kinds of people who applied for jobs in the two departments, using files from two different agencies presented no problem. In the nineteenth century, prospective clerks applied to whichever agency had openings, or to the agency where they felt they had the best political connections. Many, in fact, sent applications to both departments. Moreover, clerks often moved between departments, applying for a job in one bureau when government appropriations reduced the number of clerks in another.

My first task was to create, from these documents, a pool of names that would allow me to study federal clerks over the last four decades of the nineteenth century—a sample of men and women who were clerking in government offices in Washington, D.C., in 1860 (or 1862 in the case of women), 1870, 1880, and 1890. For the first two points in time I used the records of the Treasury Department, but since these files were arranged alphabetically, recovering clerks for specific years involved preliminary work. I collected the names of all female Treasury clerks in the 1863 and 1871 register of federal employees (published biennially in odd years) and searched for these names within the application files of the Treasury Department. In this manner I culled a group of 128 women who clerked in the Treasury Department in 1862 or 1863. (It was often impossible to determine in which of the two years the women began to work, and thus I decided to use the two years together for my first point in time.) The women whose names appeared in the 1871 register were similarly located within the Treasury Department's applications files—298 women in all.

Since there were considerably more male than female clerks, I sampled from the lists of men in the official registers rather than collecting data on each male clerk. Every other man in the 1861 register and every fifth man in the 1871 register were used in the sample. The result was a group of 212 male Treasury clerks for the year 1861 and 371 male clerks for the year 1871.

Obtaining records of government clerks for 1880 and 1890 was somewhat simpler, since I could use the chronological files of the Interior Department. I collected information on every woman (excluding charwomen) applying for a job whose records appeared in the 1880 and 1890 boxes—598 women in 1880, and 812 women in 1890. Since, again, there were so many more files of male applicants, I sampled from the men, choosing every fifth file. In the end I obtained records for 301 male applicants to the Interior Department for the year 1880, and 477 for the year 1890. The records for 1890, however, represented primarily applicants to one office within the Interior Department—the Census Office. After 1883 the Civil Service Commission began to assume the task of placing job applicants, and the records of the individual departments became more bureaucratic and much less informative. Prior to 1883, prospective clerks would write directly to the head of an agency describing their qualifications and asking for work. After the passage of the Pendleton Act in 1883, however, these letters were directed to the Civil Service Commission (which, as far as I have been able to determine, did not save them). Once applicants had taken the necessary examinations, the Civil Service Commission would then send a form to the department instructing the official to select one of three designated people (the high scorers on the test) for a specific job. These forms come increasingly to fill the files of the Department of the Interior in the late 1880s and 1890s. Fortunately for historians (if not for civil service reformers), the Census Office, a bureau within the Interior Department, did not come under the jurisdiction of the Civil Service Commission until after 1890. Consequently Interior Department records for that year are full of rich and informative applications from hundreds of prospective Census Office employees. The change in the nature of the files, however, is the reason why I did not pursue this analysis into 1900. The files for that year contain mostly form letters.

While I let this relatively systematic plan guide much of my research, my curiosity—or perhaps the voyeur in me—prompted me to read more widely within these files. For example, while including only every fifth male in the 1880 and 1890 Interior Department boxes in my sample, I nevertheless read through the dossiers of all the men whose letters rested in these boxes. I used only those in the sample for purposes of quantitative analysis, but found much important information in the other files. Similarly, I chose other years—at random—and read through all or part of the files contained within those boxes.

Indeed, these records lent themselves both to traditional and to quantitative historical analysis. They revealed a wealth of information on what happened on the "shop floor" as men and women engaged in this new kind of middle-class labor. These documents also, however, proved particularly important in helping to establish the social class background of these federal clerks, because they offered quantifiable data on former occupations of the applicants, occupations of applicants' fathers (even when they were not residing in the same place), and education—data not available in the manuscript census. After the demographic information in the federal application was coded and punched, I counted the data with the help of a computer.

As the analysis in Chapter Two reveals (see Table 2.1), I collapsed the former occupations of male clerks into eight categories. Some of them—students, the unemployed, farmers, and men connected with the army—are self-explanatory. The other four categories, however, contained a number of different occupations. Those included under the category of professionals were: doctors, lawyers, ministers, teachers or principals, judges, and engineers. Those included in the category that I labeled semiprofessionals, small businessmen, and agents were men who characterized themselves as: journalists, correspondents, editors, publishers, agents or canvassers for publishing companies, state senators, state representatives, owners of small businesses, salesmen, real estate agents, pension agents, agents, merchants, authors, lecturers, detectives, and inventors. The clerical category included: bookkeepers, accountants, stenographers, typists, sales clerks in stores, clerical workers in small businesses or banks, and government clerks. The category of manual laborer included both skilled laborers (carpenters, stonecutters, blacksmiths, brickmasons, engravers, painters, policemen, hatters, conductors, and machinists) and unskilled laborers (watchmen, cardrivers, janitors, and laborers in government offices). The analysis of the occupations of fathers of female clerks (see Tables 3.1 and 3.5) uses primarily the same categories, although I distinguished fathers who were government clerks from those who held other types of clerical jobs.

In order to augment the social and demographic data available in the application files, I also drew samples of government clerks from the federal manuscript censuses for the years 1860, 1870, 1880, and 1900. This information was used to analyze age, marital status, and household composition. The 1860 sample included every other male government clerk listed in the manuscript census for Washington, D.C. There were no female clerks employed by the government in 1860. For 1870 I sampled every fifth man and every other woman, for 1880 I sampled every seventh man and every other woman, and for 1900 I sampled every tenth man and every fifth woman. The total numbers within each sample from the manuscript census are:

Year	Men	Women
1860	719	0
1870	511	303
1880	483	489
1900	626	624

While the application files and manuscript census schedules provided the foundation for this research, other government documents—both published and unpublished—were critically important sources. Throughout the last half of the nineteenth century, Congress undertook a number of studies of the executive branch. Coming at fairly regular intervals, they revealed not only neatly quantified statistics, but rich and detailed information on the workings of the various departments within the executive branch. Similarly, the reports that the head of each executive agency wrote and submitted annually supplemented the materials found in congressional reports, applications files, and the census. Together these varied sources allowed me to recreate the world in which these late nineteenth-century middle-class men and women worked.

Notes

Abbreviations Used in Notes:

Appts. Files   Applications and Appointments Files, Appointment Division, Interior Dept.
Int. Dept.   Records of the Office of the Secretary of the Interior (Record Group 48)
Applications   Applications and Recommendations for Positions in the Washington, D.C., Offices of the Treasury Dept. (entry 210), Records of the Division of Appointments
Treas. Dept.   General Records of the Treasury Dept. (Record Group 56)
NA   National Archives Building, Washington, D.C.

Chapter One. Introduction

1. C. Wright Mills, *White Collar: The American Middle Classes* (London, 1951), ch. 4.

2. Ibid., 3–9; Burton J. Bledstein, *The Culture of Professionalism: The Middle Class and the Development of Higher Education in America* (New York, 1976); Mary P. Ryan, *The Cradle of the Middle Class: The Family in Oneida County, New York, 1790–1865* (Cambridge, 1981), ch. 4.

3. Mary Ryan has found that 28 percent of the native-born adult women in Utica, New York, were employed in 1855. While Ryan uses native-born as a measure of middle-class, the jobs that most of these women assumed—domestic service and skilled crafts—suggest that many such women came from somewhat lower status backgrounds. Ryan, *Cradle of the Middle Class*, 198–210. For a discussion of the domestic ideology see Kathryn Kish Sklar, *Catherine Beecher, A Study in American Domesticity* (New York, 1973); Nancy Cott, *The Bonds of Womanhood: "Women's Sphere" in New England, 1780–1835* (New Haven, 1977); Barbara Welter, "The Cult of True Womanhood 1820–1860," *American Quarterly* 18 (Summer 1966): 151–74.

4. Alfred D. Chandler, Jr., *Strategy and Structure: Chapters in the History of the American Industrial Enterprise* (Cambridge, Mass., 1962), 19.

5. N.S.B. Gras, *The Massachusetts First National Bank of Boston, 1784–1934,* (Cambridge, Mass., 1937), 536; Evelyn H. Knowlton, *Pepperell's Progress: History of a Cotton Textile Company, 1844–1945* (Cambridge, Mass., 1948), 206.

6. Alfred C. Chandler, Jr., *The Visible Hand: The Managerial Revolution in American Business* (Cambridge, Mass., 1977), 107, 110.

7. Walter Licht, *Working for the Railroad: The Organization of Work in the Nineteenth Century* (Princeton, 1983), 34.

8. At Christmas rush, the number employed at Macy's increased to 270. Harry E. Resseguie, "Alexander Turney Stewart and the Development of the Department Store, 1823–1876," *Business History Review* 39 (Autumn 1965): 315.

9. Alba H. Edwards, U.S. Bureau of the Census, *Sixteenth Census of the United States: 1940. Population. Comparative Occupation Statistics for the United States, 1870 to 1940* (Washington, D.C., 1943), 101.

10. Chandler, *Strategy and Structure*, 24–36; *The Visible Hand*, 383, 392.

11. The figures for 1870 and 1880 are numbers published by the U.S. Census designating people employed as "officials and employees" of the government. In 1890 the census stopped reporting that category, and instead listed "officials of the government" and another category called "clerks and copyists." It is not possible to determine which of these clerks and copyists were employed in government offices as distinguished from those employed within the private sector. In 1893, however, the Dockery Committee, a joint committee of Congress, did a massive investigation of the executive departments. In one of its reports it offers the figures cited in Table 1.1 for 1893. The published census returns for 1900 pose the same problem as those for 1890. However, the Bureau of the Census conducted a special study of the executive civil service in 1903, and the figures cited in Table 1.1 come from that report. It is important to note that this table includes employees in the executive branch, and does not include people who worked for Congress, the judiciary, or the military.

The figures in Table 1.1 include employees, not only clerical workers. It is often difficult to determine how many of these workers performed clerical labor. The 1880 published census statistics reported a category called "clerks in government offices" which revealed that 4,162 of the 6,093 male employees and 1,412 of the 1,773 female employees were clerks. In 1903, 6,065 of the 18,793 men and 2,812 of the 6,882 women employees were listed as clerical workers. There was, however, another category called "subclerical and laborers" which included an additional 4,460 men and 3,806 women. It is clear that a good many of these female employees performed clerical labor, for supervisors frequently put low-paid female "laborers" to work at clerical tasks. While this was less true for men, there were also numerous occasions when male messengers performed clerical tasks. It is, however, impossible to know how many such employees actually did clerical work and how many performed manual or custodial labor. U.S., Census Office, *Statistics on the Population of the United States at the Tenth Census (1880)*, 785, 801, 816. U.S., Department of Commerce and Labor, Bureau of the Census, *The Executive Civil Service of the United States*, Bulletin 12 (Washington, 1904), 57.

12. Janet M. Hooks, *Women's Occupation Through Seven Decades*, U.S. Department of Labor, Women's Bureau Bulletin no. 218 (Washington, 1947), 75–76; Edwards, *Comparative Occupation Statistics for the United States*, 100.

13. Margery W. Davies, *Woman's Place Is at the Typewriter: Office Work and Office Workers 1870–1930* (Philadelphia, 1982); Carole Srole, "'A Position That God Has Not Particularly Assigned to Men': The Feminization of Clerical Work, Boston 1860–1915" (Ph.D. dissertation, University of California, Los Angeles, 1984); Elyce J. Rotella, *From Home to Office: U.S. Women at Work, 1870–1930*, Studies in American History and Culture no. 25 (Ann Arbor, 1981); Anita J. Rapone, "Clerical Labor Formation: The Office Woman in Albany, 1870–1930" (Ph.D. dissertation, New York University, 1981); Mark Stuart Sandler, "Clerical Proletarianization in Capitalist Development" (Ph.D. dissertation, Michigan State University, 1979).

14. For a more complete discussion of the nature of these sources and how they were used, see the Appendix.

15. Welter, "The Cult of True Womanhood."

16. There are, of course, some important exceptions. Among the historians who have dealt with both men and women in nineteenth-century America are Ryan, *Cradle of the Middle Class;* John Mack Faragher, *Women and Men on the Overland Trail* (New Haven, 1979); Ellen K. Rothman, *Hands and Hearts: A History of Courtship in America* (New York, 1984).

Part One. Reluctant Pioneers

1. Constance McLaughlin Green, *Washington, A History of the Capital, 1800–1950,* vol. i (Princeton, 1962), 200–210. Stuart Blumin puts the population of Washington, D.C., in 1860 at 61,222, making it the twelfth largest city in the United States. New York, the largest, had 805,658 people, while Cincinnati, the seventh largest, had a population of 161,044. Stuart M. Blumin, *The Urban Threshold: Growth and Change in a Nineteenth-Century American Community* (Chicago, 1976), 223.

2. Green, *Washington,* vol. i., pp. 209, 211, 215.

3. Ibid., vol. ii, pp. 42–45, 49, 82.

4. Ibid., vol. ii, pp. 81–82.

Chapter Two. The Gentlemen

1. Application to Census Office of Fred Dickerson, 27 March 1890, (1890) #2018, Appts. Files, Int. Dept., NA.

2. See Table 1.1 of the Introduction.

3. The figures for 1861 and 1871 are computed from samples drawn from the Treasury Department files. They include men who were working in the Treasury Department in those years. The figures for 1880 and 1890 are computed from samples drawn from Interior Department files. They include men who applied for positions in the Interior Department in those years. Analyses comparing applicants to the Interior Department who succeeded in winning jobs with applicants who did not get federal positions revealed very similar profiles. The data on former occupation of only those men who succeeded in securing jobs within the Interior Department in 1880 and 1890 are:

	1880	*1890*
Professionals	10	16
Semi-professionals, small businessmen, agents	21	18
Clerical workers	43	34
Manual laborers	2	10
Unemployed	5	4
Farmers	3	4
Students	12	14
Connected with army (clerk or soldier)	3	0
	100%	100%
Number	113	275

4. For a discussion of the creation of a working class see Sean Wilentz, *Chants Democratic: New York City and the Rise of the American Working Class, 1788–1850* (New York, 1984); Alan Dawley, *Class and Community: The Industrial Revolution in Lynn* (Cambridge, Mass., 1976); David Montgomery, *Beyond Equality: Labor and the Radical Republicans, 1862–1872* (Urbana, Ill., 1981), 25–44. For a complete analysis of the development of commercial business in early nineteenth-century America see Alfred D. Chandler, Jr., *The Visible Hand: The Managerial Revolution in American Business* (Cambridge, 1977), ch. 1.

The most recent, comprehensive work on middle-class formation in the antebellum period is Mary Ryan, *The Cradle of the Middle Class: The Family in Oneida County, New York, 1790–1865* (Cambridge, 1981). Other important work includes Stuart Blumin, "The Hypothesis of Middle-Class Formation in Nineteenth-Century America: A Critique and Some Proposals," *American Historical Review* 90 (April 1985): 299–338; Stuart Blumin, "Black Coats to White Collars: Economic Change, Nonmanual Work, and the Social Structure of Industrializing America," in Stuart W. Bruchey, ed., *Small Business in American Life* (New York, 1980), 100–121; Burton J. Bledstein, *The Culture of Professionalism: The Middle Class and the Development of Higher Education in America* (New York, 1976). Clyde and Sally Griffen's book on Poughkeepsie also contains much useful information about members of an emerging middle class in that city. Clyde Griffen and Sally Griffen, *Natives and Newcomers: The Ordering of Opportunity in Mid-Nineteenth-Century Poughkeepsie* (Cambridge, 1978).

5. Blumin, "The Hypothesis of Middle-Class Formation," 302–4; Burton J. Bledstein, *The Culture of Professionalism*, 13. David Montgomery has noted that "in the 1860s the phrase 'middle class' was such a novelty that, when it appeared at all, it was enclosed in quotation marks." Montgomery, *Beyond Equality*, 14.

6. Ryan, *Cradle of the Middle Class*, chs. 4 and 5.

7. Blumin, "The Hypothesis of Middle-Class Formation," 309.

8. Alexis de Tocqueville, *Democracy in America*, trans. Henry Reeve (New York, 1961), vol. ii, p. 161.

9. Ibid., 155.

10. I have not included the data for 1861 because only six men from that sample revealed their educational background in their letters of application. Of these six men, one had received a normal school education, four had attended a college or university, and one had attended law school. The data for 1871 come from samples drawn from Treasury Department files and include men working in the Treasury Department in that year. The data for 1880 and 1890 come from samples drawn from Interior Department files and include men who applied for positions in the Interior Department in those years. As with former occupations, the educational backgrounds of men who applied for jobs and those men who succeeded in getting jobs were very similar. The educational data for only those men who obtained jobs in the Interior Department in 1880 and 1890 are:

	1880	1890
Common	36	31
High school (public)	0	14
Private	14	15
Normal or business	2	15
University or college	23	18
Graduate, medical, legal	23	3
Military, parochial	2	3
	100%	100%
Number	57	117

11. Alba M. Edwards, U.S. Bureau of the Census, *Sixteenth Census of the United States: 1940. Population. Comparative Occupation Statistics for the United States, 1870 to 1940* (Washington, D.C., 1943), 100.

12. In 1880, 88 percent of male federal clerks were native-born, and in 1900, 92 percent were native-born. In 1880, 77 percent of their fathers and 79 percent of their mothers were native-born. In 1900, 80 percent of their fathers and 83 percent of their mothers were native-born. These figures are calculated from samples drawn from the population schedules of the U.S. manuscript censuses for Washington, D.C., for 1880 and 1900. For a discussion of methods of drawing the samples, see the Appendix.

13. In 1880: 4% were under 20, 43% were ages 20–29, 30% were ages 30–39, and 22% were age 40 or older; in 1890: 12% were under the age of 20, 40% were ages 20–29; 18% were ages 30–39; and 29% were ages 40 or older. These data come from samples drawn from the Interior Department's application files. The Appendix includes a full explanation of the sources and sampling methods.

14. See Chapter Five for a more detailed discussion of persistence within the federal workplace.

15. Sixty-one percent were heads of households in 1880, 54 percent were heads of households in 1900. These figures are calculated from samples drawn from the population schedules of the 1880 and 1900 U.S. manuscript censuses for Washington, D.C. It is not possible to determine accurately comparable information for the 1860 and 1870 manuscript censuses, since in those years the enumerator did not specify the relationships between members of the household.

16. Eleven percent lived with their parents in 1880, 12 percent lived with their parents in 1900; 26 percent boarded with non-relatives in 1880, 32 percent boarded with non-relatives in 1900. Computed from samples drawn from the population schedules of the 1880 and 1900 U.S. manuscript censuses for Washington, D.C.

17. The pay scale was altered when women entered government employ, and these changes eventually affected male salaries as well. For more on women's salaries see Chapter Three, and for more on the changes in men's salaries see Chapter Four.

18. Only a tiny number of these women actually held jobs rather than contributing to their families' finances by taking in boarders. In 1880, of the two wives who held jobs, one was a government clerk, the other a small businesswoman; in 1900, ten women actually held jobs—two as teachers, two as seamstresses, four as clerks, one as a telephone operator, and one as a hairdresser. Figures were computed from samples drawn from the population schedules of the U.S. manuscript censuses for Washington, D.C., for 1880 and 1900.

19. These figures are computed from samples drawn from the population schedules of the U.S. manuscript censuses for Washington, D.C., for 1880 and 1900.

20. The vast majority of men performing manual labor in New York in 1860 earned, for example, from $7 to $18 per week—and only for the weeks they worked. Similarly, only a small number of industrial workers in Detroit during the 1890s made more than $500 per year. Montgomery, *Beyond Equality*, 41. Olivier Zunz, *The Changing Face of Inequality: Urbanization, Industrial Development, and Immigrants in Detroit, 1880–1920* (Chicago, 1982), 227, 228.

For data on salaries of clerical workers see Carole Srole, " 'A Position That God Has Not Particularly Assigned to Men': The Feminization of Clerical Work, Boston 1860–1915" (Ph.D. dissertation, University of California, Los Angeles, 1984),

101–2; Mark Stuart Sandler, "Clerical Proletarianization in Capitalist Development" (Ph.D. dissertation, Michigan State University, 1979), 146; Zunz, *The Changing Face of Inequality,* 228; Robert W. Twyman, *History of Marshall Field and Company, 1852–1906* (Philadelphia, 1954), 71–74; Ralph M. Hower, *The History of an Advertising Agency: N.W. Ayer & Son at Work, 1869–1949* (Cambridge, 1949), 516–17.

21. Carole Srole, " 'A Position That God Has Not Particularly Assigned to Men,' " 136–37.

22. In his study of Detroit, Olivier Zunz found that 18 percent of native white American men owned their own homes and another 9 percent mortgaged their homes. Zunz found that white-collar workers did considerably better (from 21 to 27 percent owned their own homes free and clear, and about 11 to 12 percent mortgaged them). Zunz, and others, have discovered that immigrants were more likely than native Americans to own their own homes. In Detroit, 50 percent of the low white-collar workers and 73 percent of the high white-collar workers were native-born white Americans in 1880. Twenty years later, 60 percent of Detroit's high white-collar workers and 43 percent of Detroit's low white-collar workers were native-born Americans. The greater percentage of white-collar workers who owned their own homes in Detroit than in Washington, D.C., may well be due, therefore, to the greater percentage of immigrants amongst the Detroit white-collar population than were present in the population of Washington government clerks. Olivier Zunz, *The Changing Face of Inequality,* 37, 152–54, 221.

23. Constance McLaughlin Green, *Washington: A History of the Capital, 1800–1950,* vol. ii (Princeton, 1962), 80. By comparison, Olivier Zunz found that in Detroit a white-collar bank employee earning $800 per year paid only $9.88 for rent and $4.99 for utilities. Zunz, *The Changing Face of Inequality,* 233.

24. M.D. Montis to John Wilson, 11 Jan. 1867, file of M.D. Montis, Applications, Treas. Dept., NA.

25. George F. Keen to P.H. Eaton, 26 Jan. 1874, file of Tasker B. Dulaney, Applications, Treas. Dept., NA.

26. J.A. Collins to Robert P. Porter, 18 March 1891, (1890) #289, Appts. Files, Int. Dept., NA.

27. File of William Mertz, Applications, Treas. Dept., NA; (1880) #1107, Appts. Files, Int. Dept., NA.

28. Lester Ward, *Young Ward's Diary,* ed. Bernhard J. Stern (New York, 1935), 172, 179, 306–7, 317.

29. For more on money-lending in the offices see Chapter Seven.

30. J.W. Clark to Danl. Clark, 1 Dec. 1861, file of John Wingate Clark, Applications, Treas. Dept., NA.

31. E.H. Merchant to Gov. Newell, 19 Aug. 1862, file of Silas Merchant, Applications, Treas. Dept., NA.

32. G.W. Williams to S.P. Chase, 14 Feb. 1862, file of George W. Williams, Applications, Treas. Dept., NA. Emphasis in the original.

33. G.W.L. Kiddell to T.L. Tullock, 20 July 1869, file of G.W.L. Kiddell, Applications, Treas. Dept., NA.

34. P.F. Causey to William H. Seward, 1 March 1861, file of Garrett Luff, Applications, Treas. Dept., NA.

35. (1880) #1284, Appts. Files, Int. Dept., NA.

36. R.E.A. Dorr to Robert Porter, 2 Dec. 1889, and Application to Census Office of Horatio Dorr, 12 Sept. 1889, (1890) #340, Appts. Files, Int. Dept., NA.

37. E. Lac Hawkins to John W. Noble, 14 July 1890, (1890) #2461, Appts. Files, Int. Dept., NA. Emphasis in the original.

38. M. Miller to Supt. of the Census, 26 June 1890, (1890) #2691, Appts. Files, Int. Dept., NA.

39. A.B. Allison to Robert Porter, 30 June 1892, (1890), #1786, Appts. Files, Int. Dept., NA.

40. Griffen and Griffen, *Natives and Newcomers,* 104, 110. For more on business failures see also Michael B. Katz, Michael J. Doucet, and Mark J. Stern, *The Social Organization of Early Industrial Capitalism* (Cambridge, 1982), 29; Michael B. Katz, *The People of Hamilton, Canada, West: Family and Class in a Mid-Nineteenth-Century City* (Cambridge, Mass., 1975), ch. 4.

41. Srole, " 'A Position That God Has Not Particularly Assigned to Men,' " 478–79; Griffen and Griffen, *Natives and Newcomers,* 105–10.

42. Between 1850 and 1880 the Griffens found that most businessmen in Poughkeepsie remained within the proprietary class, but a small minority slipped down the occupational ladder into clerical, sales, or even manual jobs. Griffen and Griffen, *Natives and Newcomers,* 60. For a discussion of the growth of large corporations employing more clerical workers see Chandler, *The Visible Hand,* ch. 7.

43. Preston Sherrard to Kirkwood, 30 June 1882, (1882) #1910, Appts. Files, Int. Dept., NA.

44. D.B. Sacket to Joseph K. McCammon, 12 May 1883, (1880) #1143, Appts. Files, Int. Dept., NA.

45. David B. Tyack, *One Best System: A History of Urban Education* (Cambridge, 1974), 61–62; Griffen and Griffen, *Natives and Newcomers,* 100.

46. See, for example, files of Dan Weed, James Reed, and Lemuel G. Brandenburg, Applications, Treas. Dept., NA.

47. John Murphy to Francis Walker, 22 June 1880, (1880) #2121, Appts. Files, Int. Dept., NA.

48. John C. Spooner to George H. Shields, 2 Jan. 1890, (1890) #24, Appts. Files, Int. Dept., NA.

49. Charles M. Wesson to John W. Noble, 12 Nov. 1890, (1890) #4145, Appts. Files, Int. Dept., NA.

50. Lawrence M. Friedman, *A History of American Law* (New York, 1973), 526, 549–50, 556–61.

51. Howard Smith to L.Q.C. Lamar, [12 Dec. 1887], Alexander Stephens to S.J. Kirkwood, 13 March 1882, (1880) #619, Appts. Files, Int. Dept., NA.

52. Harry J. Parker to Samuel J. Kirkwood, 27 April 1881, (1880) #2266, Appts. Files, Int. Dept., NA.

53. Friedman, *A History of American Law,* 537.

54. Charles Collins to Carl Schurz, 31 May 1880, (1880) #1201, Appts. Files, Int., Dept., NA.

55. Frederick Okie to John Noble, 4 Dec. 1890, (1890) #4036, Appts. Files, Int. Dept., NA.

56. See Bledstein, *The Culture of Professionalism,* chs. 5–8; Friedman, *A History of American Law,* chs. 11–12; Robert H. Wiebe, *The Search for Order 1877–1920* (New York, 1967), ch. 5; Joseph F. Kett, *The Formation of the American Medical Profession: The Role of Institutions, 1780–1860* (New Haven, 1968), chs. 1–3; Joseph F. Kett, *Rites of Passage: Adolescence in America 1790 to the Present* (New York, 1977), 154.

57. According to samples drawn from the population schedules of the U.S. manuscript censuses for Washington, D.C., in 1860 only 0.1 percent of male clerks in government offices were black, in 1870 there were no black men clerking in these offices, in 1880 black men represented 1 percent of government male clerks, and in 1900 black men represented 4 percent of government male clerks.

58. Albert Johnson to John Noble, 2 Dec. 1890, (1890) #1291, Appts. Files, Int. Dept., NA.

59. 1890 (#864), Appts. Files, Int. Dept., NA.

60. Joel Williamson, *The Crucible of Race: Black-White Relations in the American South Since Emancipation* (New York, 1984), 366–71.

61. Eugene Williams to S.J. Kirkwood, 23 Jan. 1882, (1880) #1801, Appts. Files, Int. Dept., NA.

62. Edward F. Waite to Henry M. Teller, 20 Nov. 1884, (1880) #819, Appts. Files, Int. Dept., NA.

63. George Henry Shire to Carl Schurz, 6 March 1880, (1880) #639, Appts. Files, Int. Dept., NA.

64. Wm. B. Robinson to Sec. of the Interior, 13 May 1880, (1880) #1752, Appts. Files, Int. Dept., NA.

65. Application of George Flint to Census Office, 12 May 1890, (1890) #1748, Appts. Files, Int. Dept., NA.

66. For the career patterns of middle-class, nineteenth-century men see Griffen and Griffen, *Natives and Newcomers,* 109–10.

67. Application of Joseph C. Calhoun to Census Office, 9 Aug. 1890, (1890) #3041, Appts. Files, Int. Dept., NA.

68. Application of Charles Isham to Census Office, 25 Nov. 1889, (1880) #500, Appts. Files, Int. Dept., NA.

69. Application of Allen Fowler to Census Office, 22 Sept. 1890, (1890) #3179, Appts. Files, Int. Dept., NA.

70. Application of David Floyd to Census Office, 21 Aug. 1889, and David Floyd to Superintendent of the Census, 15 July 1889, (1890) #385, Appts. Files, Int. Dept., NA.

71. Application of Carl Stark to Census Office, 23 Feb. 1890, (1890) #3773, Appts. Files, Int. Dept., NA.

72. Eric Foner, *Free Soil, Free Labor, Free Men: The Ideology of the Republican Party Before the Civil War* (New York, 1970), 17.

73. Webster Elmes to Salmon Chase, 4 Feb. 1861, file of Webster Elmes, Applications, Treas. Dept., NA.

74. A.S. Taylor to Hoke Smith, 27 June 1893, (1893) #2735, Appts. Files, Int. Dept., NA.

75. Herman Seligson to Francis Walker, 1 May 1880 (1880), #961, Appts. Files, Int. Dept., NA.

76. For a discussion of free labor ideas in the Gilded Age see Daniel T. Rodgers, *The Work Ethic in Industrial America, 1850–1920* (Chicago, 1974), ch. 2.

77. S.S. Stearns to Hugh McCulloch, 21 May 1865, file of S.S. Stearns, Applications, Treas. Dept., NA.

78. File of Henry Fried, Applications, Treas. Dept., NA.

79. Johnson remained in the Treasury Department for thirty-five years, moving gradually up to a $1600-per-year position. File of John Johnson, Applications, Treas. Dept., NA.

80. File of Milton Durnall, Applications, Treas. Dept., NA.

81. A.P. Gorman to John Sherman, 10 March 1880, (1880) #716, Appts. Files,

Int. Dept., NA.

82. M.J. Durham to L.Q.C. Lamar, 5 Oct. 1886, (1880) #614, Appts. Files, Int. Dept., NA.

83. James S. Brown to Henry M. Teller, 25 June 1882, (1880) #1354, Appts. Files, Int. Dept., NA.

84. For more on the domestic ideology and the women who worked in government offices, see Chapter Three.

85. Margery W. Davies, *Woman's Place Is at the Typewriter: Office Work and Office Workers 1870–1930* (Philadelphia, 1982), ch. 2.

86. James McCabe, *Behind the Scenes in Washington* (Philadelphia, 1873), 464.

87. Mary Clemmer Ames, *Ten Years in Washington: Life and Scenes in the National Capital as a Woman Sees Them* (Hartford, 1873), 307.

88. Harriet Earhart Monroe, *Washington, Its Sights and Insights* (New York, 1909), 74–78; McCabe, *Behind the Scenes,* 457.

89. George Hoadly to Salmon Chase, 31 Jan. 1861, file of Fred Chase, Applications, Treas. Dept., NA.

90. George H. Crumb to John Noble, 16 May 1889, (1890) #2453, Appts. Files, Int. Dept., NA.

91. Henry Stimson, "The Small Business as a School of Manhood," *Atlantic Monthly* 93 (March 1904): 337–40.

92. See Tables 4.2 and 4.3.

93. See Chapter Five for a discussion of the insecurities endemic to government work.

94. Michael Zuckerman's analysis of the fiction of Horatio Alger suggests that what these very popular stories actually reveal is the desire of nineteenth-century middle-class men for security—both domestic security and job security. Michael Zuckerman, "The Nursery Tales of Horatio Alger," *American Quarterly* 24 (May 1972): 191–209.

95. Bledstein, *The Culture of Professionalism,* 13.

96. See Chapters Four and Five for a discussion of the specific nature of the federal bureaucracy.

Chapter Three. The Ladies

1. A.H. Colquitt and J.B. Gordon to Secretary of the Interior, 9 Feb. 1894, (1890) #3880, Appts. Files, Int. Dept., NA. Portions of this chapter are from: Cindy S. Aron, " 'To Barter Their Souls for Gold': Female Clerks in Federal Government Offices, 1862–1890," *Journal of American History,* 67 (March 1981):835–53; Cindy Sondik Aron, " 'To Barter Their Souls for Gold': Female Federal Clerical Workers in Late Nineteenth-Century America" (Ph.D. dissertation, University of Maryland, 1981).

2. Kathryn Kish Sklar, *Catherine Beecher, A Study in American Domesticity* (New York, 1973); Nancy Cott, *The Bonds of Womanhood: "Women's Sphere" in New England, 1780–1835* (New Haven, 1977); Barbara Welter, "The Cult of True Womanhood 1820–1860," *American Quarterly* 18 (Summer 1966): 151–74.

3. Daniel T. Rodgers, *The Work Ethic in Industrial America 1850–1920* (Chicago, 1974), ch. 7.

4. On the lives and work experiences of working-class and immigrant women see: Alice Kessler-Harris, *Out to Work: A History of Wage-Earning Women in the*

United States (New York, 1982); Virginia Yans-McLaughlin, *Family and Community: Italian Immigrants in Buffalo 1880–1930* (Ithaca, 1977); Milton Cantor and Bruce Laurie, eds., *Class, Sex, and the Woman Worker* (Westport, Conn., 1977); Daniel J. Walkowitz, *Worker City, Company Town: Iron and Cotton-Worker Protest in Troy and Cohoes, New York, 1855–84* (Urbana, 1978); David Katzman, *Seven Days a Week: Women and Domestic Service in Industrializing America* (New York, 1978); Carl Degler, *At Odds: Women and the Family in America from the Revolution to the Present* (New York, 1980), ch. 15.

5. In 1870, 93 percent of the women clerking in government offices, 82 percent of their fathers, and 83 percent of their mothers were native-born. In 1880, 94 percent of the women, 83 percent of their fathers, and 86 percent of their mothers were native-born. In 1900, 93 percent of the women, 85 percent of their fathers, and 88 percent of their mothers had been born in the United States. These figures are calculated from samples drawn from the population schedules of the U.S. manuscript census for Washington, D.C., for each of those years. For a discussion of the sampling procedures, see the Appendix.

Nearly all the women working in government offices were white. The 1870 sample revealed no black women clerking for the government. In 1880 and 1900, less than 1 percent of the female clerks were black.

6. The statistics in this table come primarily from data culled from application files kept by the Treasury Department and the Department of the Interior. Female applicants for government jobs sometimes described their family background and mentioned their fathers' occupations. Since many women entered the labor force after their fathers had died, some of this information refers to previous occupational status of a deceased father. The women whose letters appeared in the 1880 files I traced to the U.S. manuscript census for that year. This provided an additional source of data for forty-eight women (out of 488 in the sample from the manuscript census) who were living with their fathers. For a complete discussion of the sources and the sampling procedures, see the Appendix.

7. These data are culled from the letters of female applicants found in the application files of the Treasury Department and the Department of the Interior. There were 861 women, in all, whose letters reveal their place of residence prior to applying for government jobs. Twenty-one percent had been living in Maryland, New York, Pennsylvania, New Jersey, or Virginia, 2.7 percent came from the South, 8.6 percent from the Midwest, 4.6 percent from New England, and 5.3 percent from the West.

8. The Census Office chose not even to report the percentage of people over the age of twenty attending school, since the numbers were so small. U.S. Census Office, *Report on Population of the United States at the Eleventh Census (1890)*, pt. 2, p. xxviii.

Data on education of female clerks come from the application files of the Treasury Department and the Department of the Interior. The information on age of leaving school, however, was available only from the Interior Department records for the 1880 and 1890 samples. In all there were 779 women whose applications revealed the age at which they quit school—43 of these women applied for work in 1880 and 736 applied for work in 1890. There was, however, little difference between length of education of these two groups. In the 1880 sample: 7 percent left school before the age of sixteen, 77 percent left school sometime between their sixteenth and twentieth birthdays, and 16 percent remained in school beyond the age of twenty. In the 1890 sample: 6 percent left school before the age of sixteen, 81 percent left school between the ages of sixteen and twenty, and 13 percent remained in school beyond the age of twenty.

There were 959 women who mentioned the type of schools they had attended. The following table reveals the breakdown in these educational statistics for the four sample years. I have omitted the first sample year (1862/63) because only six women in that sample revealed the nature of their education:

	1870	1880	1890
Common	53	46	47
High school (public)	11	8	19
Private	26	31	27
Normal or business	0	5	2
University or college	0	4	1
Parochial	11	6	3
	100%	100%	100%
Number	19	140	794

9. Ellen Page to Francis Walker, 26 Nov. 1879, (1880) #858, Appts. Files, Int. Dept., NA.

10. Thomas Dublin's study of women who worked in the Lowell mills in the early part of the nineteenth century indicates that primarily young women—85 percent under the age of 25—worked in the mills. Dublin explained that mill work "attracted young women seeking employment for a brief period before marriage." Thomas Dublin, *Women at Work: The Transformation of Work and Community in Lowell, Massachusetts, 1826–1860* (New York, 1979), 31. Leslie Tentler's book on working-class women in the early twentieth century finds a similar pattern among women performing a variety of manual jobs in the urban Northeast. Leslie Woodcock Tentler, *Wage-Earning Women: Industrial Work and Family Life in the United States, 1900–1930* (New York, 1979), 59–60. See also Degler, *At Odds*, 375.

11. Within the category of "clerks" I have included all the women listed in the published census reports as clerks and copyists, and stenographers and typists.

12. School teachers in the District of Columbia in the mid-1870s, for example, earned from $400 to $700 per year, with a few making as much as $800. Board of Trustees of the District of Columbia, *Third Report: 1876–1877* (Washington, 1877), 28–31, 174–80. The salary range for Chicago elementary school teachers was $500 to $875 in the last two decades of the nineteenth century. Only teachers with more than seven years' experience earned from $825 to $1000. I am grateful to Marjorie Murphy for data on salaries of school teachers in Chicago.

In David Tyack's study of urban school teachers he estimated that between 1870 and 1900, women teaching in city schools earned from $12 to $14 per week. A 1905 NEA study of 467 city school systems reported, according to Tyack, that average earnings for female elementary school teachers were $650 per year; for female high school teachers average earnings were $903 per year. David B. Tyack, *The One Best System: A History of American Urban Education* (Cambridge, Mass., 1974), 62.

13. Sallie Shane to M.G. Urner, 7 Feb. 1881, (1881) #1601, Appts. Files, Int. Dept., NA.

14. Josephine B. Placide to L.Q.C. Lamar, 7 Aug. 1886, (1881) #1384, Appts. Files, Int. Dept., NA.

15. Sue J. Jones to President Hayes, 25 Nov. 1880, (1880) #2239, Appts. Files, Int. Dept., NA.

16. Amelia Rowland to W.W. Dudley, 10 July 1881, (1881) #584, Appts. Files, Int. Dept., NA.

17. Lizzie C. Bachelder to President [U.S. Grant], 16 Jan. 1868, file of Lizzie Bachelder, Applications, Treas. Dept., NA.

18. Lillie Stratton to F. Walker, 20 March 1880, (1880) #1555, Appts. Files, Int. Dept., NA.

19. Nannie Lancaster to Walker, 24 Aug. 1880, (1880) #929, Appts. Files, Int. Dept., NA.

20. According to the information garnered from letters in application files, the percentage of women who were never married amongst applicants for government clerkships in each year were:

1862/63	64%
1870	61%
1880	65%
1890	73%

Data calculated from samples drawn from the population schedules of U.S. manuscript census for Washington, D.C., for 1880 and 1890 revealed similar findings. Sixty-five percent of women working in government offices in 1880 were single, and 67 percent of those employed in 1900 were single.

21. Ellen Neale to Secretary of the Interior, 12 Nov. 1891, (1890) #2075, Appts. Files, Int. Dept., NA.

22. Amos L. Allen to John W. Noble, 24 Oct. 1890, (1890) #3841, Appts. Files, Int. Dept., NA.

23. Cordelia Emmons to Secretary of the Treasury, 26 Dec. 1865, file of Cordelia Emmons, Applications, Treas. Dept., NA.

24. Ten percent of the women working in the government in 1870 and 1880 lived in households with their fathers, while 12 percent of female clerks in 1900 lived in households with their fathers. Data were calculated from samples drawn from population schedules of the U.S. manuscript censuses for Washington, D.C., for 1870, 1880, and 1900. The data for 1870 represent, however, an estimate, since the census schedules do not reveal the relationships between members of a household. It was therefore necessary to deduce family relationships from last names and ages.

25. Lillie Rhea to Robert Walker, 17 Sept. 1880, (1880) #1886, Appts. Files, Int. Dept., NA.

26. Laura Robinson to Mrs. Hayes, n.d., (1880) #725, Appts. Files, Int. Dept., NA.

27. John T. Heard to Robert Porter, 9 Jan. 1890, (1890) #1543, Appts. Files, Int. Dept., NA.

28. Maggie Loftus to A.F. Childs, 7 Oct. 1890, (1890) #3472, Appts. Files, Int. Dept., NA.

29. W.R. Collins to F.A. Walker, 16 Dec. 1880, (1880) #2420, Appts. Files, Int. Dept., NA.

30. Wm. W. Dudley to R.P. Porter, 1 July 1889, (1890) #2234, Appts. Files, Int. Dept., NA.

31. Addendum to application of Gertrude Bourne, 12 Dec. 1889, (1890) #1583, Appts. Files, Int. Dept., NA.

32. Unidentified note to Mr. Hill, [12 June 1894], and Marion Porter to Robert Porter, [25 July 1889], (1890) #2080, Appts. Files, Int. Dept., NA.

33. According to the information garnered from letters in application files, the percentage of widows amongst applicants for government clerkships in each year were:

1862/63	16%
1870	28%
1880	18%
1890	13%

Data calculated from samples drawn from the population schedules of the U.S. manuscript censuses for Washington, D.C., for 1880 and 1900 revealed that 28 percent and 24 percent, respectively, of the women listed as government clerks were widows.

34. Mrs. Wm. L. Pemberton to Henry M. Teller, 28 April 1882, (1879) #758, Appts. Files, Int. Dept., NA.

35. Amanda Doty to Wm. Dudley, 13 Sept. 1882, (1881) #203, Appts. Files, Int. Dept., NA.

36. Fannie Dorsey to General Walker, 10 June 1880, (1880) #760, Appts. Files, Int. Dept., NA.

37. A. Bell to Z. Chandler, 23 Dec. 1876, Miscellaneous Letters Received, Appointments Division, Int. Dept., NA.

38. Anna Sanders et al. to Appts. Clerk, 12 Feb. 1871, "Justice" to G.S. Boutwell, 7 Dec. 1869, and "Anonymous" to Secretary of the Treasury, 19 Oct. 1874, Correspondence of the Division (entry 208), Records of the Division of Appointments, Treas. Dept., NA.

39. According to the information garnered from letters in application files, the percentage of women who said they were married amongst applicants for government clerkships in each year were:

1862/63	4%
1870	3%
1880	5%
1890	8%

These figures, however, underestimate the number of married women applying for federal jobs. First, women sometimes lied. Second, there were certain women who signed their letters "Mrs." but never mentioned their marital status. Some of these women may have been widows, but since describing yourself as a widow was a definite advantage, increasing the chances of getting a job, there is a great likelihood that many of these women were, in fact, married with husbands still living. Third, some women who were single when they began to work continued in government employ after marrying; there were also a few widows and divorcées who remarried while working and continued in their jobs. When all these women are added to those who admitted to being married, the percentages of married women who were federal clerks increase to:

1862/63	18%
1870	8%
1880	15%
1890	11%

Data calculated from samples drawn from the population schedules of the U.S. manuscript census for Washington, D.C., revealed that 5 percent of female government clerks counted in the 1880 census and 8 percent of those counted in the 1900 census told the enumerator that they were married women.

40. "Justice" to Secretary of the Treasury, 24 Oct. 1874, Correspondence of the Division (entry 208), Records of the Division of Appointments, Treas. Dept., NA.

41. J.B. Burke to Benj. Butterworth, 10 Feb. 1885, (1879) #1641, Appts. Files, Int. Dept., NA.

42. For a more complete discussion of the competition for government jobs, see Chapter Five.

43. J.W. Grew to John Sherman, 17 Dec. 1877, file of Emma Fuller, Applications, Treas. Dept., NA.

44. Mrs. E.A. McPheeters to Hugh McCulloch, 6 Oct. 1867, file of Mrs. E.A. McPheeters, Applications, Treas. Dept., NA.

45. By the 1890s a relaxation in the policy of the Census Office regarding the employment of married women allowed a small number of single women who already held jobs to continue to work in that bureau after marriage. Some recently married female clerks stayed in government offices for a few months, but others remained workers for a few years. Generally these women offered no elaborate explanations for their continued employment. Indeed, what seems most noteworthy about these cases is how matter-of-factly they were treated by everyone concerned: women simply requested that their names be changed on the government's rolls. The willingness of the Census Office to comply may have been because all employees working in that office were temporary. Once the census returns had been calculated and published, the employees were dismissed and the office closed. There were sixteen single women, two widows, and one divorcée, all of whom entered the Census Office in 1890, married soon thereafter, and continued to work.

46. Nellie Grant to J.W. Noble, 15 July 1892, (1890) #3267, Appts. Files, Int. Dept., NA.

47. Mrs. Gourick to S.W. Lamoreus, 12 April 1893, (1880) #440, Appts. Files, Int. Dept., NA.

48. Thomas B. Hopkins to M.V. Montgomery, 2 April 1887, (1880) #2171, Appts. Files, Int. Dept., NA.

49. May Naylor to D.H. Browning, 3 Dec. 1868, file of Mrs. M. Naylor, Applications, Treas. Dept., NA.

50. Emma Whelply to Hugh McCulloch, 4 Nov. 1867, file of Emma Whelply, Applications, Treas. Dept., NA.

51. Francis B. Stockridge to A.B. Nettleton, 4 Oct. 1891, file of Kate Wing Hunter, Applications, Treas. Dept., NA. Emphasis in original.

52. Charlotte Cross to Captain Johnson, 4 Feb. 1868, file of Charlotte Cross, Applications, Treas. Dept., NA.

53. For a discussion of the role of women within a family economy see Louise A. Tilly and Joan W. Scott, *Women, Work and Family* (New York, 1978). For more on the role of working-class women within the family economy in the Gilded Age see Walkowitz, *Worker City, Company Town;* Yans-McLaughlin, *Family and Community;* Elizabeth H. Pleck, "A Mother's Wages: Income Earning Among Married Italian and Black Women, 1896–1911," in Michael Gordon, ed., *The American Family in Social-Historical Perspective*, 2d ed. (New York, 1978), 490–510.

54. Anna S. Parsons to J.B. Hawley, 4 Jan. 1877, file of Anna S. Parsons, Applications, Treas. Dept., NA.

55. M.L. Burroughs, to Mr. Clark, 24 March 1879, (1879) #1041, Appts. Files, Int. Dept., NA.

56. Belle Edelin to Mr. Porter, 11 Sept. 1892, (1880) #1909, Appts. Files, Int. Dept., NA.

57. A.L. Sheffey to Francis Walker, 3 June 1880, (1880) #1795, Appts. Files, Int. Dept., NA. Emphasis in original.

58. Hannah T. Meade to T.C.H. Smith, 3 July 1877, file of Hannah T. Meade, Applications, Treas. Dept., NA.

59. See Chapter Five for a discussion of federal hiring policy.

60. Jane Addams made a similar argument in the early 1900s: "There is no doubt…that many women to-day are failing properly to discharge their duties to their own families and households simply because they fail to see that as a society grows more complicated it is necessary that woman shall extend her sense of responsibility to many things outside of her own home, if only in order to preserve the home in its entirety." She argued that as society assumed many functions previously performed by the family, women would have to participate in the world outside the home if they were to influence how their children would be educated and whether their families would be able to purchase non-contaminated food and live in disease-free environments. See Jane Addams, "Women's Conscience and Social Amelioration," in *The Social Application of Religion* (Cincinnati, 1908), 41–60.

61. For a fuller discussion of women's salaries within government offices, see Chapter Four; for salaries of middle-class male clerks and school teachers see Chapter Two, and for data on salaries of female school teachers see above, note 12. Women industrial workers made much lower wages than did school teachers or clerks. An average wage for an experienced female factory worker in the late nineteenth century was about $5 or $6 for a sixty-hour week, while female domestic servants earned from $2 to $5 per week. Degler, *At Odds*, 382.

62. See Chapters Four and Five for a discussion of the bureaucratization of the federal workplace.

63. Alba M. Edwards, U.S. Bureau of the Census, *Sixteenth Census of the United States: 1940. Population. Comparative Occupation Statistics for the United States, 1870 to 1940* (Washington, D.C., 1943), 100.

64. Janice Weiss, "Educating for Clerical Work: The Nineteenth-Century Private Commercial School," *Journal of Social History* 14 (Spring 1981): 411, 417.

65. Application to Census Office of Julia A. O'Connor, 28 Oct. 1889, and Julia A. O'Connor to Robert Porter, 23 Oct. 1889, (1890) #3606, Appts. Files, Int. Dept., NA.

66. R.B. McKnight to A.T. Bliss, 16 July 1890, and Carrie A. King to Chief Clerk, 23 Jan. 1891, (1890) #3432, Appts. Files, Int. Dept., NA.

67. Lizzie Lee Shannon to Hoke Smith, 20 Feb. 1893, (1893) #2729, Appts. Files, Int. Dept., NA.

Chapter Four. Feminization, Rationalization, Mechanization

1. U.S., Congress, House of Representatives, *Retrenchment—Reorganization of the Executive Departments*, H. Rept. no. 741, 27th Cong., 2d sess., 1842, pp. 49, 149.

2. Extract from Report of the 3rd Auditor, Report of the Secretary of the Treasury, Senate Document 125, p. 26, 1st session, 32nd Congress, File of George Worthington, Applications, Treas. Dept., NA.

3. U.S., Congress, House of Representatives, *Retrenchment*, 51.

4. Ibid., 49.

5. Ibid., 149.

6. Ibid., 88, 18.

7. Between 1859 and 1861 the Department lowered the piece rates paid to these men from ten to eight cents per hundred words. U.S., Department of State, *Register of All Officers...of the United States, 1849,* p. 131; U.S., Department of State, *Register of Officers...of the United States, 1859,* p. 88; U.S., Department of the Interior, *Register of Officers...of the United States, 1861,* p. 81; U.S., Department of the Interior, *Register of All Officers...of the United States, 1863,* p. 104.

8. C.M. Walker to G. Rodman, 26 Nov. 1861, Office Files of the Division (entry 207), Records of the Division of Appointments, Treas. Dept., NA.

9. See Chapter Five for a discussion of promotion procedures within the federal government.

10. George M. Head, Statement of Facts for the Consideration of the Hon. Secretary of the Treasury, 5 April 1845, file of George Head, Applications, Treas. Dept., NA.

11. Samuel M. Bootes to Thos. Corwin, 23 Aug. 1850, file of Samuel Bootes, Applications, Treas. Dept., NA.

12. Leonard White, *The Republican Era: A Study in Administrative History* (New York, 1958), chs. 6, 9, 10; U.S., Department of the Interior, *Annual Report of the Secretary of the Interior, 1863,* p. ix; U.S., Department of the Interior, *Annual Report of the Secretary of the Interior, 1880,* vol. i, p. 56; U.S., Department of the Interior, *Annual Report of the Secretary of the Interior, 1885,* vol. i, pp. 94–95.

13. U.S., Department of the Interior, *General Land Office, Report of the Commissioner of the General Land Office, 1872,* p. 6.

14. White, *The Republican Era,* 175; Paul P. Van Riper, *History of the United States Civil Service* (Evanston, Ill., 1958), ch. 7.

15. U.S., Treasury Department, *Annual Report of the Secretary of the Treasury, 1862,* pp. 129–30.

16. U.S., Department of the Interior, *Annual Report of the Secretary of the Interior, 1875,* vol. i, pp. xiv, xv.

17. U.S., Treasury Department, *Annual Report of the Secretary of the Treasury, 1880,* p. 265.

18. See, for example, U.S., Treasury Department, *Annual Report of the Secretary of the Treasury, 1890.*

19. "General Spinner and the Women Clerks," *The Woman's Journal* (10 Jan. 1891): 16.

20. Ibid., 16.

21. Lucille Foster McMillin, *Women in the Federal Service* (Washington, D.C., 1938), 4.

22. U.S., Congress, Senate, Senator Sawyer speaking in debate on H.R. no. 974, *Congressional Globe,* 41st Cong., 2nd sess; 13 May 1870, pt. 4, p. 3450.

23. U.S. Congress, Senate, Senator Trumbull speaking in debate on H.R. no. 974, *Congressional Globe,* 41st Cong., 2nd sess; 13 May 1870, pt. 4, p. 3451.

24. Mary Dean to John Sherman, 6 Dec. 1875, file of Mary Dean, Applications, Treas. Dept., NA.

25. U.S., Congress, Senate, *Report of the Select Committee of the United States Senate, Appointed Under Senate Resolution of March 3, 1887, to Inquire into and Examine the Methods of Business and Work in the Executive Departments, etc.,* S. Rept. no. 507, 50th Cong., 1st sess., 1888, pt. 2 (Treasury Department), 46.

26. In 1870, U.S. Treasurer Francis Spinner explained that his employees "were compelled to make good all losses resulting from any mistakes [in counting] made by them." He maintained that in some cases the "counters have become so liable, in a single day, for an amount double what their present pay would amount to for a whole month." U.S., Treasury Department, *Annual Report of the Secretary of the Treasury, 1870*, p. 235.

27. Albert Day to Hugh McCullogh, 7 Aug. 1865, file of Kate McElliote, Applications, Treas. Dept., NA.

28. Mary Land to G.F. Edmuns, 24 July 1874, file of Mary Land, Applications, Treas. Dept., NA.; C. Risley to J. Sinnickson, 8 May 1878, file of Caroline Risley, Applications, Treas. Dept., NA.

29. Ellis Speak to C. Schurz, 15 Sept. 1877, Miscellaneous Letters Received, Appointments Division, Int. Dept., NA.

30. U.S., Department of the Interior, *Register of All Officers...of the United States, 1863*, p. 104.

31. In 1868 the Commissioner of Patents explained how the shortage of labor and excess of work had altered job assignments in his office, changing the duties and increasing the responsibilities of many clerks: "The Commissioner's assistant has the grade and compensation of a first assistant examiner. The gentleman who purchases the supplies of the office and upon whom its expenditure greatly depends is but a temporary clerk. More than one-half of the employees of the office are temporary clerks—an office intended by statute for copyists merely." U.S., Department of the Interior, Patent Office, *Report of the Commissioner of Patents, 1868*, vol. i, p. 8.

32. In 1854 the Patent Office hired three female copyists, one of whom was Clara Barton, and apparently allowed them to work in the office. But in 1855, Secretary of the Interior McClelland put a stop to the practice: "I have no objection to the employment of the females by the Patent Office, or any other of the Bureaus of the Department, in the performance of such duties as they are competent to discharge, and which may be executed by them at their private residences, but there is such an obvious impropriety in the mixing of the sexes within the walls of a public office, that I determined to arrest the practice...." Quoted in Mabel Deutrich and Virginia C. Purdy, eds., *Clio Was a Woman: Studies in the History of American Women* (Washington, 1980), 2.

33. U.S., Department of the Interior, Patent Office, *Report of the Commissioner of Patent, 1869*, vol. i, p. 16.

34. D.W. Haines to W.E. Chandler, 2 April 1866, file of Mrs. M.B. Whillden, Applications, Treas. Dept., NA.

35. C. Delano to George S. Boutwell, 4 June 1875, Letters Sent Book, Appointments Division, Int. Dept., NA.

36. Laura Meehan to John Sherman, 23 March 1877, file of Laura G. Meehan, Applications, Treas. Dept., NA.

37. Mr. Chesley to Mr. Solicitor, 14 June 1870, file of Mary R. Raymond, Applications, Treas. Dept., NA.

38. W.D. O'Connor to J.H. Saville, 18 June 1872, file of May E. Cole, Applications, Treas. Dept., NA. Emphasis in original.

39. Statement of the clerical duties of Miss N.D. Bishop, 16 May 1877, file of Nancy D. Bishop, Applications, Treas. Dept., NA.

40. U.S., Treasury Department, *Annual Report of the Secretary of the Treasury, 1865*, p. 118.

41. John W. Mason to John G. Carlisle, 7 Jan. 1895, file of Mary Van Vranken, Applications, Treas. Dept., NA.

42. J.R. Moore to Commissioner of the General Land Office, 10 May 1896, (1879) #1974, Appts. Files, Int. Dept., NA.

43. See Harry Braverman, *Labor and Monopoly Capital: The Degradation of Work in the Twentieth Century* (New York, 1974); Margery W. Davies, *Woman's Place Is at the Typewriter: Office Work and Office Workers 1870–1930* (Philadelphia, 1982); Valerie Kincade Oppenheimer, *The Female Labor Force in the United States: Demographic and Economic Factors Governing Its Growth and Changing Composition* (Westport, Conn., 1970), 96–120; Elyce Rotella, *From Home to Office: U.S. Women at Work, 1870–1930* (Ann Arbor, 1981); Mark Stuart Sandler, "Clerical Proletarianization in Capitalist Development" (Ph.D. dissertation, Michigan State University, 1979).

44. U.S., Congress, Senate, *Report of Work in the Executive Departments*, pts. 1, 2, and 3.

45. See U.S., Congress, House of Representatives, *Retrenchment*, 51.

46. U.S., Congress, Senate, *Report of Work in the Executive Departments*, pt. 2 (Interior Department), 347; (Treasury Department), 341–42.

47. U.S., Congress, Senate, *Report of Work in the Executive Departments*, pt. 2 (Treasury Department), 155.

48. U.S., Congress, Senate, *Report of Work in the Executive Departments*, pt. 2 (Interior Department), 223.

49. Departmental Service Record, John Johnson, 10 Sept. 1897, file of John Johnson, Applications, Treas. Dept., NA.

50. Frank Pierce MacLean to W.S. Rosecraus, 18 June 1885, (1880) #641, Appts. Files, Int. Dept., NA.

51. G.P. Hopkins to "Sir," 21 Nov. 1888, (1880) #1033, Appts. Files, Int. Dept., NA.

52. U.S., Congress, Senate, *Report of Work in the Executive Departments*, pt. 2 (Interior Department), 73.

53. U.S., Congress, Senate, *Report of Work in the Executive Departments*, pt. 2 (Treasury Department), 434.

54. Ibid., 311.

55. U.S., Congress, Senate, Senator Sawyer speaking in debate on H.R. no. 974, Congressional Globe, 41st Cont., 2nd sess; 13 May 1870, pt. 4, p. 3450.

56. U.S., Treasury Department, *Annual Report of the Secretary of the Treasury, 1870*, p. 238.

57. Seventy-two of the 88 men appointed as clerks in fiscal 1891, for example, accepted positions that paid from $600 to $900, although they had passed examinations that entitled them to higher paid jobs. U.S., Civil Service Commission, *Ninth Annual Report of the U.S. Civil Service Commission, 1892*, p. 147. Even the men who were offered first-class clerkships had to accept lower pay for a short time in any case. By the 1890s first-class clerks were required to work a six-month probationary period at $1000 before being advanced to $1200.

58. The analysis for Tables 4.2 and 4.3 comes from counting the number of permanent clerical employees at each salary level listed in the biennial register of federal employees for the years 1863, 1871, 1881, 1891, and 1901 who were employed in the Washington, D.C., offices of the Treasury and Interior Departments. I have excluded certain people from this analysis: employees of the Census Office, since these people were temporary workers (with jobs lasting from a few months to a few years) and because the salary range in the Census Office was al-

ways lower than within the permanent bureaus for both men and women; all employees of the Bureau of Printing and Engraving, a division within the Treasury Department, for these workers were often paid piece rates and their work was frequently of a non-clerical nature (many were printer's assistants or operatives); people listed as "charwomen," "janitors," "watchmen," or "carpenters"; the few people who earned more than $2900, since they were high presidential appointees or cabinet officers, not clerks; workers who were listed as *per diem* or per monthly employees, since they usually were not permanent workers but were only employed for short periods of time. I have included, however, "messengers," "skilled laborers," and "laborers," since I know that employees with such titles often performed clerical duties.

59. Commissioner of Pensions, endorsement, 4 Aug. 1879, on Mrs. C. Boughton to Secretary of the Interior, Aug. 1879, (1879) #1734, Appts. Files, Int. Dept., NA.

60. A.L. Jackson, [188?], (1890) #2466, Appts. Files, Int. Dept., NA.

61. W.A. Nestler to Mr. Noble, 4 Oct. 1890, (1890) #2607, Appts. Files, Int. Dept., NA.

62. J.W. Bentley to Secretary of the Interior, 16 Dec. 1880, (1880) #2346, Appts. Files, Int. Dept., NA.

63. Davies, *Woman's Place Is at the Typewriter*, 53–55.

64. Carole Srole, " 'A Position That God Has Not Particularly Assigned to Men': The Feminization of Clerical Work, Boston 1860–1915" (Ph.D. dissertation, University of California, Los Angeles, 1984), 226.

65. U.S., Civil Service Commission, *Ninth Annual Report*, 120; McMillin, *Women in the Federal Service*, 10–11.

66. W.M. Stone to Secretary of the Interior, 14 Jan. 1893, Miscellaneous Letters Received, Appointments Division, Int. Dept., NA.

67. W.H. Bayley to Secretary of the Interior, 23 Jan. 1893, Miscellaneous Letters Received, Appointments Division, Int. Dept., NA. Emphasis added.

68. Frank Patterson to Benj. Butterworth, 9 Jan. 1884, (1881) #2167, Appts. Files, Int. Dept., NA.

69. Frank Alexander to R.B. Belt, 24 Nov. 1890, (1890) #1374, Appts. Files, Int. Dept., NA.

70. T.J. Morgan to Secretary of the Interior, 10 June 1891, (1890) #1744, Appts. Files, Int. Dept., NA.; T.J. Morgan to Secretary of the Interior, 4 Aug. 1890, (1890) #2628, Appts. Files, Int. Dept., NA.

71. T.C. Martin, "Counting a Nation by Electricity," *The Electrical Engineer* (11 Nov. 1891): 523–4.

72. Ibid., 524.

73. Ibid., 525.

74. J. Hyde to Robert Porter, 5 Sept. 1892, (1890) #1940, Appts. Files, Int. Dept., NA; M.B. Cragg to Mr. Wardle, 11 April 1893, (1890) #3460, Appts. Files, Int. Dept., NA.

75. Robert Porter to Secretary of the Interior, 3 Feb. 1891, Miscellaneous Letters Received, Appointments Division, Int. Dept., NA.

76. U.S., Department of the Interior, *Register of the United States: 1891*, vol. 1, pp. 747–55.

77. Howard Sutherland to Mr. Wardle, 16 April 1891, (1890) #1594, Appts. Files, Int. Dept., NA.

78. J.H. LaGrange to John Noble, 20 June 1891, (1890) #1701, Appts. Files, Int. Dept., NA.

79. U.S., Department of the Interior, *Register of the United States: 1881*, vol. 1, pp. 619–32.

80. Mrs. Crandall to Supt. of the Census, 6 Nov. 1883, (1880) #2200, Appts. Files, Int. Dept., NA.

81. These figures do not include the men and women who worked for the Census Office. The Census Office included large numbers of clerks who performed routine and repetitive labor—both mechanized and non-mechanized. These employees, however, were only temporary, working for a year or two. Nevertheless, the proportion of clerks working at highly rationalized jobs certainly increased during those years when the government was busy tallying the decennial census.

82. James McCabe, *Behind the Scenes in Washington* (Philadelphia, 1873), 461.

83. Mary Clemmer Ames, *Ten Years in Washington: Life and Scenes in the National Capital as a Woman Sees Them* (Hartford, 1873), 307.

84. U.S., Congress, House of Representatives, *Retrenchment*, 50; Paul P. Van Riper, *History of the United States Civil Service*, 155.

85. U.S., Committee on Department Methods, *Report to the President on Annual Leave, Sick Leave, and Hours of Labor* (1906), 3.

Chapter Five. Getting a Job, Keeping a Job, Winning a Promotion

1. Leonard D. White, *The Republican Era: 1869–1901: A Study in Administrative History* (New York, 1958), 360.

2. F.C. Snead to Hugh McCulloch, 6 June 1867, file of Austine Snead, Applications, Treas. Dept., NA.; James C. Brown to R.J.C. Walker, 24 Jan. 1882, file of J.C. Brown, Applications, Treas. Dept., NA.

3. R.P. Spalding to John Sherman, 11 April 1879, file of Phebe Carter, Applications, Treas. Dept., NA; Note from J.W. [John Wanamaker], 15 March 1892, (1890) #3461, Appts. Files, Int. Dept., NA.

4. W. Sprague to Hugh McCulloch, 28 June 1866, file of Thomas Foster, Applications, Treas. Dept., NA.

5. V. Barnes to Abraham Lincoln, 15 Jan. 1861, file of Vincent Barnes, Applications, Treas. Dept., NA.

6. E. Dawson to J.W. Noble, 27 Oct. 1890, (1880) #1607, Appts. Files, Int. Dept., NA.

7. H.E. Nixon to Wm. Claflin, 11 Jan. 1879, (1879) #750, Appts. Files, Int. Dept., NA.

8. S.B. Loving to Mr. Porter, 5 Feb. 1890, (1890) #2382, Appts. Files, Int. Dept., NA.; Chas. W. Kenna to G.A. Jenks, 18 July 1885, (1880) #301, Appts. Files, Int. Dept., NA.

9. Edwyn W. Byrn to S.J. Kirkwood, 4 April 1881, (1881) #1174, Appts. Files, Int. Dept., NA.

10. O.H. Platt to John Noble, 15 March 1890, (1890) #1139, Appts. Files, Int. Dept., NA.

11. U.S., Civil Service Commission, *First Annual Report of the United States Civil Service Commission, 1884*, p. 25.

12. Clipping from *The Republican*, 25 March 1876, enclosed in Charlotte Cross to Chas. F. Conant, 26 March 1876, file of Charlotte Cross, Applications, Treas. Dept., NA. Emphasis in original.

13. Mrs. E.N. Chapin, *American Court Gossip—or—Life at the National Capital* (Marshalltown, Iowa, 1887), 95–96.

14. Mrs. Voute to General Walker, 21 Feb. 1880, (1880) #1004, Appts. Files, Int. Dept., NA.

15. For more on the problems these women faced as they entered the male world of the office, see Chapters Six and Seven.

16. Nannie Lancaster to Mr. Porter, 8 July 1889, (1880) #929, Appts. Files, Int. Dept., NA.

17. Maurice H. Wolfe to Jas. R. O'Breine, 1 Feb. 1883, (1880) #98, Appts. Files, Int. Dept., NA.

18. Geo. M. Rupert to William Ward, 8 Jan. 1880, (1880) #106, Appts. Files, Int. Dept., NA.; Timothy M. Sullivan to Carl Schurz, 12 Feb. 1880, (1880) #340, Appts. Files, Int. Dept., NA.

19. William D. Steadman to Secretary of the Interior, 6 Feb. 1880, (1880) #228, Appts. Files, Int. Dept., NA.

20. P.J. Cole to A. Bell, 2 June 1882, (1880) #297, Appts. Files, Int. Dept., NA.

21. L. Gambin to Jas. F. Hood, 7 Oct. 1884, (1880) #1101, Appts. Files, Int. Dept., NA. Occasionally a truly desperate man who was neither old, young, nor infirm would entreat and beg for help, but such expressions were rare.

22. Wm. W. Clapp to Francis A. Walker, 9 Aug. 1880; Mary A. Clapp to W.D. Dudley, 19 July 1881; Mary A. Clapp to Chester A. Arthur, 29 Oct. 1881, (1880) #1655, Appts. Files, Int. Dept., NA.

23. Joseph Cooke to John Noble, 12 Feb. 1893, (1890) #3084, Appts. Files, Int. Dept., NA.

24. L. Crittenden to George Harrington, 9 July 1863, Letters Received from the Register of the Treasury (entry 171), Correspondence of the Office of the Secretary of the Treasury, Treas. Dept., NA.

25. Mary L. Balch to Secretary Kirkwood, 21 June 1881, (1881) #296, Appts. Files, Int. Dept., NA.

26. A. Bell to Mrs. M.C. Knowles, 5 April 1881, (1881) #512, Appts. Files, Int. Dept., NA.

27. Walter Licht, *Working for the Railroad: The Organization of Work in the Nineteenth Century* (Princeton, N.J., 1983), 49–59.

28. Stephen Skowronek, *Building a New American State: The Expansion of National Administrative Capacities, 1877–1920* (Cambridge, 1982), 50–59. For more on the constituency of the civil service reform movement see Ari Hoogenboom, *Outlawing the Spoils: A History of the Civil Service Reform Movement, 1865–1883* (Urbana, Ill., 1961); Paul P. Van Riper, *History of the United States Civil Service* (Evanston, Ill., 1958); Carl Russel Fish, *The Civil Service and the Patronage* (New York, 1963); White, *The Republican Era.*

29. Skowronek, *Building a New American State*, 65–67; Van Riper, *United States Civil Service*, 88–94.

30. *The Statutes at Large of the United States of America*, vol. xxii (Washington, D.C., 1883), 403–7.

31. Robert Porter to the Secretary of the Interior, 3 Feb. 1891, Miscellaneous Letters Received, Appointments Division, Int. Dept., NA.

32. A.M. Dockery to Hoke Smith, 2 Oct. 1893, Miscellaneous Letters Received, Appointments Division, Int. Dept., NA. Between 1893 and 1896 the size and scope of the classified service was increased considerably. U.S., Civil Service Commission, *Fourteenth Report of the United States Civil Service Commission July 1, 1896 to June 30, 1897*, pp. 136–40.

33. Van Riper, *United States Civil Service,* 150–51.

34. Ibid., 151*n.* It was a common practice for outgoing Presidents to place more federal workers within the classified system before they left office, thereby reducing the number of patronage positions available for the incoming party.

35. White, *The Republican Era,* 360–61.

36. U.S., Civil Service Commission, *Second Annual Report of the United States Civil Service Commission, 1885,* pp. 24–25.

37. U.S., Civil Service Commission, *First Annual Report,* 25. The law to which this report refers was an 1870 statute allowing department heads to request women for any position. Previous to that time there had been a statutory limit of $900 on women's salaries. This 1870 statute did not, however, require officials to pay women salaries commensurate with their duties, but left it up to the individual officer. Not until the Classification Act of 1923 were women employed in the government entitled to equal pay for equal work.

38. R.D. Graham to Secretary Teller, 16 July 1884, Miscellaneous Letters Received, Appointments Division, Int. Dept., NA.

39. The data in this table come from the annual reports published by the U.S. Civil Service Commission. The table requires some explanation. The first column of figures lists the number of people who successfully passed the clerk and/or copyist examinations for entrance into the federal civil service in the given years. The Civil Service commission, however, offered two other major categories of examinations, called "supplemental" and "special." The supplemental examination included areas such as typewriting, stenography, and proofreading, among others. An applicant who wished to qualify for one of these positions needed first to pass the general (i.e., clerk) exam and then pass a supplemental exam in one of the supplemental fields. The special examination covered more technical, and usually more high-status jobs, such as pension examiner, bookkeeper, and draughtsman (although a few low-status jobs, such as printer's assistant, were also included in this category). Applicants for these jobs needed to take only the special exam and not the general examination as well. I have not included in the first column of figures the people who competed in either the special or supplemental examinations. The Civil Service Commission often changed the boundaries of the categories, and an examination which one year was included in the supplemental category was the next year put into the special category. Also, those applicants who competed in the supplemental exam had also competed in the general exam, and thus had already been counted. It was, as well, difficult to know if some of the people who took the special examination had also taken the general exam, perhaps to increase their chances of being appointed. Moreover, until the mid-1890s, the numbers of people competing in special and/or supplemental exams remained low. In 1891, for example, 2,927 people sat for the clerk/copyist exam, 1,997 of whom passed. Only 364 people took the special exam, 128 of whom passed.

The second column in Table 5.1 includes the number of men and women appointed to civil service positions in the given years. These figures also require some explanation. I have included in these figures all appointments except those to the position of printer's assistant (a low-status, low-paid, manual job given only to women and a job which required only its own special exam and not the general clerical exam). Many of the people accounted for in the second column received other than strictly clerical and/or copyist jobs—these figures include people who received special and supplemental jobs, as well as those appointed to what were labeled "non-competitive" jobs. (The Civil Service exempted certain jobs from competition, requiring only a non-competitive, "pass" exam.) Thus, this table for the most part underestimates the number of clerical applicants and overstates the number of clerical appointments. In fact, the competition for federal clerkships was even greater than this table suggests.

I have carried this analysis only until 1894 because the statistics reported by the Civil Service Commission changed in the last years of the century. After 1894 the figures become less useful for our purposes because the Commission expanded the definition of the departmental service to include numerous non-clerical, manual jobs as well as certain positions outside Washington, D.C.

40. The data for this table were computed from the annual civil service reports. The number of men and women passing exams and the number of men and women appointed to jobs include the same people as did Table 5.1. These figures exclude (as did those from Table 5.1) the women appointed to positions as printer's assistants, but include all other men and women receiving classified civil service appointments.

41. U.S., Civil Service Commission, *Ninth Annual Report of the United States Civil Service Commission, 1892*, pp. 332.

42. F. Dudley Carson to L.Q.C. Lamar, 16 Oct. 1887, (1880) #697, Appts. Files, Int. Dept., NA.

43. Ida Edson to J.H. Blodgett, 26 Oct. 1891, (1890) #356, Appts. Files, Int. Dept., NA.

44. Those applicants who still tried to use political connections to acquire civil service jobs usually exercised considerable discretion. In 1894, May Williams noted that work on the census would soon be completed and requested a permanent position from the Secretary of the Interior in one of the other offices of his agency: "I rely principally upon my official record and hence do not disobey the letter or spirit of your general order...by referring you to my Representative and Texas friends, John Thomas M. Paschal, Hon. G.D. Sayer, and others, as to my family, social and other ex-official record and merit." Lest this "subtle" reference to her political connections pass unnoticed, a member of Congress from Texas also communicated with the Secretary of the Interior, informing him that Williams possessed "the very best political antecedents and connections....She and her family, like many other Southern families, are without resources, and she depends solely upon her own labor." May C. Williams to Hoke Smith, 9 May 1894, and T.M. Paschal to Hoke Smith, 10 May 1894, (1890) #1940, Appts. Files, Int. Dept., NA.

45. The only exception was the short-lived civil service system begun under the Grant administration. In 1871, Congress authorized President Grant to establish a Civil Service Commission which, for three years, instituted competitive examinations for entrance to federal clerkships. But even this commission, rather than assuming control of all testing for the federal service, left the examining process to individual agencies. The Grant Commission, as it was known, folded in 1875 when Congress refused to appropriate funds for its continuance, and departments thereafter reverted to the examination practices of the 1850s and 1860s. Van Riper, *United States Civil Service*, 51–52.

46. White, *The Republican Era*, 228.

47. U.S., Civil Service Commission, *Second Annual Report*, 10, 94–98.

48. See (1880) #719, Appts. Files, Int. Dept., NA.

49. W.H. Alexander to Board of Examiners, 1 Feb. 1890, (1890) #188, Appts. Files, Int. Dept., NA.

50. Eleanor Bryan to G.B. Nudinghaus, 6 May 1890, (1890) #1996, Appts. Files, Int. Dept., NA.

51. Mitta Newell to Robert Porter, 22 Oct. 1889, (1890) #582, Appts. Files, Int. Dept., NA.

52. E.S. Wicklin to D.B. Henderson, 1 March 1890, (1890) #889, Appts. Files, Int. Dept., NA.

53. Daniel Calhoun, *The Intelligence of a People* (Princeton, N.J., 1973), 76–77.

54. Mrs. R.B. Harrington to Senator Paddock, n.d., (1890) #483, Appts. Files, Int. Dept., NA.

55. Throughout the late 1880s and 1890s the Civil Service Commission repeatedly condemned the illegal assignment of clerical responsibilities to non-classified employees hired as "laborers," but the practice apparently continued. In 1894 the Commissioner of Patents, upon request of the Civil Service Commission, submitted a list of the men and women in his office outside the classified service (i.e., earning less than $720 per year) who performed clerical tasks. He explained: "In submitting this list I desire to say that when I assumed the duties of this office I found the practice had prevailed under each of my predecessors, since the enactment of the Civil Service law, of assigning to clerical duty persons employed as messengers and laborers, without any examination under the Civil Service Rules as therein required." The Commissioner of Patents tried to excuse such actions by stating that the increasing work load made it absolutely essential to assign laborers to clerical tasks. John Seymour to Secretary of the Interior, 6 March 1894, Miscellaneous Letters Received, Appointments Division, Int. Dept., NA.

56. Maggie Loftus to A.F. Childs, 7 Oct. 1890, (1890) #3472, Appts. Files, Int. Dept., NA.

57. U.S., Congress, House of Representatives, *Report of the Select Committee of the House of Representatives, Investigating the Methods and Management and Practices of the Bureau of Pensions,* H. Rept. no. 1868, 52nd Cong., 1st sess., 1892, part 1, pp. 3–21.

58. See Skowronek, *Building a New American State;* Hoogenboom, *Outlawing the Spoils;* Van Riper, *United States Civil Service;* Fish, *Civil Service and Patronage.*

59. Jurgen Kocka, *White Collar Workers in America 1890–1940: A Social-Political History in International Perspective* (London, 1980), 122.

60. For a discussion of the importance of university education for the new professional middle class see Bledstein, *The Culture of Professionalism: The Middle Class and the Development of Higher Education in America* (New York, 1976).

61. William Mathews, *Getting on in the World; or, Hints on Success in Life* (Chicago, 1874), 83.

62. The data in this table were computed from information drawn from the application files of men and women who were clerking in the Treasury Department in the year 1871. They do not reveal how long these clerks had worked for the government as of 1871, but how long they had worked and would continue to work. (See Appendix for a discussion of how the sample was drawn.) Determining persistency rates for federal clerks is, however, a difficult and cumbersome task, and the final figures can only be taken as estimates. Some of the files were incomplete and did not reveal exactly when a clerk entered or left the department. Determining job-persistency for these clerks required that their names be searched through successive volumes of the biennial registers of federal employees. This register, however, had no index until 1877, and searching through the entire register would have been impossible. Thus, if a clerk who worked in the 1860s or early 1870s was not listed in the same office where he or she had previously been employed, then it was assumed that that clerk was not employed by the government at all. Clerks who switched from one office to another were there-

fore counted as having left the government. While the figures in Table 5.3 are not exact, their bias is consistent. They consistently underestimate the length of service within the department. These figures, however, make the federal service seem more stable than it was in one regard—they do not include the large number of temporary employees who entered and left the bureaucracy during some years. At certain times in certain agencies, such as the counting of the decennial census, temporary clerks could number well over a thousand.

63. Emma Della Seta to Senator Chilcott, 17 June 1882, (1879) #1441, Appts. Files, Int. Dept., NA.

64. N.L. Jeffries to Secretary of the Treasury, 25 Nov. 1868, Letters Received from the Register of the Treasury (entry 171), Correspondence of the Office of the Secretary of the Treasury, Treas. Dept., NA.

65. J. Gilfillan to John Sherman, 30 June 1880, Letters Received from the Treasurer (entry 177), Correspondence of the Office of the Secretary of the Treasury, Treas. Dept., NA.

66. Mrs. L.B. Chandler to Mr. Sherman, 30 Aug. 1876, file of Lucy B. Chandler, Treas. Dept., NA.

67. H.G. Jacobs to Mr. Bell, 20 Aug. 1879, (1879) #1852, Appts. Files, Int. Dept., NA.

68. Nanci E. Coxe to John W. Noble, 24 Nov. 1892, (1890) #2367, Appts. Files, Int. Dept., NA.

69. G.J. Hodgson to Hoke Smith, 24 May 1893, (1890) #2274, Appts. Files, Int. Dept., NA.

70. Van Riper, *United States Civil Service*, 144.

71. The information in Table 5.4 reveals how long these clerks had worked up until 1907, the date when the figures were compiled.

72. *Statutes at Large*, vol. xxii, p. 406.

73. Geo. W. Richards, 1 Dec. 1880, endorsement on letter from A.J. Carrier to C. Schurz, 27 Nov. 1880, (1880) #1331, Appts. Files, Int. Dept., NA.

74. Jas. Crawford to R.P. Porter, 20 June 1891, (1890) #2011, Appts. Files, Int. Dept., NA.

75. J.D. Bradley to Hugh McCulloch, 30 April 1866, file of James D. Bradley, Applications, Treas. Dept., NA.

76. Virginia Dunnavant to H.L. Vanderbilt, 18 July 1874, file of Virginia Dunnavant, Applications, Treas. Dept., NA.

77. Edmund Rise, Memorandum in the case of Mrs. Kate Hoffman, 7 Jan. 1888, file of Catherine Hoffman, Applications, Treas. Dept., NA.

78. E.B. Curtis to J.M. Brodhead, 30 Sept. 1869, file of Bernard May, Applications, Treas. Dept., NA.

79. O.F. Dana to J.W. Douglass, 17 March 1875, file of Joseph B. Marvin, Applications, Treas. Dept., NA.

80. Theo. French to S.J. Kirkwood, 23 March 1881, (1881) #808, Appts. Files, Int. Dept., NA.

81. Charles C. Snow to J.H. Franklin, 10 Dec. 1890, file of Enna B. Wilson, Applications, Treas. Dept., NA.

82. For more on social interaction in the offices see Chapters Six and Seven.

83. Israel P. Smith to Charles J. Folger, 29 Nov. 1882, file of Israel P. Smith, Applications, Treas. Dept., NA.

84. John R. French to "Dear Sir," 1861, file of John R. French, Applications, Treas. Dept., NA.

85. Elizabeth Denham to S.J. Kirkwood, 13 June 1881, and Elizabeth Den-

ham to M.E. Cults, 9 May 1881, (1881) #936, Appts. Files, Int. Dept., NA.

86. See note 12, Chapter Three for data on salaries of women school teachers.

87. Jane W. Gemmill to H.S. Vanderbilt, 5 April 1872, file of Jane W. Gemmill, Applications, Treas. Dept., NA.

88. Julia Henderson to Hoke Smith, 4 Oct. 1893, (1879) #1718, Appts. Files, Int. Dept., NA.

89. Louise P. Brown to Geo. F. Edmunds, 14 Feb. 1881, (1880) #1642, Appts. Files, Int. Dept., NA.

90. John Noble to Appointment Clerk, 31 July 1890, Miscellaneous Letters Received, Appointments Division, Int. Dept., NA.

91. W.D. Harlan to Commissioner of the General Land Office, 22 Sept. 1899, and Filibert Roth to Chief Clerk, General Land office, 20 May 1902, (1879) #1974, Appts. Files, Int. Dept., NA.

92. Throughout the post-Civil War decades, Congress periodically created committees to investigate the executive departments and determine if they were being run efficiently. In the mid-1870s the Boutwell Committee, in 1887 the Cockrell Committee, and in 1893 the Dockery Committee all conducted such investigations. White, *The Republican Era*, ch. 4.

93. Quoted in White, *The Republican Era*, 356.

94. J.A. Bentley to Carl Schurz, 26 July 1879, Miscellaneous Letters Received, Appointments Division, Int. Dept., NA.

95. Ibid.

96. U.S. Congress, Senate, *Report of the Select Committee of the United States Senate, Appointed under Senate Resolution of March 3, 1887, to Inquire into and Examine the Methods of Business and Work in the Executive Departments, etc.*, S. Rept. no. 507, 50th Cong., 1st sess., 1888, pt. 2 (Interior Department), 149.

97. In 1882, for example, the Pension Office instituted a program that was intended to "increase the efficiency of the office and to give clerks an official notice of their standing." The plan instructed supervisors to rate their clerks each month on a scale of seven (perfect) to zero (worthless) in each of the following areas: punctuality, habits, industry, accuracy, and rapidity. The Commissioner of Pensions noted that "a record lower than 4 for three consecutive months, will cause a dropping of the name of the clerk making such record from the rolls of this Office." Despite the intended objectivity of such a scheme, a supervisor with the power not only to rate, but to place the clerk on a certain kind of work, could certainly affect the outcome of that clerk's evaluation record. Department of the Interior Circular, Pension Office, 8 Aug. 1882, Miscellaneous Letters Received, Appointments Division, Int. Dept., NA.

98. Department of the Interior, circular, "Efficiency Record in Compliance with the President's Instructions of December 4, 1891," 2 Jan. 1892, Miscellaneous Letters Received, Appointments Division, Int. Dept., NA.

99. Department of the Interior, circular, "Efficiency Record in Compliance with the President's Instructions of December 4, 1891," 2 Jan. 1892, Treasury Department, circular, "Relative to Competitive Examinations for Promotion," 24 Dec. 1891, Miscellaneous Letters Received, Appointments Division, Int. Dept., NA.

100. W.H. Bayly to Chiefs of Division, 19 May 1892, Miscellaneous Letters Received, Appointments Division, Int. Dept., NA. Emphasis in original.

101. J.T. Newton to Josephus Daniels, 31 May 1894, Miscellaneous Letters Received, Appointments Division, Int. Dept., NA.

102. Ibid.

103. "Clerk" to Secretary of the Treasury, 26 March 1901, clipping enclosed, "The Plan To Be Adopted in Recommending Treasury Promotions," [1901], Correspondence of the Division (entry 208), Records of the Division of Appointments, Treas. Dept., NA.

104. Margery W. Davies, *Woman's Place Is at the Typewriter: Office Work and Office Workers, 1870–1930* (Philadelphia, 1982), ch. 6; Harry Braverman, *Labor and Monopoly Capital: The Degradation of Work in the Twentieth Century* (New York, 1974), 304–15.

105. Ann R. Story to Lyman S. Gage, 7 June 1897, file of Ann Story, Applications, Treas. Dept., NA.

106. File of Mary Willard, Applications, Treas. Dept., NA.

107. File of J.G. Bruff, Applications, Treas. Dept., NA.

108. Deposition of Kate Norwood, 7 July 1893, (1880) #1554, Appts. Files, Int. Dept., NA.

109. In 1866, for example, Mary Key Reily, a $900 employee in the Treasurer's Office, submitted a doctor's certificate and requested that she be reimbursed for pay withheld during her six-week absence. Treasurer Francis Spinner, noting that she really was sick and unable to "attend to her office duty," recommended that she receive the money. But Helen Sayles had a much different experience. In 1876, after ten years' employment within the Treasury Department, Sayles fell ill and her physician requested "leave for a few days" for her to "go North and regain [her] strength." Her supervisor consented only to her taking leave without pay. Nevertheless, she reported: "I sent in my application [for leave] and in return received my dismissal." Male clerks had similar experiences: some supervisors allowed them considerable leave time while others kept closely to the written letter of the law. F. Spinner, endorsement, [Oct. 1866], on Mary Key Reily to Hugh McCulloch, 6 Oct. 1866, file of Mary Key Reily, Applications, Treas. Dept., NA; Helen M. Sayles to Senator Howe, 24 Jan. 1877, file of Helen M. Sayles, Applications, Treas. Dept., NA.

110. Carole Srole, " 'A Position That God Has Not Particularly Assigned to Men': The Feminization of Clerical Work, Boston, 1860–1915" (Ph.D. dissertation, University of California, Los Angeles, 1984), ch. 4; Miriam Cohen, "Italian-American Women in New York City, 1900–1950: Work and School," in Milton Cantor and Bruce Laurie, eds., *Class, Sex and the Woman Worker* (Westport, Conn., 1977).

111. Francis A. Page to S.J. Kirkwood, 15 June 1881, (1880) #1598, Appts. Files, Int. Dept., NA.

112. Robert Porter to Secretary of the Interior, 26 Dec. 1890, and J.W. Noble to Superintendent of the Census, 27 Dec. 1890, (1890) #2188, Appts. Files, Int. Dept., NA.

113. See the following files: (1890) #3757, (1890) #3669, (1890) #3375, (1890) #1643, and (1890) #370, Appts. Files, Int. Dept., NA.

114. William Graebner's study of retirement reveals that as late as 1920 the federal bureaucracy was still functioning in much the same way. The bonds that had developed between clerks and supervisors made officials reluctant to dismiss aged workers: "Even in the mid-1920s, the federal bureaucracy was not yet the fully rationalized instrument that some desired. It was still laced with personal ties and informal bonds that often transcended increasing pressures for purely contractual relationships." William Graebner, *A History of Retirement: The Meaning and Function of an American Institution, 1885–1978* (New Haven, 1980), 87.

115. Licht, *Working for the Railroad*, 124, 254–55.

Chapter Six. Adapting to a New Style of Middle-Class Work

1. "One Who Knows" to Secretary of the Interior, n.d., (1880) #1554, Appts. Files, Int. Dept., NA.

2. Deposition of Minnie Reed, 10 July 1893, (1880) #1554, Appts. Files, Int. Dept., NA.

3. Ibid.

4. Minnie Reed to Wm. Lochren, 14 Sept. 1890, Wm. Lochren to Hoke Smith, 2 Oct. 1893, (1880) #1554, Appts. Files, Int. Dept., NA.

5. Deposition of Kate Norwood, 7 July 1893, (1880) #1554, Appts. Files, Int. Dept., NA.

6. Deposition of Minnie Reed, 11 July 1893, (1880) #1554, Appts. Files, Int. Dept., NA.

7. Geo. F. Worthington to S.P. Chase, 31 Jan. 1862, file of George Worthington, Applications, Treas. Dept., NA.

8. S.H. Goodman to Geo. S. Boutwell, 3 June 1869, file of Samuel Goodman, Applications, Treas. Dept., NA.

9. Robert Patterson to Geo. S. Boutwell, 2 July 1870, file of Robert Patterson, Applications, Treas. Dept., NA.

10. L.J. Anderson to Chas. H. Cragin, 23 April 1869, file of L.J. Anderson, Applications, Treas. Dept., NA.

11. A.B. Jamison to Theo. F. Swayze, 3 April 1897, file of A.B. Jamison, Applications, Treas. Dept., NA.

12. U.S. Congress, House of Representatives, *Report of the Select Committee of the House of Representatives, Investigating the Methods and Management and Practices of the Bureau of Pensions*, H. Rept. no. 1868, part 2, 52d Cong., 1st sess., 1892, p. 1059.

13. U.S., House of Representatives, *Report on the Bureau of Pensions*, part 1, p. 395, part 2, p. 1049.

14. U.S. House of Representatives, *Report on the Bureau of Pensions*, part 2, pp. 743–47.

15. William Mathews, *Getting on in the World; or, Hints on Success in Life* (Chicago, 1874), 4.

16. E. Anthony Rotundo, "Manhood in America: The Northern Middle Class, 1770–1920" (Ph.D. dissertation, Brandeis University, 1982), 143, 148.

17. Ibid., 263.

18. Lizzie Bachelder to Wm. Tullock, 13 July 1869, file of Lizzie Bachelder, Applications, Treas. Dept., NA.

19. Mary Ruckman to Mrs. John W. Noble, 14 April 1891, (1890) #3703, Appts. Files, Int. Dept., NA.

20. John Buxman to Abraham Lincoln, 25 Sept. 1861, file of John Buxman, Applications, Treas. Dept., NA.

21. Almond Woodward to John Noble, 7 Oct. 1891, (1890) #2132, Appts. Files, Int. Dept., NA.

22. Ann R. Story to Chas. G. Folger, 9 Aug. 1884, file of Ann Story, Applications, Treas. Dept., NA.

23. Fannie E. Wadleigh to U.S. Grant, 16 Feb. 1876, file of Fannie Wadleigh, Applications, Treas. Dept., NA.

24. Emily Neyland to John W. Noble, 3 Aug. 1890, (1879) #1322, Appts. Files, Int. Dept., NA.

25. Mrs. M.V. Brown to Joseph Washington, 11 Sept. 1889, and Joseph Washington to Secretary of the Interior, 28 Aug. 1889, (1880) #986, Appts. Files, Int. Dept., NA.

26. "Anonymous," [1869], Office Files of the Division (entry 207), Records of the Division of Appointments, Treas. Dept., NA.

27. "A List of Women Who Are Rebs...," [1869], Office Files of the Division (entry 207), Records of the Division of Appointments, Treas. Dept., NA.

28. "Watchful" to T.L. Tullock, 10 June 1869, and [no signature] to J.H. Alendering, [1869], Office Files of the Division (entry 207), Records of the Division of Appointments, Treas. Dept., NA.

29. Interrogatories by Emmet Womack, answers by John O'Connell, n.d., (1879) #1610, Appts. Files, Int. Dept., NA.

30. Henry F. Picking to Secretary of the Treasury, 21 Nov. 1884, file of Lesa Shelby, Applications, Treas. Dept., NA.

31. Albert Day to Hugh McCulloch, 7 Aug. 1865, file of Kate McElliote, Applications, Treas. Dept., NA.

32. P.E. Wilson to Commissioner of Patents, 16 Feb. 1880, and Transcript of Conversation between Major Lockwood and Mrs. Shaw, 25 March 1880, (1880) #645, Appts. Files, Int. Dept., NA.

33. Lester Ward, *Young Ward's Diary*, ed. Bernhard J. Stern (New York, 1935), 281, 225.

34. U.S., House of Representatives, *Report on the Bureau of Pensions*, part 2, pp. 1227–29.

35. Ward, *Young Ward's Diary*, 189, 194, 204.

36. U.S., House of Representatives, *Report on the Bureau of Pensions*, part 2, p. 990.

37. Emily Neyland to John Noble, 3 Aug. 1890, (1879) #1322, Appts. Files, Int. Dept., NA.

38. Emma James to Commissioner of Patents, 1 July 1885, (1880) #1554, Appts. Files, Int. Dept., NA.

39. F. Spinner to Hugh McCulloch, 9 July 1867, Letters Received from the Treasurer (entry 177), Correspondence of the Office of the Secretary of the Treasury, Treas. Dept., NA.

40. Geo. W. Barry to G.S. Boutwell, 21 Aug. 1869, file of George Barry, Applications, Treas. Dept., NA.

41. S.B. Kennaugh to Robt. L. Miller, 20 April 1887, file of Catherine Hoffman, Applications, Treas. Dept., NA.

42. R.V. Robinson to C.S. Fairchild, 10 April 1887, file of R. Virginia Robinson, Applications, Treas. Dept., NA.

43. M.L. Higgins to S.J. W. Tabor, 24 Feb. 1865, file of Benjamin Messer, Applications, Treas. Dept., NA.

44. Jno. Baxter to P.G. Hopkins, 1 July 1874, file of P.G. Hopkins, Applications, Treas. Dept., NA.

45. William Elder to Wm. E. Chandler, 27 Sept. 1866, and William Elder to H. McCulloch, 27 Sept. 1866, file of Harman C. Westervelt, Applications, Treas. Dept., NA.

46. Austin Fowler to S.P. Chase, 31 May 1862, file of John F. Bentley, Applications, Treas. Dept., NA.

47. Josiah Bellows to J.J. Martin, 26 May 1869, file of Robert Patterson, Applications, Treas. Dept., NA.

48. D.A. Pierce et al., 10 June 1869, file of Josiah F. Harding, Applications, Treas. Dept., NA.

49. B.F. Rittenhouse et al. to George Barry, 3 March 1862, file of George Barry, Applications, Treas. Dept., NA.

50. J.S. Moffat et al. to B.H. Bristow, 29 June 1875, file of F.I. Seybolt, Applications, Treas. Dept., NA.

51. Samuel H. Janney et al. to S.P. Chase, 31 May 1861, file of Henry K. Randall, Applications, Treas. Dept., NA.

52. Frank I. Tedford et al. to C.J. Folger, 28 Aug. 1882, file of William Gunnison, Applications, Treas. Dept., NA.

53. Wm. B. Randolph et al. to James Guthrie, 28 Sept. 1853, file of Henry B. Croggon, Applications, Treas. Dept., NA.

54. Wm. Hemphill Jones et al. to James Guthrie, 1 July 1853, file of George W. Fales, Applications, Treas. Dept., NA.

55. Zachariah Chandler, Order, 20 Oct. 1875, Orders and Circulars, 1852–1908, Appointments Division, Int. Dept., NA.

56. The order prohibited Interior Department clerks from making recommendations or giving out information about positions only within their own agency. Apparently clerks continued to make recommendations and relay information concerning jobs in other departments of the government. In 1893 the Secretary of the Interior amended the order to prohibit these actions as well. Hoke Smith, Order, 13 Sept. 1893, Miscellaneous Letters Received, Appointments Division, Int. Dept., NA.

57. Frances Forrester Cougle to Commissioner of Pensions, [April 1885], and Frances F. Cougle to Gen'l. Black, 9 May 1885, (1880) #1912, Appts. Files, Int. Dept., NA.

58. Statement of Frank E. Anderson, n.d., (1881) #1974, Appts. Files, Int. Dept., NA.

59. Joseph Nimrod to John Sherman, 13 Aug. 1880, file of Carrie Sheads, Applications, Treas. Dept., NA.

60. Gitt to General Black, [29 April 1885], (1880) #1912, Appts. Files, Int. Dept., NA.

61. Statement of Mr. J. O'C. Roberts, n.d., (1881) #1974, Appts. Files, Int. Dept., NA.

62. U.S., Congress, Senate, *Petition of Officers of the Civil Service of the Government,* S. Misc. Doc. no. 119, 38th Cong., 1st sess., 1864, pp. 1–5. Emphasis in original.

63. J.M. Blanchard et al. to O.H. Browning, 12 Nov. 1867, Miscellaneous Letters Received, Appointments Division, Int. Dept., NA.

64. Victoria A. Forrest et al. to Hugh McCullogh, 17 March 1865, Letters Received from the Treasurer (entry 177), Correspondence of the Office of the Secretary of the Treasury, Treas. Dept., NA.

65. M.L. Dunlevy et al. to Benjamin Butterworth, [June 1884], (1881) #402, Appts. Files, Int. Dept., NA. Emphasis in original.

66. Louis Falk et al., 15 Jan. 1872, Letters Received from the Treasurer (entry 177), Correspondence of the Office of the Secretary of the Treasury, Treas. Dept., NA.

67. Jno. R.M. Connell et al. to Secretary of Interior, 3 Feb. 1893, Miscellaneous Letters Received, Appointments Division, Int. Dept., NA.

68. William Graebner, *A History of Retirement: The Meaning and Function of An American Institution, 1885–1978* (New Haven, 1980), ch. 3.

Chapter Seven. Manners, Morals, and Money

1. See Linda Kerber, "Defining Our Terms: Separate Spheres—1600–1865," paper presented to the Organization of American Historians, Los Angeles, California, April 1984; Mary Ryan, *The Cradle of the Middle Class: The Family in Oneida County, New York, 1790–1865* (Cambridge, 1981); Kathryn Kish Sklar, *Catherine Beecher, A Study in American Domesticity* (New York, 1973); Nancy Cott, *The Bonds of Womanhood: "Women's Sphere" in New England, 1780–1835* (New Haven, 1977); Eleanor Flexner, *Century of Struggle: The Woman's Rights Movement in the United States* (New York, 1972).

2. Maurice Francis Egan, *A Gentleman* (New York, 1893), 60. See also Miss [Eliza] Leslie, *The Behaviour Book: A Manual for Ladies* (Philadelphia, 1855), ch. 5.

3. Egan, *A Gentleman,* 45.

4. Quoted in Arthur M. Schlesinger, *Learning How to Behave: A Historical Study of American Etiquette Books* (New York, 1946), 38–39.

5. Egan, *A Gentleman,* 76.

6. U.S., Congress, Senate, *Report on the Conditions of the General Land Office,* S. Rept. no. 362, 47th Cong., 1st sess., 1882, follows p. 94.

7. Wm. H. Barker to A.W. Fisher, Nov. 1890, (1890) #4024, Appts. Files, Int. Dept., NA; W.R. Laskaw to Secretary of the Interior, 12 Nov. 1889, (1880) #1511, Appts. Files, Int. Dept., NA.

8. U.S., Congress, House of Representatives, *Report of the Select Committee of the House of Representatives, Investigating the Methods and Management and Practices of the Bureau of Pensions,* H. Rept. No. 1868, part 1, 52nd Cong., 1st sess., 1892, p. 441.

9. Mary Ruckman to Mrs. John W. Noble, 14 April 1891, (1890) #3703, Appts. Files, Int. Dept., NA.

10. Frances Forrester Cougle to Commissioner of Pensions, n.d., (1880) #1912, Appts. Files, Int. Dept., NA.

11. Hoke Smith, Order, 2 Jan. 1896, Miscellaneous Letters Received, Appointments Division, Int. Dept., NA.

12. For a discussion of nineteenth-century views of female sexuality see Linda Gordon, *Woman's Body, Woman's Rights: A Social History of Birth Control in America* (New York, 1976); John S. Haller and Robin M. Haller, *The Physician and Sexuality in Victorian America* (Urbana, Ill., 1974).

13. Shellabarger and Wilson to Robert Porter, 2 April 1891, and Robert Porter to Secretary of the Interior, 30 March 1891, (1890) #557, Appts. Files, Int. Dept., NA.

14. Fannie M. Simpson to H.M. Teller, 25 July 1883, and William Dudley, Endorsement, 27 July 1883, (1881) #1502, Appts. Files, Int. Dept., NA.

15. U.S., Congress, House of Representatives, *Report of the Select Committee...To Investigate Certain Charges Against the Treasury Department,* H. Rept. no. 140, 38th Cong., 1st sess., 1864, pp. 414–15.

16. Ibid., 406–7.

17. John Ellis, *The Sights and Secrets of the National Capital* (Chicago, 1869), 385–86.

18. Ibid., 385–87.

19. "The Lady of the Treasury," *The Washington Capital* (12 March 1871): 1.

20. Mary Clemmer Ames, *Ten Years in Washington: Life and Scenes in the National*

Capital as a Woman Sees Them (Hartford, 1873), 358–60; Mrs. John Logan, *Thirty Years in Washington: Or, Life and Scenes in Our National Capital* (Minneapolis, 1908), 208.

21. Logan, *Thirty Years in Washington*, 255–57; James McCabe, *Behind the Scenes in Washington* (Philadelphia, 1873), 465–79.

22. Ames, *Ten Years in Washington*, 357–58.

23. "Women as Government Clerks: Their Work and Their Play—Play Fair," *The Washington Capital* (4 Nov. 1871): 1.

24. Quoted in Constance McLaughlin Green, *Washington: A History of the Capital, 1800–1950*, vol. ii (Princeton, 1962), 168.

25. Ellis, *Sights and Secrets*, 385.

26. Addie Tyrrell to Secretary of the Treasury, 7 Jan. 1868, Letters Received from the Register of the Treasury (entry 171), Correspondence of the Office of the Secretary of the Treasury, Treas. Dept., NA.

27. See Cornelia Mills to Senator Edmunds, 1 May 1875, Affidavit of Mrs. Amelia Carroll, 17 April 1875, Affidavit of G.S. Thompson, 26 April 1875, Affidavits of Nellie F. Mills, 17 April 1875, file of Cornelia Mills, Applications, Treas. Dept., NA.

28. U.S., House of Representatives, *Report on Bureau of Pensions*, part 1, pp. 361–63.

29. Ibid., part 2, p. 1480.

30. J.M. Burkhard to B.H. Bristow, 16 June 1875, file of Bernard May, Applications, Treas. Dept., NA; Memo of Information, [14 July 1883], (1880) #1503, Appts. Files, Int. Dept., NA.

31. S.C. de Hart to Carl Schurz, 11 March 1880, (1880) #737, Appts. Files, Int. Dept., NA.

32. Geo. W. Black to Secretary of the Interior, 23 March 1901, (1880) #2194, Appts. Files, Int. Dept., NA.

33. Application of Anna E. Douglass, [27 Aug. 1889], and D.S. Alexander to Benj. Harrison, 27 March 1889, (1890) #341, Appts. Files, Int. Dept., NA.

34. Lewis Vital Bogy, *In Office, A Story of Washington Life and Society* (Chicago, 1891), 43–52.

35. U.S., House of Representatives, *Report on Bureau of Pensions*, part 1, p. 361.

36. Newspaper clipping in (1884) #362, Appts. Files, Int. Dept., NA.

37. Charles C. Snow to A.M. Dockery, 13 March 1893, file of Enna B. Wilson, Applications, Treas. Dept., NA.

38. U.S., House of Representatives, *Report on Bureau of Pensions*, part 2, p. 1053.

39. New York *World* (18 April 1892): 1; U.S., House of Representatives, *Report on Bureau of Pensions*, part 2, pp. 1016–17.

40. A newspaper reporter described Ford as "a married man with a wife and grown children. He is between fifty-five and sixty years of age, with iron gray hair, and most people would regard him as fine looking." New York *Herald* (18 April 1892): 6.

41. U.S., House of Representatives, *Report on Bureau of Pensions*, part 2, pp. 1050–51.

42. Ibid., 1341.

43. New York *World* (19 April 1892): 1.

44. New York *World* (18 April 1892): 1.

45. U.S., House of Representatives, *Report on Bureau of Pensions*, part 2, p. 1052.

46. Ibid., part 2, p. 1053.

47. Ibid., part 1, p. xv.

48. See Chapter Two for a discussion of the money problems and continual debt that plagued government clerks.

49. U.S., House of Representatives, *Report on Bureau of Pensions*, part 2, p. 969.

50. Ibid., 804, 806–7.

51. Ibid., 818–19.

52. Ibid., 1283.

53. Ibid., 1286.

54. Ibid., 985–86, 761–70.

55. S.L. Taggart to Green B. Raum, 24 Jan. 1890, (1882) #3701, Appts. Files, Int. Dept., NA.

56. Commissioner of Pensions to Secretary of the Interior, 18 April 1809, and Chas. Lyman to Secretary of the Interior, 28 April 1890, (1882) #3701, Appts. Files. Int. Dept., NA.

57. U.S. House of Representatives, *Report on Bureau of Pensions*, part 2, pp. 445–47.

58. Mrs. M.A. Fithian to Secretary of the Interior, 16 Oct. 1882, (1882) #3701, Appts. Files, Int. Dept., NA.

Chapter Eight. Conclusion

1. E. Anthony Rotundo, "Manhood in America: The Northern Middle Class, 1770–1920" (Ph.D. dissertation, Brandeis University, 1982).

2. Alba H. Edwards, U.S. Bureau of the Census, *Sixteenth Census of the United States: 1940. Population. Comparative Occupation Statistics for the United States, 1870 to 1940* (Washington, D.C., 1943), 100.

3. C. Wright Mills, *White Collar: The American Middle Classes* (London, 1951), ch. 13; Harry Braverman, *Labor and Monopoly Capital: The Degradation of Work in the Twentieth Century* (New York, 1974), ch. 15.

4. For an excellent review of the literature concerning the debate on the class position of white-collar workers, see Mark Stuart Sandler, "Clerical Proletarianization in Capitalist Development" (Ph.D. dissertation, Michigan State University, 1979), ch. 2.

Index